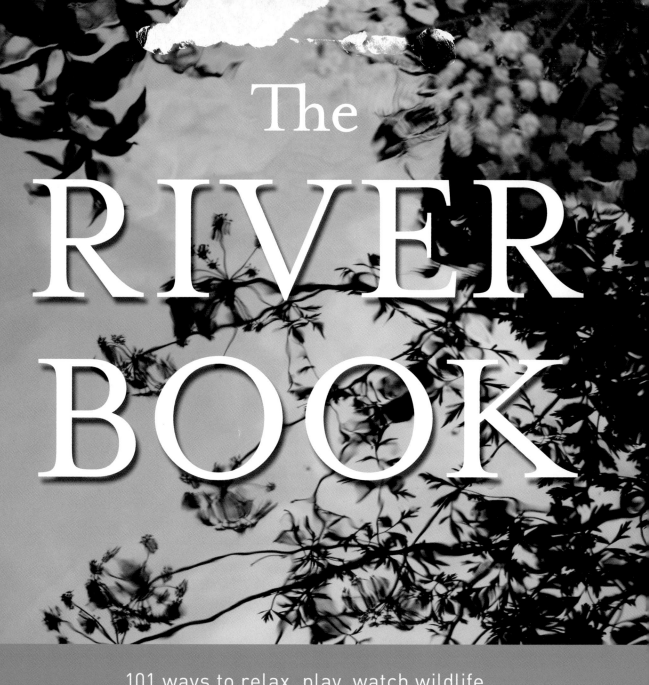

The
RIVER
BOOK

101 ways to relax, play, watch wildlife
and have adventures at the river's edge

TESSA WARDLEY

Published 2012 by Bloomsbury Publishing Plc, 50 Bedford Square, London WC1B 3DP

ISBN (print) 978-1-4081-5866-1

A CIP catalogue record for this book is available from the British Library

Commissioning editor: Lisa Thomas
Design: Nicola Liddiard, Nimbus Design

Printed in China by C & C Offset Printing Co Ltd
10 9 8 7 6 5 4 3 2 1

Visit *www.acblack.com/naturalhistory* to find out more about our authors and their books. You will find extracts, author interviews and our blog, and you can sign up for newsletters to be the first to hear about our latest releases and special offers.

We are grateful to the following for permission to use the following copyright photographs: p.39 Gordon Bell/shutterstock; p.82l Attila Jandi/shutterstock; p.82r 1000 Words/shutterstock; p.83t kurt_G/ shutterstock; p.83b Denis Barbulat/shutterstock; p.97tl olena2552/shutterstock; p.97trJ Funk/shutterstock; p.97bl dabjola/shutterstock; p.97bc Phoric/shutterstock; p.97br StonePhotos/shutterstock; p.102r Martin Fowler/shutterstock; p.103l Ruud Morijn Photographer/shutterstock; p.103c Zlatko Guzmic/shutterstock; p.103r bluecrayola/shutterstock; p.105 ImageBroker/Imagebroker/FLPA; p.106t Ingo Arndt/Minden Pictures/FLPA; p.111 Alwyn J Roberts/FLPA; p.115 El Choclo/shutterstock; p.120 Gail Johnson/shutterstock; p.122r John P. Ashmore/shutterstock p.131 Paul Hobson/FLPA; p.132 Mircea Bezergheanu/shutterstock; p.133 Mirek Srb/shutterstock; p.134l Vasily Vishnevskiy/shutterstock; p.134r Alexey Sokolov/shutterstock; p.135l Vasily Vishnevskiy/shutterstock; p.140 Mark Bridger/shutterstock; p.141t Lightpoet/shutterstock; p.141b Andras Harsanyi/shutterstock; p.144t nialat/shutterstock; p.144b H.Häring/shutterstock; p.145 Andy Poole/shutterstock

The extract on page 3 is reproduced with the permission of the Robert Gibbings Estate and the Heather Chalcroft Literary Agency.

For my inspirational parents
who introduced me to rivers.

JOT and JEMT

'THERE IS NOTHING UNUSUAL IN THIS LOVE OF WATER... I THINK IT IS
THE UNBROKEN SEQUENCES OF FLOWING WATER, THE UNCHANGING
DESTINIES OF STREAMS, THAT SEEM TO KNIT A MAN'S SOUL WITH THE
ETERNITIES. THE RHYTHMS OF EDDYING POOLS, THE RHYMES OF
LAPPING WAVELETS, BRING PEACE THROUGH EYE AND EAR,
EMPHASIZING BY THEIR UNCEASING FLOW THE UNIMPORTANCE OF OUR
PASSING LIVES. ON AND ON THEY GLIDE, NOT MERELY FOR THE BRIEF
MOMENTS OF OUR ATTENTION BUT THROUGH EVERY HOUR OF NIGHT OR
DAY, VARYING YET CONSTANT. THE DANCING OF A MOUNTAIN STREAM
MAY BE AS ENTRANCING AS A BALLET, BUT THE QUIET OF AN AGE-OLD
RIVER IS LIKE THE SLOW TURNING OF PAGES IN A WELL LOVED BOOK.'

Robert Gibbings *Till I End My Song*

Contents

Introduction

My earliest memories of rivers are like the rivers themselves, pristine, clear and unblemished.

At Easter each year we would change our riverscape from the slow-flowing murk of the Norfolk Broads to the dancing moorland streams of Exmoor where we visited my Aunt and Uncle at their hotel. This was always an opportunity for my father to indulge his passion for fly-fishing. Walking through the beech woods, the six of us, with fishing tackle and waders, backpacks full of picnic and binoculars and dogs in tow, we made rather a motley caravan. It was a short walk down to the banks of the River Barle. My father chose his spot to unravel his paraphernalia while the rest of us were banished upstream. We could play for hours as our mother set up camp and lookout up on the bank, then sketched and watched birds as we played. With industry and imagination we spent the days inventing games and building dams and channels in the streams. Ian as the eldest was general-in-charge, Christopher chief engineer, Ruth chief scout on the lookout for invaders in the surrounding hillsides and as the youngest I was general dogsbody - collecting a steady supply of stones for construction, as instructed. It wasn't long before our feet were squelching in our inundated wellies. The dogs would paddle and snuffle around us chasing stones in the hope of a tasty morsel until, following multiple disappointments they would sneeze the water out of their noses and harrumph down next to Mum, head on paws, waiting patiently for us to move off.

In spite of the hours spent rearranging the flow, I have no memory of achingly cold, frozen hands but they must have been. I do remember the look of our alien feet at the end of a day in flooded wellies, white and shrivelled like bunches of albino prunes.

They were simple, happy days. Many different places and many different activities but so often there was a river, a moving constant, in the background or foreground, dark and silent or sparkling and babbling.

Rivers have wound their way through my life but the way I have perceived them and interacted with them has changed. As a child I was playing; always looking for adventure, investigating, busy, I wanted to keep moving. As a young adult I studied rivers; I was always working, looking for information, aiming to achieve something, still investigating and still looking for adventure, never stationary.

Finding myself with four young children, I started to perceive the familiar differently. I slowed down and reflected. I took time to notice the details and used all my senses; I listened, saw, touched, tasted and smelled everything anew. Alongside my developing children I experienced everything I had been seeing and learning about for so many years from a different perspective, with a certain childlike wonder and a greater sense of value.

Complemented by my years of accumulated knowledge I found a new way to take delight in the river. I still love and search out the

adventures but I have learned to slow down and enjoy the journey. I am able to appreciate what I have learned and the understanding I have developed over years of immersion – literal, literary and scientific.

Our lives are fantastic journeys and it has taken me until now to realise that the memories I have gathered from the riverbank are jewels that stand out bright and many faceted while others fade away. These memories are what I want to remember when I am in my dotage, rocking in my chair. These memories are the reason I wanted to write this book.

It was shortly after reading the wild swimming bible *Waterlog* by Roger Deakins that I decided to write this book. *Waterlog* has spawned a wild swimming revival in the UK with websites, books and swimming groups all over the country. Suddenly a whole generation have been inspired to swim in our rivers but there is so much more to see and understand. I wanted to explore all the fun you could have at the river, to help people to slow down, step off the treadmill of life and enjoy the details.

As I started planning I realised that in spite of all my years around rivers I needed to look at them with the book in mind. After five years dominated by home life, I needed to change focus; so I began a period of research. It was a great excuse to reacquaint myself with rivers on which I had worked and played over the years – and to pop in to see friends, cadging bed and board along the way. During the spring and summer I travelled throughout the UK, two days a week, to indulge my love of rivers. It was a complete luxury going at my own speed and having largely solo adventures.

But I wasn't happy just going to the rivers on my own. I was now able to justify my usual desire to visit rivers every weekend and holiday and as my 'research' spilled over into the rest of my life we had lots of great days out with family and friends. We played and investigated and relaxed and had adventures in new and old haunts, peering in to rivers, sometimes clear and sparkling, sometimes with the appeal of Kipling's great grey-green greasy Limpopo. Many adventures have been had in the name of research over the last four years and some of those have made their way into this book, many have not – many more from before the days of the book have also been included but they have all gone a long way to feeding my passion for water and feeding into this book.

How to use the book

Within the book there are five sections full of activities to suit the way you feel, whether you want to relax, play, investigate, have an adventure or answer some questions.

Each activity starts with a journal extract where I convey the images that I captured and that captured my imagination. In most cases this is followed up with 'how to' sections that give more detailed information, which should enable you to try out or refine the activities that may or may not be familiar to you. Where relevant there are also notebook sections which provide all sorts of information about the river environment – the wildlife, geography, mythology, natural history or just stories that will enrich the experience.

Each section has some suggestions for easily accessible places known to me on UK rivers that are well suited to the activity; details on how to find the sites with grid references are included in the river sites section at the end of the book. However, don't be limited by the sites that I suggest. Throughout this country there are literally thousands of rivers and streams: arm yourself with a map and read through the section on 'finding your river' at the beginning of the book and you will be set to get out there and find your own river haven.

The underlying philosophy of this book, if there is one, is one of simplicity. Strip out all the unnecessary clutter of life, just go out to a river for the day and have fun with what you find there. None of the activities in the book require specialist equipment. There is always something at the river on which to build a game, investigation or adventure without the need for hours of planning and bags of kit.

Visiting rivers is a fantastic way to get out into the great outdoors, challenge the ties of technology and get some fresh air, a bit of exercise, nourish your senses and be inspired. The fact that it is easy on the pocket and the environment is a bonus.

The River Book will give you the confidence to side step the work hard, play hard, walk fast mentality; to indulge your inner fish, and just go to the river for the river's sake. Revel in the freedom and savour the slightly illicit sensation that it gives. It is free, simple, environmentally friendly and therapeutic.

Finding your river

Planning adventures on English rivers can be a daunting process. When you look at maps there is lots of information but how do you unravel the information to find the useful bits that will help you have a great time? The blue lines are everywhere and the possibilities are endless.

Where to start?

Each section of river will suit some activities but not be ideal for others. If you are happy to take the river as you find it and just engage in whichever activities seem possible then almost any bit of accessible river will do. If you have a clear idea of what you want to do, such as a day-long swimming safari or building channels, then there are more constraints on the rivers and streams that will meet your needs. It really depends on your expectations and requirements. The pleasure in finding your own private haven is great. You may rely on serendipity, the best days often come this way, but if a group of people are involved and relying on you, it is probably worth doing a bit of research to increase your chances of a great day out.

You can take several different approaches when in search of your river:

● Talk to people. Friends who have visited an area before and especially locals all have their favourite spot; people with dogs are a good bet if you fancy a walk, people with young children often know the good picnic and shallow play spots and if you are after an adrenaline rush, the young lads in an area always know where the ride-able rapids and weirs are, as well as the best bit of blue string! Wild swimmers, kayakers and anglers often know of some great

out of the way tranquil spots – even if you are not planning to swim, kayak or fish yourself, they may suit your activity.

● Have a look on the Internet and in guide books. There are several Internet sites and guide books for walking, canoeing and swimming in particular which will give you some good starting points. The Wild Swimming website has linked with Google maps to identify good swim sites but also have a look at the websites for the Outdoor Swimming Society, RALSA and the UK Rivers Guidebook aimed at Kayakers. See the Links section on page 222.

● Go exploring. Go for a drive and peer off bridges. There are loads of places where the rivers are crossed by roads. How does the river look for size? Is there a footpath? You may find somewhere that looks hopeful. Go for a walk; walk down towpaths and riverside footpaths and just see where they take you.

● Look at a map. Even once you have spoken to people and looked in books and the Internet it is always worth having a look at a map. The best place to start is by finding the blue lines – these are the rivers: run your finger along its length and work out access points at bridges and along footpaths. Also look at the place names, the history and dependence of people on the rivers is reflected in place names everywhere for example: Oxford, Millbrook, Troutbeck, Sadlers Wells, Bath.

Looking at maps

The anticipatory excitement of looking at a map to plan a day's fun is unbeatable. Find a big table or even better the floor, spread the map out and have a good peruse. Pore over the map and see the possibilities, think about the activities you could get involved in at different places on the river.

So, how are you going to locate the best bit of river for you? Along its length almost any river will have the perfect playing spot, the perfect place for a bit of tranquility and a good stretch or at least a deep pool for a swim, you just need to identify where they are.

If you don't have much experience of looking at maps and particularly finding good river spots here are some tips that will help you find your own adventures...

To start with

● For paper maps a scale of 1:25 000 Outdoor Leisure Series (yellow cover) or Explorer Series (orange) map will give you the best kind of detail but the 1:50,000 OS Landranger maps (fuchsia pink cover) will do too. Maps for all of the UK are available in bookshops and local maps in stationers, newsagents, service stations and other outlets.

● If you don't have paper maps then all OS maps are available online: www.multimap.com provides free 1:50,000 OS mapping or www.ordnancesurvey.co.uk/getamap for 1:25,000 OS mapping. www.streetmap.co.uk also uses OS mapping and can help you pinpoint your location using grid references, postcodes or place names. It can also very usefully convert between the different types of coordinates and zoom up to 1:2500 scale.

● Have a look at the key to the map you are using and make sure you are familiar with the symbols used. The most important features you will be looking for are:

- Blue lines – rivers.
- Brown lines – contour lines indicating vertical height above sea level.
- Marks on the blue lines such as:
- a single black line crossing the river – a weir;
  - double black lines – a footbridge;
  - a V crossing the river – a lock.
- A variety of red, green, orange or black dashed lines indicate the foot and bridle paths.
- On more recent maps also look out for the wide yellow line that encircles open access land where you have the right to roam away from footpaths (see more in the Access section on page 219).
- Think about your plans for the day. Do you have some definite activities that you want to find a river to suit? Or are you just going to find the nicest bit of river in the area and will adapt the activities to the river as you find it?

Look at the river

To match the river to your planned visit the most important factors to consider are how fast the water is moving and how deep it is. While it is not possible to read this information directly from the map, you can infer quite a lot from the map if you look at the information that is there and put this together with what you know about rivers and how they behave. The map will tell you to some extent how wide the river is, the slope the river is flowing down – the gradient of the river, the shape or course of the river and the nature and aspect of the valley that it is flowing through. You can also see how big the river catchment is, how deep the valleys are and how far you are from the river's source – all of it important information that will allow you to build a mental picture of the river that you will find on the ground.

HOW WIDE IS THE RIVER?

On the 1:50,000 Landranger map series a river will be shown as a thin blue line, a thick blue line or a double blue line as the river gets bigger on the ground, while on the 1:25,000 Explorer or Outdoor Leisure map series rivers are either a thin blue line or a double blue line, with a pale blue colour filling in between. The double blue lines on the 1:25,000 scale appear once a river is greater than 8m wide and from that width and wider they are drawn to scale. This means that as the river widens on the ground, it also widens on the map.

HOW STEEP IS THE RIVER?

The gradient of the river channel can tell us a lot about the speed of the water in the river. Contour lines are drawn in brown on all OS maps; on the 1:50,000 maps they are drawn at 10m intervals and every fifth one is a shade darker (e.g. 50m, 100m 150m) while at the 1:25,0000 scale they are drawn at 5m intervals and again every fifth one is a shade darker (25m, 50m, 75m, 100m). Look at a 1km length of your river and see how many contour lines are crossed; you need to look very closely as they can be hard to see. Remember 1km at 1:50,000 will be 2cm on the map and at 1:25,000, 4cm on the map.

There is a huge range of gradients for rivers. In lowland areas such as the Thames Valley you may be looking at a 10m fall every 10km or so, while in upland areas such as the

Lake District you may expect to see a 10m fall every 2km for a main river in the bottom of a large valley or up to a 10m fall every 100m for a mountain stream.

Looking along the length of the River Severn its source is around 670m above sea level. It drops 520m in its first 12 miles and only 150m in its remaining 208 miles. This kind of profile with a rapid initial descent is typical of many rivers.

When the river crosses a clustering of contour lines this would suggest a rapid drop in height, which indicates a significant waterfall, a series of waterfalls or rapids.

WHAT SHAPE IS THE RIVER CHANNEL?

A long, straight river channel will give very uniform conditions and it is likely that the depth and flow will be very constant. A more complex river shape will result in more complex river depths as well as variable water speeds in different bits of the river. So, around a bend or meander in the river channel there is faster flow around the outside of the bend. This results in greater erosion of this part of the river and deeper water – useful to remember if you want to swim or paddle a boat. On the inside of the bend there will be a shelving beach that will gradually deepen and often rapidly drop into the deeper pool on the outside of the bend. The shelving beach is great for getting in, picnicking or playing but remember the rapid drop if you don't want to get wet or are supervising non-swimmers.

Beware of engineered river channels, as they may not conform to your expectations. Some rivers are dredged for navigation or flood defence reasons so may not have the expected shallow and deep areas. Look for unnaturally straight edges as these are often characteristic of managed rivers.

WHAT IS THE LIKELY DEPTH AND SPEED OF THE WATER?

From the width of the river and particularly changes in the width of the river, we can infer a lot about the depth at various points. Assuming that there is not a sudden input of water, for example from a tributary or sewage treatment works, then a wider channel should mean shallower water and likewise, assuming there is no sudden loss of water, a narrower channel means deeper water.

Features to notice may be a widening in the blue line, often downstream of bridges or other structures where the river has a chance to spread out and slow down – this is likely to be a shallow riffly area – good for playing and paddling but not for swimming. Along with widening there may be braiding where the river divides into many shallow channels – these rivers can be great for playing in.

Conversely look out too for a rapid narrowing; this means the water is squeezed and is likely to be deeper and probably faster flowing; depending on how fast and how deep, this may be hazardous or fun – but needs consideration in either case.

While looking at the river width it is worth looking at the gradient as well. The slope that the water travels down is an important factor in the speed of the water.

While it is not possible to calculate accurate water velocities from the information on the map it is possible to have an idea of the nature of the river and therefore the gradient that may suit certain activities. In general if want to swim, a 10m drop for every 1 to 2km or less is ideal (a gradient of less than 1:100); a dip or private spa in mountain pools, then look for a drop of 10m over 100 to 400m (a gradient of greater than 1:40). If you want to play, then almost any gradient can work, but it depends on the activity. A very shallow stream with a rapid drop (1:40) can be great for water wheels and boat races but slow flowing, knee deep water (1:200) could be better for mini-beast hunting and skipping stones.

THE IMPACT OF THE WEATHER

One important variable when it comes to water depth and speed in rivers is the recent weather conditions. Remember that in mountain areas rivers are prone to spate (high flow) conditions. Water levels rise and fall dramatically and very rapidly; therefore the weather conditions over the previous 12 to 24 hours are very important. The first rush of water off the mountains will go past in the first 12 hours after heavy rain but the streams will be fuller than usual for a couple of days or so. In lowland areas that first spate will be slower off the catchment and may take 24 hours to raise the levels of the rivers significantly but they may stay up for several days after heavy rainfall. See more in the Safety section on pages 219-221.

OTHER RIVER FEATURES

Weirs, waterfalls, stepping-stones, footbridges, fords, locks and sluices are generally all marked on the map. These can all be useful features and add interest to a day by the river. Stepping-stones and fords are not always marked but a footpath crossing a river with no bridge suggests one or the other. Stepping-stones may be submerged after high rainfall but in almost all cases where there are stepping-stones there will be a bridge nearby as an alternative crossing for those who don't want to risk wet feet or want a more secure crossing.

Weirs are marked on maps as a single black line across the river channel, sometimes it is written on too. They will generally have a good stretch of river upstream or a pool downstream for swimming and can sometimes be good for chutes or jumping – but you should exercise extreme caution here as they can also be dangerous. Box- or U-shaped weirs should always be avoided as the water flowing over three sides at once sets up complex currents, which can be very hazardous.

Access to the river

If you have found a bit of river that suits your needs, you need to know whether you can get to it legally. Following the Countryside Rights of Way Act 2000 (CRoW Act), in open access areas you have the right to roam away from footpaths; if it is not open access land then you need a footpath or bridleway to take you to the river's edge. At 1:50,000 scale paths are marked as red dashed or grey dashed lines. At 1:25,0000 paths are green, orange or grey dashed lines with some national trails marked as green dotted or green diamond lines.

How much access do you require? If you are

swimming you may need to be able to get in and out at a few points so a footpath along the river could be useful. If you are just going to play then a single access point at the right kind of place may be sufficient.

Public access to navigation of the rivers is not covered by the CRoW Act so swimming and boating may not be strictly legal. See the resources section page 219 for more on the legality of access to and on rivers.

Consider other people's access to the river as well as your own. If you want a tranquil swim hundreds of ramblers tramping along the river bank may spoil the mood somewhat. Conversely a path alongside the river means you can get in and out at many points along the river providing good safety and flexibility. You may need to balance out your requirements when choosing your access point.

Look at the river bank

The nature of the river bank and the conditions you want to find there are important to your enjoyment of a really special day. While it is not possible to anticipate the presence of flocks of geese and their extensive poo-ing habits or a fishing contest or a bank full of nettles, all of which could mar your day, some conditions can be anticipated.

Consider the aspect of the river and the nature of its valley. If it is a really hot, wet or windy day then some tree shelter may be welcome but in general a deeply wooded river channel can be a bit dank for picnics and sunning yourself, so avoid densely wooded areas — on the map these are coloured green with the types of tree drawn on (coniferous,

non-coniferous or coppiced).

If you want a nice sunny bank for picnicking or sunbathing, look at the direction faced by the river banks. To get an accurate idea of the aspect of the river valley lay a pencil or other straight edged object perpendicular (at exactly a 90° angle) to the contour lines. The direction in which the downhill end points is the direction you will be facing when you sit on that slope. South facing will get daytime sun in summer; east will get the morning sun and west the sunset. Remember in high summer the sun rises in the north-east and sets in the south-west, much further round than you would imagine, and adjust your planning accordingly — you don't want to be left holding a bottle of champagne, waiting for the sun to set when it has snuck around behind you!

A steep-sided valley running east to west won't get much sun in the middle of the day so if you are hoping for a sunbathe you could be unlucky. You could be headed for a shady dip and need to find somewhere to warm up.

The wind can be chilling if it funnels down a valley or whips over hills or drives over plains. In general in this country the prevailing winds are from the south west so bear this is mind but have a feel of the wind direction on your day of travel, you may be able to shelter round a bend in the river if the wind is in an inconvenient quarter. Once you get to the river have a look around, if the trees are permanently bent over, it is not a good sign.

Think about what your view will be — or whose view you will be. In general on the river bank you will be lower than the surrounding area, so often well hidden, but the shape of the slope is significant. On a convex slope people at the top won't see you at the bottom but on a concave slope they will. A convex slope has progressively more tightly packed contour lines as you descend it. A concave slope will have closely packed contour lines at the top becoming progressively less tightly packed towards the bottom. It is often surprising how hidden you can be on the river bank. Just a small dip or a convex slope can provide good protection.

There may be power stations, industrial towns, warehouses, major roads, train tracks etc that you don't want to look over – or maybe you do – so check them out on the map. Check 360° around the point where you will be sitting to see if there is anything you want to avoid. If there is, see if there may be a handy woodland or hill shielding it from view. If not consider how much it will impact on your day – you may need to look for a better place.

Other activities you want to tie in

There may be many other activities that you would like to tie in with your day by the river so have a look at the surroundings and see what the area offers up.

● A blue tent is the symbol for camping if you want to extend your stay.

● A blue tankard indicates a hostelry on the 1:25,000 maps while PH is the marker on the 1:50,000 maps. A nice pub lunch to warm you up after your (possibly wet) activities could just round off the day nicely.

● National Trust properties and sites often have food facilities, and toilets, as do other tourist attractions, so consider these.

● The Outdoor Leisure and explorer maps have all sorts of useful tourist information on them so check the key and look for the symbols in the area you are going to: fishing, castles, viewpoints, rock climbing, horse riding and cycle trails; there are lots of activities you may want to tie in with your time by the river which are often marked on these maps.

Be brave, get out there and find your river

It can be hard when you first look at a map to have a clear picture in your head of how the land and water will look when you see them. You can never get the whole picture from a map: there are some features you will never imagine and may take you by surprise when you get to your chosen site.

A map won't show river banks fenced in by landowners, private fishing rights, angling competitions, fields full of feisty bullocks or river banks chock full of waist high nettles. In the national parks and other open access areas, access should be quite straightforward but in lowland Britain where there are many private landowners and intensive farming, access can be a real problem. If you can, identify a few sections of river to try or a whole length that may have potential so that if your first choice proves to be unsuitable you can try again.

The more you look at maps and see how they relate to the nature of the water on the ground the clearer your mental picture will be. You will get better at picking suitable sites from your sofa and you will have a greater chance of success and greater confidence in yourself when choosing locations for your days out.

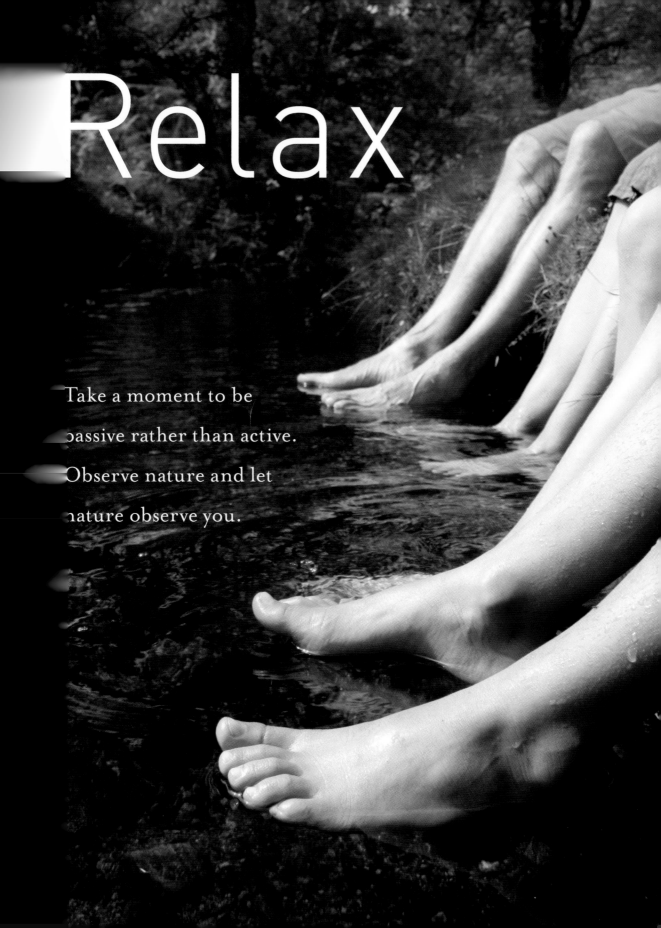

Relax

Take a moment to be
passive rather than active.
Observe nature and let
nature observe you.

16 Lie back and listen

Riuferrer, Arles-sur-Tech, Pyrenees Orientale, France ... August

... I managed to escape today. I picked my way down the steep wooded track to the river that winds its way around large granite boulders, jumping down small waterfalls and sliding over rock chutes. The banks are covered in buddleia bushes and so the river margins shimmer with the busy life of butterflies, dragonflies and damselflies.

I found myself a sun warmed rock mid flow and settled down to read but it was so perfect I didn't want to escape, so I just listened. I opened my ears to the river and heard music.

The bass was played by the water itself, continually rushing past; below this the hollow boom of a rolling, bumping boulder caught under a small waterfall formed the rhythm section: the heartbeat of the music.

The melody added variation, coming and going, birds shrieked their conversations as they flew overhead, insects whirred in and out of earshot and shrieks and splashes reached me from my family and friends up at the house.

I felt I could stay forever but eventually heat and curiosity took over and I slipped into the water to spend time with the fish and explore the waterfall pool where the boulder boomed and clunked rhythmically as it circulated, bouncing and rebounding around the rock hewn pool in perpetual motion. Another short spell lying on the rock and my bubble was burst by the arrival of the screaming hordes but that was fine, I was ready for some more noisy fun ...

How to lie back and listen

Being able to lie back and listen without the aural disruption of the acoustic jumble of noise that we usually block out is a rare treat for many of us.

Whenever you find yourself on the river bank try to find a few moments when you can lose your companions, or, along with very quiet ones, lie back on the bank and concentrate on what you can hear: the soundscape.

You can try this wherever your river is but ideally find a river away from roads and air transport and the electronic noise with which we fill our lives. Once you remove these distractions you may be treated to some much needed tranquility that will allow you to listen out for some real sounds. The sounds of nature. Real music.

Play with your acoustic environment. If you move around closer to and further from the river you can change the balance of the sounds and control the music you hear. Try listening to the same river in different ways and at different times.

Every river has its own unique music that changes with the seasons. A slower lowland river will slide by so silently that you can hear subtle noises from wildlife; the plop and splash of fish, birds, voles and frogs, the rustle of wind in the reeds or trees. In spring the riot of noise from birds and insects as they mate and nest and feed can dominate the noise of the water. People and boats add their own music, so lie back and enjoy your river's symphony.

Camp overnight and you will experience a different auditory spectacle. The darkness reduces the visual distractions and you can focus more easily on what you hear. Animals reveal themselves; you may hear the whistling call of the otter, heron moving off from their hunting ground with the 'whomping' of their wings, foxes barking and calling as they hunt, the plop of small animals as they drop in to the water. In spring you may be treated to the croaking of frogs trying to find a mate and at dawn you will be torn from your sleep by the intensity of the sonic bombardment as the birds wake up and start their displays in a bid for territories and mates.

Once you have exhausted the range of music above the water, lie back with your feet hooked under a tree root and get your ears under the water. In this new alien world it is hard to distinguish whether the sounds are created within your head or are actually in the river.

The noise of flowing water at the river is actually caused by the entrapment of air in the water as it moves. The air that is trapped, but not absorbed into the water, eventually breaks free and makes the unique and beautiful music of the river. At fast-flowing rivers more air is caught up in the water so what we hear is as loud as a roar while in slow flowing sections it is no more than a whisper.

ANIMAL SOUNDS Riverside animals are perfectly adapted for living in harmony with the river. The melodic song of the water birds has evolved alongside the river so that even by a fast-flowing stream they can convey their important news. The Dipper's song, for example, has evolved into a series of sharp high frequency notes that are much higher than the frequency of the water's music in the fast flowing streams that the birds tend to colonise.

UNDERWATER SOUNDS The sounds we hear when we are underwater are so different from the same sounds above the water because sound travels through water more than four times faster than it moves through air (1435m/s in water compared to 330m/s in air). Sounds above the water that roll and extend, sound sharp and harsh under the water, as the sound waves concertina into your ear.

Not only do underwater sounds travel faster than in air but they travel further than sounds in air. The pressure waves travel on until they bump into something; either the riverbed, where they are absorbed, or the surface of the water, where they are reflected. Underwater animals use this property of sound through water as a means of communication, navigation and hunting and man has also caught on to its value. As far back as the 6th century BC the Greeks – Aristotle and Pythagorus – were investigating the wave-like movement of sound, while Leonardo da Vinci in 1490 was the first to note that by lowering a tube into the water he could hear ships some distance away – an early form of echolocation.

Why not try...

a river with an interesting soundscape and somewhere comfortable to sit, away from everyday noise.

Horner Water, Horner, Exmoor **(5)**

River Teign, Fingle Bridge, Dartmoor **(11)**

River Ouse, Barcombe Mills, East Sussex **(27)**

Elmley Marshes, Isle of Sheppey, Kent **(33)**

River Thames, Wallingford, Oxfordshire **(49)**

River Glaven, Letheringsett Mill, Norfolk **(67)**

River Wye, Monnington Fallls, Bycross Farm campsite, Herefordshire **(69)**

Goredale Beck, Janet's Foss, Yorkshire Dales **(83)**

River Caldew, Swineside, Cumbria **(98)**

Easedale Beck, Grassmere, Lake District **(104)**

(x) numbers relate to site listings in the resources section

Easdale Valley, Lake District ... October (104)

... The Lake District in autumn is unbeatable. My memories are all of crisp clear autumn days, a multi-coloured patchwork of leaves blanketing the tamped-down earth of the paths while the remaining leaves of the trees are a vibrant mix of fiery oranges, deep glowing reds and dayglo yellows. I remember clearly one autumn day as a child, with cloud level down to the valley bottom. I was being dragged against my will up 'The Band' — a wide grassy path in the Langdale Valley. I moaned and muttered and sulked as I stomped up the slope, periodically sitting on rocks and refusing to move. Visibility was down to about 5 metres and since we were engulfed in cloud there was a persistent drizzle. I was just opening my mouth to launch into another protracted moan, when looming out of the mist came my aged school teacher and her even more aged retired school teacher chum. Being a sports-loving, model student I instantly changed tack mid-whine and pretended to be having a wonderful time, jollying along my poor, long-suffering parents and siblings.

Now it is my turn to cajole my children in the midst of long protracted moans. Today never achieved full daylight and we had wind, rain, cold and low cloud. There was only one outdoor option and that was to go and look at waterfalls — with all that water they would surely be impressive. We headed up towards Easdale Tarn to have a look at Sour Milk Gill. I had Lottie on my shoulders most of the way. The others headed up, happily chatting and making up songs while munching on Werther's Originals.

The whole valley had turned into a water feature, every rock had water sluicing off it, the grass and mosses were sponges full to capacity and the paths were all streams; even the dry stone wall against the slope had water spouting from every nook and cranny. The falls at Sour Milk Gill were as impressive as predicted. At the water's edge where the froth and spume churned and boiled into a riot of spray, we couldn't begin to hear ourselves speak. At this point we discovered that neither Thea nor Poppy's waterproofs were actually waterproof so we headed home with promises of hot chocolates and crumpets ...

How to find a waterfall

All of the hill, moor, dale or mountain regions in the UK are blessed with the most wonderful waterfalls. These range from dramatic 30m drops through collections of small cascades right down to a single modest drop of a less than a metre.

To find your waterfall on a map you need to have a look at how steep the ground is — the steeper the land the greater the probability of waterfalls. The gradient of the river channel can tell us a lot about the speed of the water in the river. Look at a 1km length of your river and see how many contour lines are crossed, you need to look very closely as they can be hard to see.

A clustering of contour lines suggests a rapid drop in height for the river and this indicates a significant waterfall, series of waterfalls or rapids. Don't be fooled though, it can be hard to identify waterfalls from contour lines; this is because while even a 5m drop may produce a dramatic waterfall it may only register as one extra contour line on the map. To help clarify this significant waterfalls are generally marked on the map. As you explore rivers in upland areas, particularly after a period of high rain, you will find many more large and small falls, often temporary ones, than you will ever see marked on a map.

If you find yourself in the flatlands and craving the noise and action of a waterfall, the best you can hope for is an artificial weir. Although not as dramatic as a natural waterfall they still provide some interest and are marked on the map by a small black line crossing the river; very often they are marked with the word 'weir' as well.

Why not try...

upland rivers with a steep gradient

East Lyn River and Hoar Oak Water, Watersmeet, Exmoor **(8)**

Becka Brook, Becky Falls, Dartmoor **(12)**

River Conwy, Fairy Glen, Betws-y-coed, Wales **(81)**

River Llugwy, Swallow Falls, Betws-y-coed, Wales **(82)**

Goredale Beck, Janet's Foss, Yorkshire Dales **(83)**

Stainforth Beck, Catrigg Foss, Stainforth, Yorkshire Dales **(87)**

Cald Beck, The Howk, Fairy Kettle, Cumbria **(96)**

Stonethwaite Beck, Galleny Force, Lake District **(101)**

River Brathay, Skelwith Force, Ambleside, Lake District **(105)**

River Tees, High Force, Barnard Castle, County Durham **(112)**

(x) numbers relate to site listings in the resources section

The nature of a waterfall changes with the weather; something that may be a trickle one day, can become a dramatic cascade following heavy rain.

Watching the way the water foams and sprays, shooting its spume into the air like a breaching whale can lift you into the sublime. The all-encompassing sound pounds in your chest so that you feel organically part of the surroundings.

Go to see the same waterfall in the depths of a cold spell and the spume is frozen into ropes of cloudy white and green glass, the contrasting silence as well as the cold can be quite chilling.

Explore behind the falling water. Many waterfalls are overhanging at the top and therefore allow passage behind the water. From this vantage point you will see the world through the curtain of water, deafened by the sound and aware only of shattered light coming through the rushing water. There are many tales of smugglers and other criminals making use of these places of refuge.

THE IMPACT OF WATER   While you are contemplating your waterfall have a look at the impact that all that water has on the rocks. While water can sometimes feel like the softest of elements, the relentless ribbons of water habour enormous power. The never-ending work of the water can cut and channel through solid rock creating gorges and waterfalls. The pools carved out at the base of a waterfall can be great for swimming; the depth of the pool directly under the fall of the water will amaze

you. If you get right in under the water for a quick shower, all you will be aware of is the immensity of the weight of the water pounding down on you, even quite small waterfalls rapidly become unbearable – there's a calculation in 'Some Questions Answered' on page 198 so you can find out the power involved.

TAKE CARE   Think carefully before swimming under a waterfall as strong currents are set up by the force of the falling water. You can be pushed beneath the surface and may have to wait some time to be spat out of the plunge pool and back up to the surface.

Water faeries are an interesting bunch, they are variously known as asrai, kelpies, sprites, naiads or non-specifically – nymphs. True to the double nature of rivers they range from the beautiful to the deadly; inspiring fear and romance in equal measures. The kelpies and asrai are thought to be corporeal (have bodies) while the sprites and naiads are more elemental and intangible.

THE ASRAI While by the riverbank, listen out for the crooning of the faeries of the water – the asrai. These are the freshwater sirens, beautiful seductresses who lure men with their enchanting songs, before sending them to their untimely deaths with a kiss.

There are many asrai tales from all over the country and all have a similar musical theme. In one tale from Shropshire, a man, on his way to work one morning, saw a woman waving to him from the water. She was beautiful, with a fish's tail and long, silky green hair. She sang to the man with a voice as sweet and gentle as the waves lapping the bank. The man was drawn to her song and she further tempted him with gold and jewels and then disappeared.

The man could not forget the asrai. He went on his way but could not clear her image from his head and her song kept ringing in his ears as he worked. Being slowly driven wild by his thoughts of her the man went back with a boat

and a net. He rowed quickly to the middle of the lake, threw the net overboard and trawled her up. He headed for the shore as fast as he could while she wept and wailed. Eventually she freed a hand from the net, touched his arm with her icy hand and pointed to the moon. The man, bemused, turned and once more headed to the shore. It took him an age to row the short distance and when he finally reached the bank the beautiful maiden had gone. All he had left was a damp patch at the bottom of his boat and the icy cold feeling on his arm where she had touched him. Distraught at his loss the man was unable to settle to anything and spent the rest of his days searching in vain for the lost asrai.

An encounter with a nymph was believed to be enough to drive a man mad with desire and is the root of the word 'nymphomaniac'.

KELPIES The kelpies are malevolent Scottish water spirits. They can change their form between water and horse and delight in drowning their victims. Their victims are generally children who they lure on to their backs. Once on, the children become stuck and can no longer escape. If you can capture a

kelpie you can use their powers to help you but beware, they are extremely powerful and don't like being tamed. A captured kelpie is bound to obey its owner but if they regain their freedom they will turn against their captor.

SPRITES AND NAIADS   The sprites and naiads are a much more playful group. They may play puckish tricks on people but nothing too deadly. The nymphs of the freshwaters were called naiads in Greek mythology. Each spring or stream would have its own naiad presiding over it. The very essence of the naiad was bound up with its water body and if it should dry up then the naiad would die. They were credited with their own special powers and worshipped because of this. Drinking their water could have creative, cleansing, medicinal and nourishing properties. They could, however, occasionally use their powers negatively and in Greek mythology are typically jealous. Hylas, one of Jason's crewmen on the Argo, was taken by some naiads who were drawn to his beauty. While in Thoecritus' story another Naiad, Nomia, blinded her husband Daphnis for his unfaithfulness.

Do some yoga

River Thames, Wallingford Bridge, Wallingford ... May (49)

... After work today, I went down beside the river in Wallingford. One of the good things about working in the water industry is that our clients' offices are often near water. Although the Thames at Wallingford runs close to the busy town centre, I have found it is really easy to escape just a step away from the footpath. If you drop down the river bank just one metre, to one of the many fishermen's stances, you are cut off from the passing multitudes. I could still hear people, on their lunch breaks, jogging past and chatting, their feet level with my head, but I was in my own little world, screened off by the alder trees on either side and the grasses growing up the bank. I had just enough room to sit for a while and then do my reviving yoga sequence. It just hits the spot, a full body stretch that is relaxing and revitalising. Only the cows on the far bank gave me a few bemused looks as they lazily chewed the cud ...

Do some yoga

Yoga aims to enable us to experience a greater harmony with ourselves and the world. The natural environment as a setting, with the background sights and sounds of water and river therefore complements these aims perfectly.

SURYA NAMASKAR – THE SUN SALUTATION

The sun salutation is a classic yoga sequence that invigorates and energises. It is often used at the start of a yoga session but is a great sequence to salute the day and get you going at the riverbank – maybe before you launch in to the water?

The sequence is repeated twice in each set alternating between the left and right foot leading. For the full benefit you should try to complete three sets.

❶ Stand, hands in prayer pose
❷ Stretch arms overhead, palms touching.
❸ Bend forward from the hips, rest hands on shins, ankles or toes depending on flexibility.

④ Bring palms flat on floor (bending knees if necessary). Extend left leg back, knee resting on floor, right knee at right angle. Bring right foot back to join left foot (plank pose).

⑤ Lift hips to ceiling to form downward facing dog. Then, bend arms, lower hips and curve body upwards, knees and hips on floor (the cobra).

⑥ Repeat in reverse until you are back in prayer pose.

⑦ Repeat extending right leg back first in number 4.

⑧ Repeat instructions 1 to 7 through two more complete cycles.

Why not try...

anywhere with a peaceful setting where you can be by the river with your own thoughts.

River Barle, Wheal Eliza, Simondsbath, Exmoor **(4)**

River Itchen, Winchester St Cross and College, Hampshire **(21)**

River Thames, Duxford, Oxfordshire **(45)**

River Stour, Sudbury, Suffolk **(57)**

River Ant, How Hill, Ludham, Norfolk **(65)**

River Windrush, Minster Lovell Hall, Oxfordshire **(73)**

River Lugg, Lugg Meadows, Hereford, Herefordshire **(78)**

River Llugwy, Swallow Falls, Betws-y-Coed, Wales **(82)**

River Skirfare, Arncliffe Church, Yorkshire Dales **(90)**

River Rothay, Rothay Park, Ambleside, Lake District **(106)**

(x) numbers relate to site listings in the resources section.

Make a sculpture

Grizedale Beck, Grizedale Forest, Lake District ... October (109)

... We are now all mini Andy Goldsworthys. We spent the day making land art alongside the river in Grizedale Forest. Being autumn there was an abundance of brightly coloured fallen leaves in a myriad of shapes and shades of colour which we used creatively in our sculptures. My daughter Anousha and nieces Hannah and Rachael coated a river rock in damped down copper beech leaves. The bright red rock stood out brilliantly mid-stream as the iron-grey water ran smoothly past. Duncan and Poppy and Thea made a great spiral of leaves descending from a tree trunk. The spiral showed a whole rainbow of autumn leaves, the different colour bands merged into each other along the length of the spiral. Ruth made what looked like a great yellow centipede along a long branch with the leaves fixed together by threading each stalk through the subsequent leaf, while Mark and Jacob made a big manly sculpture from fallen branches which looked rather like the skeletal hull of a boat, propped between two upright trees ...

How to make a sculpture

Look at your surroundings with an artist's eye to get your creative juices flowing. Be alert to the colours and textures, light and darkness; search out the movements of the wind and how the plants move around you as you pass through.

Using nothing but the natural materials from the riverbank and bed available throughout the seasons you can make wonderful temporary works of art.

Explore the margins of the river and see what nature has provided. Use river-washed stones, bright autumn leaves, empty snail shells, twigs stripped of bark, sticky river bank mud and clay and any other available flotsam and jetsam to create a work of art. Take inspiration from your surroundings and the work of other land artists (see box). You may want to recreate the patterns you observe in nature – criss-crossing tree branches, a spiralling spider's web or unfurling fern fronds. Or you may want to create otherworldly beings or structures: fairy homes and alien monsters. You can create something beautiful in just a few minutes and leave it to change and decay as time and weather take their toll.

You can use many of nature's resources in so many ways but the following will give you some ideas to get you started:

● Link together leaves of different colours and shades and shapes by poking the stem through a hole in the leaf.

Use river-washed stones, bright autumn leaves, empty snail shells, twigs stripped of bark, river bank mud and clay and other flotsam and jetsam to create your own work of art.

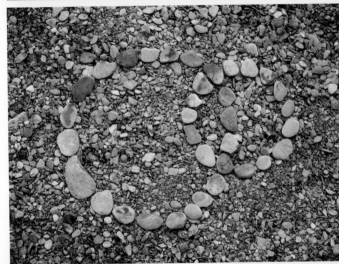

- Coat a rock in dampened leaves.
- Use the riverbed clay as glue to join leaves or pine cones to fallen branches.
- Use the spikes from gorse or blackthorn to join rushes in spirals and fix leaves together.
- Select smooth stones to make stone towers.
- Make stone spirals on a bed of moss.
- Fill an eddy with stripped twigs.
- Make patterns with stripped twigs, flower heads... the list is endless.

Getting your hands cold and dirty, feeling the different textures of mud, leaves, stones and

Why not try...

rivers with lots of natural resources.

River Barle, Landacre Bridge, Exmoor (3)

River Beaulieu, Longwater Lawn, New Forest (14)

River Adur, Shermanbury to Wineham, West Sussex (26)

Pooh Sticks Bridge, Ashdown Forest, Hartfield, East Sussex (31)

River Mole, Norbury Park, Leatherhead, Surrey (35)

River Lugg, Lugg Meadows, Hereford, Herefordshire (78)

River Usk, Crickhowell, Wales (80)

River Skirfare, Littondale, Yorkshire Dales (89)

River Derwent, Grange, Lake District (103)

Yewdale Beck, under Raven Crag, Coniston, Lake District (107)

(x) numbers relate to site listings in the resources section

The land art movement

THERE IS A GROWING BAND OF ARTISTS WHO HAVE ESCHEWED THE STUDIO AND WORK OUT IN NATURE USING ONLY NATURE'S BOUNTY. ARTISTS SUCH AS ANDY GOLDSWORTHY, MARTIN HILL, NILS UDO, RICHARD SHILLING AND MARC POUYET ARE AMONG THE WELL-KNOWN LAND ARTISTS WORKING TODAY. HAVE A LOOK AT THEIR BOOKS AND WEBSITES TO INSPIRE YOU FURTHER EITHER BEFORE OR AFTER YOU HAVE HAD A GO. IF YOU WANT SOME MORE IDEAS OF THE MATERIALS YOU CAN USE AND THE ART YOU CAN MAKE, TAKE A LOOK AT WWW.RICHARDSHILLING.CO.UK – THIS IS HIS LAND ART WEBSITE WHICH INCLUDES LINKS TO THE OTHER GREAT LAND ARTIST WEBSITES.

thorns will bring you fully into contact with your river and its environs. You will feel closer and more connected with your river than if you just watch it as a tourist. The sense of achievement as you create a work of art and the satisfaction as you leave it, in the knowledge that it will return ultimately and undamagingly to the river, is rounding. Your sculpture may last a few seconds or for days. If you are able, it can be fun to return over time, to photograph it and see how the wild world has treated it and how the colours and shapes have changed.

Remember to take a camera to record your artwork for posterity so you can enjoy the memory of the experience and your creativity for longer.

Peer off a bridge

River Windrush ... March

... We've started a new job on the River Windrush, a beautiful
tributary of the Thames and today we drove over the catchment with
the client, to have a look at sites of interest and discuss the project. It was a
great chance to peer off bridges and get an overview of the river.

Unfortunately, today I felt very queasy. I am about ten weeks into my, as yet
undeclared, pregnancy and in a permanent state of travel sickness. The only
way to keep it in check is to eat. Like Paddington Bear I find marmalade
sandwiches just about do the trick. Every time we stopped to have a closer look
at the river, inevitably at a bridge crossing, I laid my head on the bridge
parapet. The cool stones of the bridge as I looked down into the flowing water
rebalanced me. From here I was then able to pass on my pearls of wisdom in a
coherent manner. I hope the client wasn't too concerned ...

Why not try...

any river crossing on any river!

River Teign, Fingle Bridge, Devon **(11)**

River Itchen, Martyr Worthy, Hampshire **(20)**

River Mole, Box Hill Stepping Stones, Surrey **(34)**

River Thames, Chimney Meadows, Oxfordshire **(44)**

River Thames, Abingdon, Oxfordshire **(47)**

Lower River Thames bridges through London **(55)**

River Stour, Dedham, Essex **(56)**

River Lune, Devils Bridge, Kirby Lonsdale, Yorkshire Dales **(88)**

River Wharfe, Loup Scar, Yorkshire Dales **(94)**

Cald Beck, St Mungo's Well, Caldbeck **(97)**

(x) numbers relate to site listings in the resources section

Follow any watercourse for a distance and before long you will come across some kind of bridge. Similarly, if you drive or cycle around the countryside it will not be long before you find yourself crossing a river on a bridge. Bridges are marked on all Ordnance Survey maps – footbridges as double black lines and a road bridge as parallel black lines with angled lines off them.

Bridges provide a wonderful vantage point from which you can observe all river life. With little effort or risk of getting wet you transport yourself to the middle of the river and get a different view of stream life. Staring over the edge into the reflections below is as absorbing as staring into flames.

HAVE A LOOK   Whenever you cross a bridge try to stop and take a moment to peer in; all river life is concentrated around the crossing points and whether it is bridge-jumping, kayaking, fishing, wildlife or ever changing reflections you will see all sorts of things to lift your mood. You may even discover, standing on the bottom rung of the bridge, that suddenly, like Winnie the Pooh, you know everything there is to be known.

As you look at the water surface you will start to see through the reflections and pick out the fish life. On the water there is often a bit of a duck soap opera to watch. Bridges provide a great focal point on a walk with children. Re-enacting the 'Three Billy Goats Gruff' trip-trapping across has always been a favourite of ours and there is always Pooh Sticks (see page 67).

BRIDGES AT BOUNDARIES   Since rivers form a natural barrier, they have historically formed territorial boundaries, and still do. Because the river was the boundary the bridges and fords were strategically important as the places most vulnerable to attack. Fortifications are often still visible near bridges and fords throughout the country to protect these territories. Heron were once thought of as being bad luck, for the very reason that because they hunt in shallow water, invaders seeing a heron hunting would know that they had found a possible fording place where they could progress their attack.

As you travel around consider how many river boundaries you cross every day. Without the bridges you would have to travel huge distances zigzagging around whole catchments to get from one place to another.

Many cultures believe that a river forms the barrier between the worlds of the living and the dead. In Greek mythology, rivers flow over and around, as well as under the earth. The River Styx – the best known of the rivers of Hell, had to be crossed before the deceased's wandering soul could find rest in the afterlife. People were often buried with money to pay the ferryman Charon so they could progress to the afterlife.

In the earliest known written story, the Babylonian epic of Gilgamesh, Gilgamesh rowed across the waters of death to the mouth of all rivers in search of immortality. He never achieved this goal and his body was ultimately buried beneath the waters of the Euphrates. Polynesian souls must swim or canoe a gulf to reach their afterlife, while the Karen of Burma's ghosts must find their graves beyond rivers.

In England, near Stonehenge in Wiltshire, recent excavations have exposed a Neolithic village within which is a woodhenge. From this wooden circle an avenue leads down to the River Avon. There are theories that the dead were floated onto the waters, in the manner of Hindu rituals on the Ganges in India, and then possibly taken from the river to Stonehenge for burial.

The river also represents a barrier in the mythical world. It is a central theme in English legends that faeries would not dare cross holy water or running water. It was believed that they were repelled by water and so crossing a river would keep you safe from the 'little people'.

Search for sacred springs

Swallowhead Springs, River Kennet, Avebury ... May (16)

... I am working on the River Kennet, carrying out plant surveys that can only be done in summer when the plants are growing and flowering. Today I set off especially early to have a look at the Swallow Head Springs that feed into the River Kennet. Approaching the car park the truncated cone mound of Silbury Hill rose out of nowhere through the early morning mists. No-one really knows why it was built but it probably dates from around 2500BC. I walked along the dew-laden path leaving a clear trail behind me. To my left the view was sharply divided into three colour bands; duck-egg clear blue sky, bright new spring leaf green and the vibrant yellow of the rape field. To the right the top of the mystical mound floated above the layer of early morning mist.

When I reached the springs it sent a tingle down my spine. They join the main flow on a sharp corner by some old stepping-stones. People come on pilgrimage leaving an array of offerings from flowers, pots and jars to slightly macabre plastic dolls. These lie around the base of the old willow tree which bears many ribbons and strips of material in its branches.

In the past it was thought that spring waters had magical powers and they were celebrated for their healing properties. The range of ailments treated ranged from warts and infertility to eyesight problems, broken bones, rheumatism and deafness. The rags at were often torn from the clothing of the afflicted, dipped in the water and tied to the tree or bush. As the rag rotted away, the ailment declined, until both rag and ailment were completely gone ...

Why not try...

exploring your river's sacred past?

Cald Beck, St Mungo's Well, Caldbeck, Lake District **(97)**

Coventina's Well, North Tyne, Chesters Fort, Northumberland **(115)**

Alsia's Well, St Buryan, Cornwall **(116)**

Flaxley Brook, Wizards Well, Alderley Edge, Cheshire **(117)**

St Dyfnog's Well, Llanhaedr, North Wales **(118)**

St Seriol's Well, Porth Penmon, Angelsey **(119)**

River Skell, Robin Hood's Well, Fountains Abbey, Yorkshire **(120)**

(x) numbers relate to site listings in the resources section

In the days before water was piped clear and sparkling directly into our homes, considerable effort was required to gather water for daily life. Imagine the impact, in those days, of coming across a spring of clear water bubbling up from the ground. It is easy to see how those springs became spiritual gateways linked to deities and magical beings, their waters attributed with great powers which have since been revered and celebrated.

Early pastoral settlers worshipped the springs for the fertility they brought to the land. With the Roman occupation of Britain, Celtic goddesses were replaced by their Roman counterparts. A good example of this is evident at Coventina's well at Brocilitia on Hadrian's Wall. Coventina was a Celtic goddess but the Romans enclosed the well in a temple where Coventina is depicted as a nymph in the well carvings. Later, the Christian church discouraged this worshipping of false gods, however, Christian missionaries often rededicated the sacred springs to Christian saints which then became the focus of Christian pilgrimages.

At some unmarked springs it is still possible to find rags hanging in the trees and find offerings of shells, feathers and notes. The gifts were and are still left to appease the spirits or deities presiding over the springs.

WELL DRESSINGS At some of the more developed springs there are formal well dressing ceremonies. Well dressing originates from those early times when the spirits of the spring were given gifts so that they would allow the water to flow, ensuring a good harvest. The Romans then introduced the festival of Fontinalia, dedicated to Fontus – the God of the springs. The Christian church discouraged this but once the springs were rededicated to saints the traditions slowly returned. Modern dressings often include a religious-themed picture made out of petals and pulses. These adorn the well for a week, amidst festivities along with Christian services and blessings.

Some spring waters have particular mineral properties, natural heat or effervescence. The therapeutic benefits of these waters became famous towards the end of the seventeenth century and into the eighteenth century. This was the heyday of the spa towns, several famous spas are still open for visits today including: Droitwich, Royal Tunbridge Wells, Harrogate, Bath, Malvern, Buxton, Royal Leamington Spa and Cheltenham.

Soak your feet

Goredale Beck, Yorkshire Dales ... May (84)

... It has been raining heavily for a few days and the rivers are high, but today was a perfect spring day. Amidst clear blue skies, Goredale Beck high up on the moor was stunning. A bubbling bouncing brook, it is unusual in these parts as it doesn't have the usual peaty orange, 'permatan' colouring to the water. The water was clear, and flowing over the limestone bedrock, sparkled in the sunlight. After walking and scrambling up on the moor for a couple of hours I came down to the edge of the Beck before it jumps off Goredale Scar in its dramatic waterfall. Here the beck falls down a series of rock chutes making a whole chain of perfect, Jacuzzi-style pools.

I didn't feel quite brave enough for the full dip, but my feet were cramped and sweaty, having been in boots all day so I released them and dunked them into a perfect bubbling foot spa. In amongst the champagne bubbles it was achingly cold and I could only hold them in there for a couple of minutes before they were screaming to come out. After just a couple of dips I was quite happy to put them back into thick socks and boots. I felt refreshed and energised, as if I was floating on air when I walked on ...

Why not try...

cooling, accessible streams, possibly on long walks.

River Barle, Tarr Steps, Exmoor **(1)**

Hoar Oak Water, Brendan Two Gates, Exmoor **(7)**

Becka Brook, Becky Falls, Dartmoor **(12)**

Tillingbourne, Abinger Hammer, Surrey **(36)**

River Conwy, Fairy Glen, Beyws-y-coed, Wales **(81)**

River Aire, Newfield Bridge, Gargrave, Yorkshire Dales **(85)**

River Caldew, Swineside, Mosedale, Lake District **(98)**

Yewdale Beck, low Tilberthwaite, Lake District **(108)**

River Rawthay, Sedburgh, Cumbria **(111)**

North Tyne, Chesters Fort, Hadrian's Wall, Northumberland **(115)**

(x) numbers relate to site listings in the resources section

The champagne bubbles of the Beck were achingly cold and I could only hold my feet in the water for a couple of minutes. But when I went on I was walking on air.

Have a picnic

Easdale Beck, Lake District ... August (104)

... Driving up to our holiday cottage in Easdale, nestling under the dark mass of Helm Crag we couldn't believe our luck. Having had a week of rain we arrived to clear blue skies, deep luxurious riverside grass, a sparkling brook bouncing away merrily, artistically dividing the lush green water meadows from the austere craggy mountains and the frothing white of Sour Milk Gill: drama and beauty in one vista. We were too early to get into the house so we took a short muddy walk through a kissing gate and over wobbling stepping-stones. It brought us to the picturesque slate stone bridge and thick grass alongside the rushing beck. With picnic blanket spread out and food available to all, everyone found their own niche; balanced on the wide stone parapet overlooking the stream, immersed in the long grass watching the view, cradled in the low branches of the stream-side alder or stretched out on towels and blankets. Bread and hunks of cheese never tasted so good. And then we had an afternoon of duck racing, exploring, dragonfly hunting and paddling provided the perfect antidote to a week in the rain ...

How to find the perfect picnic spot

What makes the perfect picnic often comes down to location, location, location. A riverside meadow with deep soft grass is perfect on a summer's day. The trick is finding it. There are tips on finding your perfect picnic location in 'Finding your river' (pages 7–14). So, have a look at the map before you go to see what your options are.

Pay particular attention to the direction that the river flows and the shape and direction of the bank slopes. Think about wind direction as well as what you will be looking at and who will be looking at you, as these will all have an impact on the quality of your picnic spot.

PERFECT PICNIC FOOD

The picnic itself can be as elaborate or as simple as you wish. Take a camp stove and cook up some pasta with a tin of tuna. Forage for wild foods or take a romantic hamper and use the river as your natural cooler. Anything packed into watertight containers can be kept cool at the edge of the river. Just remember to make sure the containers really are watertight and wedge or tether items if the flow is high or the food light.

Picnics are a great way to feed groups of friends in a large informal gathering. Everyone brings their own bits and pieces to throw in to the mix, there is no worrying over mess and food quantities and who will eat what.

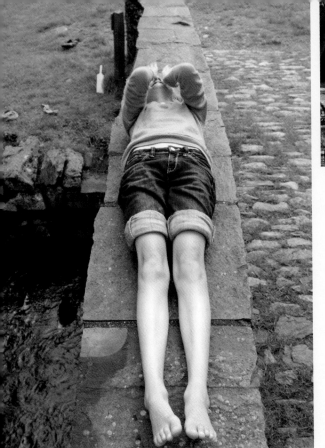

The perfect picnic is dependent on the perfect location. Check the slope of the river bank, the way the river flows and the direction of the wind before you go.

It's a cliché but food really does taste better in the fresh air, particularly after a walk, run around or swim.

Probably the most useful picnic equipment we have is our picnic rug. The tartan rug with waterproof underside is the first thing to go into the bag on a day out, one of the most well-used and long-lived wedding presents ever. Its presence ensures that the most serendipitous picnics will be carried out with dry bottoms and in the event of unplanned rain it can be turned upside down and immediately converts into a waterproof shelter.

The food you take is really a personal preference and we tend to go through phases, fluctuating between Tupperware boxes filled with pasta creations, to individually designated sandwiches or alternatively — for me the most perfect picnic — we just take some nice bread, a slab of cheddar cheese, tomatoes and a melon for a rustic meal. After a good yomp or play in the fresh air it beats fancy dining any time — and if you forget the knife you just tear it up! On other occasions it can be fun to take a camping stove and make lunch while you are there. Cook up some pasta, or hard-boiled eggs and brew up some tea, forage for wild garlic and sorrel to supplement the eggs and water mint for the tea — it doesn't have to be elaborate but it can still be tasty and fun.

COOL WEATHER PICNICS

Picnics don't just have to be for the lazy, hazy days of summer; however, if you are not going to take a stove always think about filling a thermos. A picnic in the cold can be great fun as you huddle up, wrapped in the picnic blanket, to keep warm while a cup of hot chocolate or soup steaming gently can make the day.

Of course there are times when you want to be more romantic or make special plans and cook up a gourmet feast. Whatever your plans the food will have to be transported either pre- or post cooking so think carefully about what you plan to serve up.

Foods that travel well include:
- Whole cooked chicken or wings or legs
- A cooked gammon joint
- Pork pies and pasties
- Filled breads — make your bread dough, roll it out and layer on your choice of filling then roll the dough to enclose the filling. Bake as usual. Fillings such as chorizo, bacon, cheese,

pine nuts, onion and tomato all work well.
- Any pasta salad all bundled together – the bonus here is that it doesn't matter how much the container is buffeted.
- Soups hot and cold in a food thermos – when my children were very small and still in backpacks, we would just take this with a slab of bread and we were done.
- Whole melon – don't forget the knife.
- Fruit salad – like the pasta salad as long as you have a tightly sealed plastic container it doesn't matter how much it gets jumbled around.
- Good hearty biscuits tend to survive better than cake – but a nice slab of cake is lovely eaten outside. Just make sure it is well-wedged into its container otherwise you will just be eating crumbs.

The picnic is almost a pre-requisite of any day out by the river and all the activities in this book will blend perfectly with a picnic either as appetisers or aperitifs. There are other activities that, while not strictly river related, also go hand in hand with a good riverside picnic. They need little introduction or description but include:

- Making daisy chains
- Cloud watching
- Catching butterflies (particularly if you already have your pond net handy)
- Lying in the long grass
- Hide and seek in the long grass
- Straw or grass sucking
- Searching for four leafed clover
- Leap frog.

Why not try...

good banks for sitting and relaxing.

River Barle, Landacre Bridge, Exmoor **(3)**

River Dart, Deeper Marsh, Dartmoor **(10)**

River Lymington, Balmer Lawn, Brockenhurst, New Forest **(13)**

Tillingbourne, Abinger Hammer, Surrey **(36)**

River Wey, Tilford, Surrey **(39)**

River Bure, Buxton and Lammas, Norfolk **(64)**

River Wye, Wilton Bridge, Ross-on-Wye, Herefordshire **(70)**

River Lugg, Lugg Meadows, Hereford, Herefordshire **(78)**

River Aire, Newfield Bridge, Gargrave, Yorkshire Dales **(85)**

River Caldew, Swineside, Mosedale, Lake District **(98)**

(x) numbers relate to site listings in the resources section

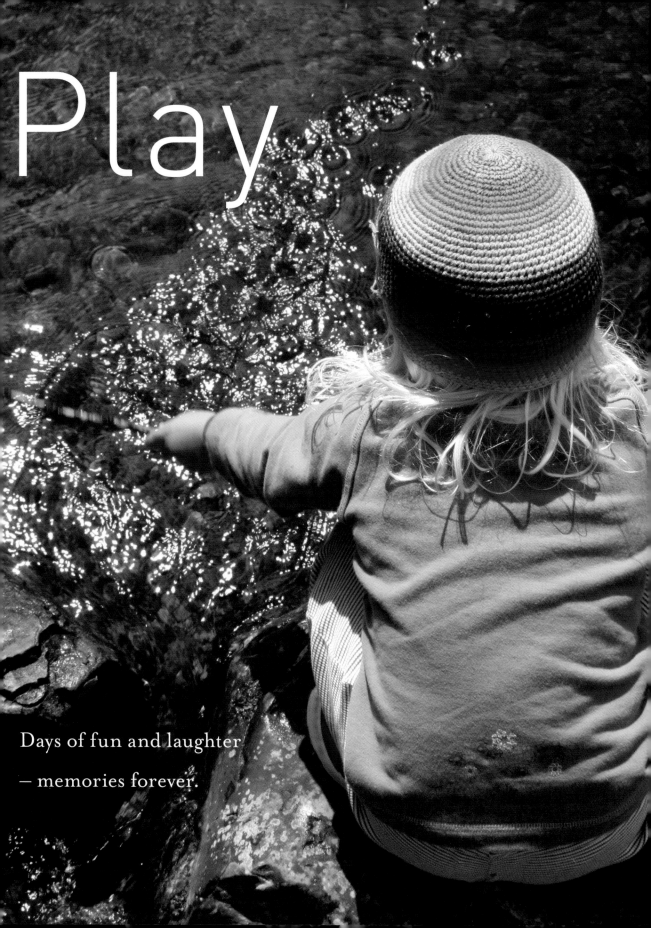

Play

Days of fun and laughter
— memories forever.

Words and games

Becka Brook, Dartmoor ... October (12)

… Walking back from the stream today, Anousha suddenly spotted two trees that made the letter 'A'. They were in an ancient hedge and apart, they didn't look anything special, but they merged as we went past and combined to make a rather spiky 'A'. This set us off on a game where we had to spot the letters of the alphabet in our surroundings. With a bit of artistic licence it was surprisingly easy, using mostly the hedgerow, trees, gates and farmyard, we were able to get the whole alphabet. This 'i' in the tree trunk was truly inspirational (below).

We play a lot of word games as we walk. It is a good way to take your mind off tired legs and it often ends in hilarity. Sitting back beside a river when you are done with playing or contemplating is another great time to play some word games — writers and poets the world over have been inspired by the river — from Wordsworth to Burns to Shelley and Iris Murdoch so give it a go and see if you find your creative mojo …

Some word games

There are thousands of word games but these are a few of our favourites:

Two word stories This is best played with a small group. The first player starts a story but with just two words. The next player adds to the story with their two words and so it goes on, the story grows but never in the way you expected when you made your contribution.

One day I went to the river and in my bag I put … The first person repeats the phrase and adds something that goes in the bag beginning with A. The next person repeats the phrase with the object beginning with A and adds something beginning with B. This process repeats until all the alphabet has been done or the players

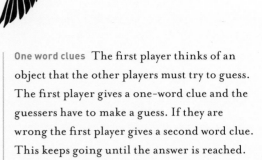

Why not try...

walks that may need some additional distraction.

can no longer remember the sequence. Make this more difficult by adding an adjective to your object but beginning with the same letter, for example: for E it could be Eerie Eggplants. You can even make it into a whole sentence for example Eerie Eggplants making Echoes.

Number gibberish / alliteration The first person says One... and adds an adjective and noun starting with O, the next person repeats the first phrase and follows on with Two... and adds an adjective and noun beginning with T. Keep going up through the numbers and go on as long as you can remember the sequence. For example: One orange orang-utan, two tweeting turtles, three thirsty throngs and so on until you run out of memory.

One word clues The first player thinks of an object that the other players must try to guess. The first player gives a one-word clue and the guessers have to make a guess. If they are wrong the first player gives a second word clue. This keeps going until the answer is reached. For example, if the word is DOG – clue 1 is hairy, clue 2 animal, clue 3 barks and so on.

Chuckle The aim of the game is not to laugh. The first person turns to his neighbour and says 'Ha!', she then turns to her neighbour and says 'Ha! Hee!', he turn to his neighbour and says 'Ha!Hee!Ha!'. Silly voices and facial expressions should be employed to try to make other players laugh and anyone who can't resist a chuckle is out. The last man standing is the winner.

Fortunately / unfortunately The aim of this game is simply to tell a story one sentence at a time. The first player introduces the story with a sentence: play progresses with each person adding a sentence in turn; each player starts their sentence alternately with 'fortunately' or 'unfortunately' so that the story progresses through a series of disasters and happy coincidences. For example: Player one says: One day a boy went for a walk. Player two adds: Unfortunately he fell into a deep dark chasm. Player three adds: Fortunately there was a big trampoline in the bottom and he bounced straight out again. Person four: Unfortunately an eagle was flying past and grabbed him in its talons. Person five: Fortunately the boy was too heavy and it dropped him into a soft haystack... and so on, the more outrageous the better.

Build channels and dams

Yewdale Beck, Below Eagle Crag, Lake District ... October(107)

… We arrived today to find some great stone towers that a previous visitor had made, just asking to be worked on. Diggory got settled in to making channels and dams, while the girls went boulder-hopping upstream. The Beck at this point is perfect for dam and channel construction. It has a shallow, wide channel that is already quite braided, there is a vast supply of rocks and stones perfect for moving around. Diggory was the main protagonist but all the adults and some of the other children joined in at one time or another, moving stones to make a smooth flowing set of channels. Testing with log boats, refining bits where the boat had faltered until the perfect canal system had been worked out – and we hadn't even noticed how cold our hands were …

Building channels and dams

Hours of fun can be had in even the smallest of trickles: in fact the smallest of streams or very shallow braided streams generally make the best locations for channel building.

It seems to be a human instinct to create dams. Watch a child beside a small stream and before long they have created a wall of stones across the water to hold back the flow and create a pond. Keep watching as they break down the wall and watch the water flood away. Moving around stones of all shapes and sizes to contain and control the water can be so satisfying; it is quite easy to see why engineers still aspire to the construction of large-scale dams and canals.

As you link bits of flow with pools of dammed water the river sediment mixes in so that you end up with sections of fast and slow flowing water with the swirling effect of the sediment-laden currents making interesting swirls and eddies as it seeks to reach its equilibrium. Use small logs as 'boats' to test the waterways and see how they require alterations to keep the 'boat' moving smoothly. Whole days can be whiled away building and perfecting channels and testing them with small log boats. But don't be surprised if a big, hairy, over-enthusiastic dog comes along and trashes them.

Add to the complexity of your engineering works by taking a length of hosepipe with you. You can move the water from one pool over obstructions and into another pool or containers by creating siphons. As long as the point where it flows out of the tube is downhill from where it went in you can move the water where you want and open up a whole new set of options.

HOW TO MAKE A SIPHON

❶ Take a length of hosepipe or other plastic tubing. Any length can work but 1 to 3 metres is probably most manageable.

It seems to be a human instinct to create dams. A child playing by a stream will create a wall of stones to hold back the flow of the water and make a pond.

❷ Fill the tube entirely with water. This can be done by fully submerging the tube and waiting for all the air to be replaced by water — you can see the bubbles of air escaping and when they stop you know the job is done. Another way to achieve this is by sucking the water through the tube. Consider the cleanliness of the water before you use this technique as it is hard to stop when the tube is full before getting at least some of it in your mouth.

❸ Once the tube is completely filled with water, with no airlocks, you can leave one end submerged in the pool of water and the water will continue to flow out of the tube as long as the outlet is lower than the inlet. The intermediate length of tube can go over the bank or stones to pour water into riverside mud parks or containers.

....

This technique is used quite regularly to empty tanks of fuel when there is no drain tap. We used to have a sailing dinghy with a waterproof cover on it that would sit outside our house on its trailer and fill with water between trips out sailing. Our early

morning entertainment on sailing days was setting up siphons to empty the water out of the cover and use it to water the nearby flowerbeds.

Endless hours of fun can be had with a river and combining some of these engineering techniques.

Why not try...

shallow water with a good supply of stones, and a gradient for siphons.

River Barle, Landacre Bridge, Exmoor **(3)**

Tillingbourne, Abinger Hammer, Surrey **(36)**

River Bure, Buxton and Lammas, Norfolk **(64)**

River Lugg, Lugg Meadows, Hereford, Herefordshire **(78)**

River Aire, Newfield Bridge, Gargrave **(85)**

River Derwent, Grange, Lake District **(103)**

Yewdale Beck, Low Tilberthwaite, Lake District **(108)**

Grizedale Beck, Grizedale Forest, Lake District **(109)**

River Coquet, Linshiels, Northumberland **(114)**

(x) numbers relate to site listings in the resources section.

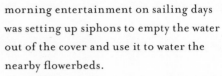

Badgeworthy Water, Cloud Farm, Exmoor ... July (6)

... Badgeworthy is a great stream to play in. Large enough to have a nice noise and great wildlife but not so big that you can't have fun on it. Large boulders in the channel add to the interest and the water flows at a good pace, verging on white water. From where we are camping we can wade across the stream to get to the woods and on up to the moor on the other side and we can throw our shoes over the water so we have our hands free as we wade across – although I have already lost one shoe in the water that way – luckily, along with the flip flop and picnic bowl, it wedged downstream waiting to be retrieved.

We've been making water wheels today. We did cheat a bit as we used a large wodge of plasticine I found sticking to some toys in the bottom of the car as the hub. We found five forked sticks, stuck them into the plasticine hub and then a long thin stick that we pushed right through the centre of the hub as the axle. Just like that and balanced between two convenient rocks it actually turned. We tried refining it a bit by peeling the bark off the sticks and lacing large leaves onto the forked sticks but it didn't make much difference. The girls were most sceptical when we started, so it was very satisfying that it worked so easily ...

HOW TO MAKE A RUSTIC WATER WHEEL
Making water wheels with just the materials you find on the river bank is easily manageable with a bit of searching around for the right twigs. Unless, like me, you find a handy lump of plasticine for your hub, you will probably need a penknife to be successful.

There are all sorts of designs for water wheels but we will keep it simple and go for the most basic, rustic design.

❶ Find an old branch at least 15cm long and the girth of your wrist to be your hub

❷ Cut six slits evenly spaced around the circumference of the hub.

❸ Find six forked sticks that, cut or broken to a similar length, will act as the paddles of the wheel. Sharpen the unforked end of the sticks and push them into the slits cut in the hub.

❹ Find bearings on which the water wheel will balance and be able to turn. The bearings may be either two handy rocks with a good flow of water between them, or alternatively find two more sturdy forked sticks to push in to the stream bed: the forked end will act as the bearings.

❺ Taper the ends of the hub and balance it on the bearings to get a reasonably smooth turn between the two wooden surfaces. Alternatively drive nails in to the ends of the hub to balance on the bearings. This will give better

Making water wheels using only items found at the river's edge needs a little searching for the right twigs and branches. Keep it simple and go for basic, rustic designs.

Once you have established the basic construction there are lots of different techniques and designs you can use to customise and perfect your water wheel. For a very simple, more temporary water wheel, try cardboard paddles stuck into an empty toilet roll tube, with your fingers sticking into the ends of the tube as the bearings. It doesn't last long in the water but it is quick and easy and amazingly satisfying as it works perfectly well.

You can also make a very simple nailed together version if you take some nails with you or make it at home. A square wooden shaft with four board paddles nailed on each side works very well (see illustration left).

TESTING YOUR WATER WHEEL

Once you have made your water wheel the best stream on which to test run your models will have a moderate water speed, to overcome any friction in your highly engineered system. The ideal channel on which to test it is a rocky fast flowing stream with a reasonable gradient where there are thin channels of good flow between rocks that are conveniently spaced to support the axle of the water wheel. If you don't have this convenient set-up then it is possible to spend many happy hours altering the flow in your stream to create the perfect channel, much as would have been done in the full size mill system in the creation of mill leats. Even quite a slow flowing stream will have enough power to drive a simple water wheel. To make the most of the energy in the slow flowing water your water wheel may need much bigger paddles and a smoother construction to eliminate friction.

movement as having different materials between axle and bearing produces less friction and therefore a smoother motion. If the flow is sufficient the wheel should turn but for greater efficiency fix pieces of leaf, paper or foil to the forked paddles to catch more water.

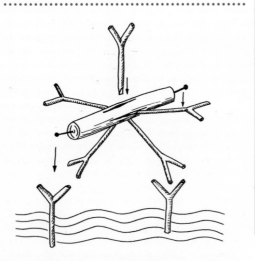

Why not try...

rivers with a good supply of materials and flowing water to make the wheels turn.

Horner Water, Horner, Exmoor **(5)**

River Dart Country Park, Ashburton, Dartmoor **(9)**

Becka Brook, Becky Falls, Bovey Tracey, Dartmoor **(12)**

Beaulieu River, Beaulieu, New Forest **(15)**

River Adur, Shermanbury to Wineham, West Sussex **(26)**

Pooh Sticks Bridge, Hartfield, Ashdown Forest, East Sussex **(31)**

River Wey, Hankley Common, Surrey **(40)**

River Glaven, Letheringsett Mill, Holt, Norfolk **(67)**

River Teme, Leintwardine, Herefordshire **(77)**

River Rawthay, Sedburgh, Cumbria **(111)**

(x) numbers relate to site listings in the resources section.

Once you have mastered the basic water wheel construction you can get more and more elaborate as you grow in confidence. The finished product – a water wheel being driven round by the speed of the water – is immensely satisfying. Before you know it you'll be coupling your wheel to all sorts of devices and toys to make use of your new power source. You could combine your siphon to extract a small side flow of water which powers your wheel and then returns to the main flow.

WATER WHEELS IN ACTION

If you find you are becoming obsessed with water wheels you may want to go and see some full scale operating systems. While at the beginning of the 18th century there were an estimated 10,000 working water mills in the UK there are very few operational ones today. The website www.ukmills.com has a list of all the existing mills in the UK. Alternatively there are plenty of water mill remains dotted along the rivers throughout the country where you can piece together the channels and ponds that were created and used historically to operate the wheels.

Leatherhead Leisure Centre Cafe

... How many different versions of 'It' have you ever played? I've just had a coffee with some friends and we were talking about all the various versions of 'It' we have played over the years. There were also lots of places that 'It' had been played, including in the water but the winner was probably a friend who started a game on the steps up the Eiffel Tower which then caught the attention of a Japanese tour group who all joined in.

I don't know where the name 'It' comes from but it always makes me think of the E. Nesbit classic, *Five Children and It,* so I've drawn a picture of the 'It' in that book — I believe it is a sand fairy or Psammead, a mythical creature that E. Nesbit invented.

As a family we tend to break into impromptu games of 'It' wherever we are, often at most inappropriate times but also often when it is cold and people need warming up, breaking out of lethargy or just to be kept busy ...

'It' and all its variations

All of these games can also be played in the water, with the most successful games being 'it', 'stuck in the mud' and 'sinking lemons'. You will recognise many of these variations-on-a-theme from playground days.

'It' One person is 'it' until they tag someone at which point the 'itter' is free and the tagged person is 'it' and tries to tag someone else.

Water 'It' Using a water pistol or sports top water bottle a person must be squirted to be 'it'. Pass the bottle on to the new 'it'.

Home Players cannot be 'itted' if they are touching an agreed 'home'; only one person at a time is allowed on 'home'.

My Gang If 'itted' you join the 'itter's' gang so that there are now two 'itters'. This continues until just one person is left free — the winner. He/she starts the next game as 'it'.

Chain gang Once 'itted' you hold hands with the 'itter' until everyone has joined the chain — last one free is the winner.

Statues A number of people are designated as statues and must be stationary but are immune

Why not try...

rivers with open smooth banks for running around madly.

River Barle, Withypool, Exmoor **(2)**

River Dart, Deeper Marsh, Ashburton, Dartmoor **(10)**

Latchmore Brook, Ogdens, New Forest **(14)**

Tillingbourne, Abinger Hammer, Surrey **(36)**

River Wey, Tilford, Surrey **(39)**

River Thames, Lechlade, Gloucestershire **(42)**

River Stour, Sudbury, Suffolk **(57)**

River Ant, How Hill, Ludham, Norfolk **(65)**

River Windrush, Wash Meadow, Minster Lovell, Oxfordshire **(72)**

River Wharfe, Bolton Abbey, Yorkshire Dales **(91)**

(x) numbers relate to site listings in the resources section.

from being 'it'. Other players can get a rest from the game by tagging and changing places with a statue. The released statue can be 'itted'.

Stuck in the mud Once 'itted' you are stuck in the mud and must remain stationary until another player frees you by crawling through your legs. If all the players get stuck in the mud the 'itter' has won. This game transfers particularly well into the water where you swim under the stuck in the mud's legs to free them.

Sinking lemons The name is a mystery to me but the rules are similar to 'Stuck in the mud' but once 'itted' and therefore stuck, you gradually sink. The challenge for the other players is to tag you to release you before you reach the ground or water surface. Once you have sunk to the ground or under the water, in the water version, you are out.

The good thing about these games is that as everyone is moving all the time, there is no time to get cold.

Make miniature boats

Becka Brook, Dartmoor .. October (12)

... I am always buying packs of brightly coloured paper which then tend to sit around in drawers and boxes at home while everyone wonders what they are for. Well, today we found out. I have been reading about the water-loving poet Percy Bysshe Shelley, who apparently, when he lived on the banks of the River Elan in Wales, developed a passion for launching flotillas of paper boats. He would use whatever paper was to hand, often the pages torn from a book and make boat after boat after boat. He would launch them filled with a cargo of coins, watching entranced until they disintegrated and deposited their cargo on the riverbed.

Today we took out my stash of brightly coloured paper and folded a multi-coloured flotilla of paper boats. We made a little dam at the side of the river to hold the boats in so we could release them all at the same time. Each boat was given a cargo of a small stone to help it float upright in the water and was lovingly placed in the 'harbour'. We stationed ourselves down the river with pond nets for rescues and cameras for filming and then the dam was breached and the boats released.

The multi-coloured flotilla looked great as it was tossed and buffeted on its way down the stream; the boats were rapidly inundated as they went through some mini rapids so that only about half the fleet made it to the first pool. The spectacle didn't last long and the soggy jewels had to be salvaged from the river bed but it looked wonderful and was fun while it lasted ...

HOW TO MAKE MINIATURE BOATS

There is no right or wrong way to make a boat. They can be as simple or as complex as you like; our motto is: 'as long as it floats, it counts as a boat'. We have had entrants that consisted of an empty nutshell and a single leaf. When it comes to floating and racing they often turn out to be the winners; however, they may lose marks in the aesthetics category!

The secret to the best fun when making boats is to collect natural materials on your walk to the river. Remember to be adaptable, as your materials may not work the way you expect them to and you will have to alter your design ideas as you work. Some perfectionists may find this activity a challenge!

There is no right or wrong way to make a boat – we've used something as simple as a nutshell and a single leaf as well as more complex woven structures made from reeds.

Riverside grasses and rushes are great for weaving and tying twigs together to make the hull of your boat. You will quickly become expert at choosing the more flexible varieties and working out which are strongest — be careful with some of the grasses as they have sharp edges and can cut!

Large leaves like sweet chestnuts make great sails. Rose thorns as well as blackthorn and gorse spikes can all be used to fasten bits of your construction together.

Bits of bark and empty shells, twigs, can all be used in their entirety and work as a complete hull with no further construction required.

EMULATE FAMOUS BOAT BUILDERS OF THE PAST

Moses was famously set adrift in an ark or

basket made from bulrushes and daubed with clay. You could try this technique but I wouldn't launch your small child in it.

Loggers in Canada make great rafts out of the trunks of the trees they have felled and ride on them down the river until they reach the sawmills. Miniature rafts of this kind – twigs tied together with grasses and rushes – are one of my favourite constructions and work well.

The Norwegian sailor Thor Heyerdahl, built the 'Kontiki' of two balsa wood logs and sailed it across the Pacific Ocean. He built 'Ra' and 'Ra II', out of reeds and attempted to sail across the Atlantic from Morocco, reaching Barbados with 'Ra II'. Reeds grow on river margins throughout the UK and while you may not want to try a full-sized vessel, a miniature version could be good fun.

MAKE IT A CONTEST

The main aim of making boats is for enjoyment but you can turn it into a contest with judges and criteria on which the boats can be judged. All boats need to be launched in the water and involved in a race – the ultimate test. Criteria we have used for judging include:

Aesthetics Does it look nice? Has care been taken over the appearance?

Craftsmanship How refined is the weaving or any other skills employed.

Innovation Use of unusual materials, a novel approach to boat craft.

Floatability Does the boat float? Does it float upright? Can it carry a passenger – usually a small stone or similarly inert object?

Speed A straight head to head race usually finishes off the proceedings. Sometimes

entrants are so proud of their craft that they don't wish to risk it in the water, it is up to the judges as to how this is viewed, and marked.

I know some people like to make more professional constructions in the tool shed and extend their pleasure beyond the day at the river but that is akin to whittling and smoothing your entrant before playing Pooh sticks, an element of professionalism I'm not sure I can condone. That said, anything goes and you can make your own rules.

Why not try...

rivers with a good supply of materials and inspiration.

(x) numbers relate to site listings in the resources section.

Easdale Beck, Lake District ... July (104)

... We've just had a great day, helped by perfect weather and an idyllic setting. I brought all our duck supplies from home: we have a set of heat sensitive ducks which change colour with the water temperature, a Moroccan-style painted duck I was given for my birthday and a motley collection of standard issue yellow ducks in varying sizes. We started off with everyone launching their ducks off the bridge and then two catchers with nets were set to catch and identify the ducks at the finishing line. After the first race, everyone realised that the best fun was being in the river, retrieving ducks stuck in eddies or behind tree branches, dive bombing them with stones and water squirts from bottles and catching them with the pond nets and generally getting 'hands on'. By the end just one person was launching ducks when they were returned to the start; everyone else was in the river taking whatever role they fancied ...

Have races with anything that floats

Of course you don't need recognisable boats or plastic ducks for races. You can use anything that floats — it may be your miniature boats, just twigs or pine cones (along the lines of Pooh sticks), any plastic bath toys, half empty water bottles, picnic cups. Ducks are a classic and still my favourite. The sight of a flotilla of plastic ducks bobbing their way down the river is somehow immensely pleasurable.

A varied course with small waterfalls, eddies and straight fast sections all add to the interest; but races can take place in any stretch of flowing water. You can even rig up parallel sections of guttering in a garden to emulate a flowing river. Ensure your catcher(s) are ready at the finish line, with nets, if you are using ducks or anything you brought to the river!

PIRATES

If a straight race becomes too mundane then it's easy to spice it up a bit. Boat owners may be allowed to make attacks on other boats to hamper their progress. Piratical activities may include bombing opponents' ships with stones or trying to drown them with squirts from sports top water bottles or even water pistols.

There are lots of variations on this theme but try floating picnic glasses or plastic pots, with non-precious cargo on board, daisy or dandelion heads for example. The aim is to upset your opponents' cargo but for your own to reach the end intact. These contests can get dirty so do anticipate carnage and make sure no-one is going to get upset if the boats are completely destroyed.

Why not try...

nicely flowing streams accessible along the race length.

Hoar Oak Water, Brendan Two Gates, Exmoor **(7)**

Dockens Water, Linwood, New Forest **(13)**

Pooh Sticks Bridge, Hartfield, Ashdown Forest,East Sussex **(31)**

Tillingbourne, Abinger Hammer, Surrey **(36)**

Little Ouse, Santon Downham, Thetford, Norfolk **(58)**

Goredale Beck, Malham, Yorkshire Dales **(84)**

River Caldew, Swineside, Mosedale, Lake District **(98)**

Grizedale Beck, Grizedale Forest, Lake District **(109)**

River Rawthay, Sedburgh, Cumbria **(111)**

River Coquet, Linshiels, Northumberland **(114)**

(x) numbers relate to site listings in the resources section.

Water fights

Priory Park ... May

... Lottie and I took a picnic down to the park after playgroup today. We went down to the pond, to watch the birds, the dog walkers, the joggers and to have a relaxed munch. Lottie always finds some way to entertain me so it is never dull. Today a family walked past – a mum, two biggish boys and a toddler with a toy dog on wheels. One of the bigger boys flicked his water bottle half-heartedly at the other one who gave a hearty squirt from his own bottle. A volley of attacks followed with dodging behind mum, younger brother and trees, going on too. Suddenly the largest boy grabbed the toy dog off little brother, ran to the water and held the dog under the water for a few seconds. As he did so, he was soaked by his brother but only until he lifted up the saturated dog and started whirling it round, creating a large arc of sparkling water which reached right over his mother, big brother and baby brother, who all scattered screaming. I had to hold on to Lottie who was laughing so hard she nearly fell off the bench ...

How to get the most out of water fights

Water fights can take any form as long as you have some kind of technique by which the water can be sprayed at people. This can just be scooping the water with your hands direct from the river at your target or kicking the water with your feet. However, since part of the aim is usually to stay dry yourself and your target is likely to just run away from you at the water's edge then a mobile water source is by far the best – a bag with holes in it, sports top drink bottle, water pistols, cups, buckets, shoes. The most enjoyable water fight as far as I'm concerned is the impromptu soaking meted out on a scorching day when retaliation is inevitable and escalation occurs. There are times when a more planned approach is good and certain rules and more organised games can formalise a good old-fashioned soaking.

A particularly satisfying but challenging weapon is a real live dog. Persuade a dog into the water and then try to position it near your target as it goes for its post swim shake. Sunbathing or picnicking friends and relatives are ideal targets for this kind of ambush. There are of course risks associated with this kind of weapon; dogs are notoriously unreliable and frequently discharge before they are accurately located in the vicinity of the target. You will find that yourself as operative and innocent bystanders often do not come out of the attack well and are often hit by friendly fire. Dogs tend to be overexcited by the game and crumble under the pressure of expectation; a typical response is to start jumping, laughing and yelping, liberally

Why not try...

anywhere with space to run around, good access to the water and not too many people to upset.

River Barle, Landacre Bridge, Exmoor **(3)**

River Dart Country Park, Ashburton, Dartmoor **(9)**

Latchmore Brook, Ogdens, New Forest **(14)**

Cuckmere River, Cuckmere Meanders, Seaford, East Sussex **(29)**

River Thames, Duxford, Oxfordshire **(45)**

River Thames/Isis, Portmeadow, Oxford, Oxfordshire **(46)**

River Bure, Buxton and Lammas, Norfolk **(64)**

River Lugg, Lugg Meadows, Hereford, Herefordshire **(78)**

River Monnow, Skenfrith Castle, Monmouth, Monmouthshire, Wales **(79)**

River Aire, Newfield Bridge, Gargrave, Yorkshire Dales **(85)**

(x) numbers relate to site listings in the resources section.

spraying all and sundry with no distinction between their target and their operative.

SCORING GAMES

At the core of all water fights is the aim that the other person gets soaked while you stay dry. If you want some more organised games try:

At the end of a timed contest combatants are assessed in terms of relative wetness,

To assess wetness look for:

- Area of wetness on formerly dry clothes, or
- Players can have some kind of soluble target e.g. made out of tissue paper. The removal or destruction of this soluble target is the aim of the other players.
- If you trust the combatants, each player counts the number of direct hits and therefore points scored in a game, or

If hit then a player is out of the game for a fixed time say 20 seconds on the bench.

What counts as a direct hit is a matter for debate in most of these games but a fist-sized hit seems to be a standard measure, or else any contact with water other than just mist.

Games can be devised where teams are trying to reach their opponents' home without being hit. A direct hit means you are out of the game. The team that reaches their opponents' home first, wins.

A simple game of 'it' can be played where being hit with the water equates to being 'itted' as in normal 'It'.

All these games work well around the water but are most fun on a warm day or when warm dry conditions and spare clothes are available. Otherwise you risk a decline into misery when the adrenaline of the game wears off.

If you are ever stuck for games to play and you need some action then obstacle courses can be devised anywhere with a bit of imagination. Once you start you will find everyone joins in with ideas, without any encouragement.

Wet or dry the natural environment provides lots of potential for imaginative obstacle course setters. There may be stiles to climb over, fallen trees to balance on, or climb under, or over, branches to swing on, stepping stones to cross rivers on, small streams to leap. Have a look around and use your imagination, see what the opportunities are and how you can use the natural environment. Use the water as a hazard to be crossed or waded up for a section of the race; alternatively make it part of the requirement that each competitor must carry a cup full of water and not spill any, otherwise

they have to go back to the start of the course, or stand and count to five or ten as a time penalty.

It may be that part of the course incorporates filling a pot with water.

Each competitor or team has a pot or container to fill and a smaller pot or container with which to fill it e.g. kettle and spoon, saucepan and small cup. The large pot is placed some way away from the water and the competitors race backwards and forwards between the river and the pot to fill it using the smaller receptacle. If you can only muster one set of pot and filler then time how long it takes to fill or how much you can fill it in a given time. Add complexity by making a more challenging course to reach the river or adding obstacles – climbing over tree roots, under low

Why not try...

Smallish, complex rivers with interesting banks and open access on both banks.

Badgworthy Water, Malmesmead, Exmoor **(6)**

Becka Brook, Bovey Tracey, Dartmoor **(12)**

Dockens Water, Linwood, New Forest **(13)**

River Mole, Norbury Park, Leatherhead, Surrey **(35)**

River Waveney, Outney Common, Bungay, Suffolk **(61)**

Wellow Brook, Wellow, Bath, Somerset **(76)**

Styhead Gill, Seatwaite, Lake District **(99)**

Yewdale Beck, Tilberthwaite, Lake District **(107 and 108)**

Scandal Beck, Smardale Viaduct, Kirby Stephen, Cumbria **(110)**

North Tyne, Chesters Fort, Hadrian's Wall, Northumberland **(115)**

(x) numbers relate to site listings in the resources section.

branches etc. Adults may need to do it left handed or crawling, if playing with children.

Or each competitor starts with an empty cup, goes through the obstacle course with it empty, fills it from the river then has to negotiate the obstacles with it full to empty it in a pot before passing it on to the next player. First team to fill their pot is the winner or the team with the fullest pot after the whole team has had a turn is the winner.

Competitors can be timed on the course with the fastest time winning or it could be a team game with individuals doing a relay over the course in teams. Maybe passing the cup of water between racers like a baton.

There is no set formula for a good obstacle course — just use the available resources and your imagination and you will be fine.

Scavenger and treasure hunts

River Wey, Guildford ... June (38)

... Lottie and I met up with an old friend and her daughter today. We went for a nice walk down the River Wey in Guildford. It should have been lovely but the kids, for whatever reason, decided to be in conflict mode. Ali and I spent most of the time practising our mediation and distraction techniques. On the plus side, Lottie found a drake's tail feather. Who would have thought it? A perfectly formed curved over tail feather, so perfect in its formation that it is a little hard to believe. The mallard drake has just the two central tail feathers that have the curve of its trademark tail. One of those little miracles of nature that make your heart sing.

We brought it home and it is now sitting on my shelf of found treasures, along with the purest white swan's feather and a nattily spotted guinea fowl feather, dragonfly larvae cases and special stones: witches' ones with holes in, some with fossils and others that just look nice ...

Scavenger hunts

A scavenger hunt is a really good way of slowing you down and making you look a bit more closely at your surroundings.

Write out a list of things for the hunters to track down. The hunters either get the list or bring back each item when they have found it to be given the next thing to find. The objects that the hunters have to find may be very specific, such as 'a duck's feather' or they may be very general, such as 'something rough'. It could be a mix of both.

Another variation is to give a letter and the challenge is to find as many things as you can which start with that letter. Work your way through the alphabet or the letters of your name or the name of the river if you want to make a longer game.

The objects that you find in the scavenger hunt could be kept and taken home as the day's treasure to make a collage or to draw in a journal to help remember the day.

Treasure hunts

Devising and setting up treasure hunts as well as doing them can fill many happy hours. You probably have your own favourite way to do treasure hunts but a treasure hunt by the river is a great opportunity to have a really good look around and extend your enjoyment of the river environment for longer.

A simple treasure hunt may just be a map with an X marks the spot but the more challenges you have to overcome on the way to the treasure the better.

Try making a map with lots of Xs, each one

My shelf of treasures includes a mallard tail feather, a white swan's feather, a spotted guinea fowl feather, the cast cases of dragonfly larvae and many special stones.

with a clue which when they are all put together leads the hunters to the treasure.

You could have a bag of clues so the hunters follow one clue, find part of the treasure and come back for another clue for more treasure.

Alternatively each clue may lead to another clue and the trail goes on until the treasure at the end is found.

Young hunters may find it easier to follow a trail — this can be made from distinctive stones, arrows made from twigs, blobs of flour, whatever comes to hand.

It can be as much fun setting up treasure hunts as doing them so if you want to keep people occupied set them the challenge of devising a fiendish treasure hunt for you. This could win you a few minutes of peaceful contemplation if that is what you crave.

Make it as tricky or complicated as you wish but make sure there is enough treasure at the end for all taking part (including the setters) if you want a happy crew.

Why not try...

anywhere with interesting river banks or where you can walk along the river.

East Lyn River and Hoar Oak Water, Watersmeet, Exmoor (8)

Beaulieu River, Beaulieu, New Forest (15)

River Wey, Shalford, Surrey (37)

River Wey, Guildford, Surrey (38)

River Thames, Teddington Lock, London (54)

Little Ouse, Santon Downham, Thetford, Norfolk (58)

River Waveney, Hoxne Weir, Suffolk (62)

Wellow Brook, Wellow, Bath, Somerset (76)

Cald Beck, The Howk, Caldbeck, Lake District (96)

River East Allen, Allendale, County Durham (113)

(x) numbers relate to site listings in the resources section.

Pooh sticks

Beck near Skelwith Bridge, Lake District ... October

... We managed a reasonably long walk with the kids today. We went past Tarn Hows and over the low fells towards Skelwith Bridge. We did finally make Skelwith Bridge but only after we had been distracted by tea and cakes at Park Farm. We were then further delayed by a highly competitive game of Pooh sticks. Just beyond the farm a very small stream crossed our path, it was too small to even warrant a bridge but to get under the path it had been routed through a pipe, so disappeared from view for about two metres. This proved to be perfect for an adaptation of the classic Pooh sticks that we usually play. We were using twigs and leaves and a good supply of empty beech nut cases that were nearby. Once launched, they disappeared for about 10 seconds, just enough time to run to the emerging stream and to build up the anticipation. The order that the beechnuts went in seemed to have very little bearing on the order in which they came out, which only added to the highly addictive nature of the game. By the time we moved on the daylight had almost gone and we arrived at Skelwith Bridge in the pitch black ...

How to play Pooh sticks

Crossing bridges and anticipating a game of Pooh sticks is a great incentive if you are on a walk with children — you can collect suitably distinctive twigs or pine cones on the way to add further to the anticipation and draw out the fun.

Virtually any piece of flowing water is good for Pooh sticks. While the strictest of rules would require that you play from a bridge, we have found that that is not always necessary. It is best if the river disappears temporarily to add to the excitement of the game but this could be going through a pipe or just behind some trees if you play it running down beside the river or stream.

It is also usual for the game to involve two or more competitors but I have noticed that some people with excessive Pooh stick stamina will play happily on their own – left hand against right hand or even by counting seconds or using a timer to beat their previous best time.

If you do play on a bridge just remember two important safety aspects:

Make sure it is not a road bridge – dodging cars is not part of the game, and

Make sure there are no swimmers, boaters or other river users in the water before launching your sticks.

THE RULES

Each competitor chooses an easily identifiable stick or pine cone.

The sticks are released from the bridge at the same time, usually after the official starter calls 'ready, steady, go'; 'one, two, three', 'go' or other accepted starting cry.

The sticks should be dropped rather than thrown or propelled forwards in any way. The strategic choice of dropping point is allowed in order for the players to gain maximum advantage from the variable water velocity in the stream.

Why not try...

non-road bridges with width but not height.

River Barle, Tarr Steps, Exmoor **(1)**

Beaulieu River, Beaulieu, New Forest **(15)**

River Itchen, Martyr Worthy, Hampshire **(20)**

Pooh Sticks Bridge, Hartfield, Ashdown Forest, East Sussex **(31)**

River Mole, Box Hill Stepping Stones, Surrey **(34)**

Cald Beck, St Mungo's Well, Caldbeck, Lake District **(97)**

Easdale Beck, Grassmere, Lake District **(104)**

River Rothay, Rothay Park, Ambleside, Lake District **(106)**

Scandal Beck, Smardale Bridge, Kirby Stephen, Cumbria **(110)**

River East Allen, Allendale, County Durham **(113)**

(x) numbers relate to site listings in the resources section.

Golden Bay, South Island, New Zealand

… Duncan and I have met up with three other couples, old university friends, to celebrate the New Year. The others are all working and travelling over here in different parts of New Zealand. We went off for a walk down the almost dry rocky riverbed and came across the perfect waterhole with a beach of smooth pebbles on one side and a cliff over deep water just askin~~ ~~climbed on the other. Without breaking step we crunched over *~~ ~~*ached stones to the water's edge, collecting good skim~~ ~~ton~~ ~~nt. Like wine tasters rolling wine around their mout~~ ~~warm stones in our hands, sizing up the weight and balance of the stone and rubbing the warm, smooth edges through our fingers. At the water's edge we released the stones in a cascade of singing, bouncing arcs across the pool, breaking the previously still, reflective water into a riot of shattered images and shards of sunlight glancing off the expanding rings. Why that should have been so satisfying I don't know, but it was …

How to skip stones

Skipping or skimming stones is an ancient waterside activity that is also known as 'Ducks and Drakes'.

Back in Roman times Ducks and Drakes would have been played with tiles. Years later the poet Percy Bysshe Shelley used to spend hours splitting slate rocks apart to produce nice flat stones which he then rounded off by chipping away at the edges. Once he had a good supply he would while away his time skipping these specially made stones across the water and counting the number of bounds they made, with great pleasure.

The skipping stones ritual, for those of us who are not carving our own missiles, starts with the search for the perfect stone. What are the qualities of a champion skipper? Water worn so it is smooth to the touch, nestling perfectly into the palm of your hand, slightly flattened to maximise skimming potential. Someone, somewhere must have unravelled the formula which dictates the dimensions of the ultimate skipping pebble.

Once you have it cool and smooth in your hand, gripped between crooked finger and thumb, stand sideways, lean back, recoil and whip your arm round to launch it across a smooth expanse of water. An angle of 20° between stone trajectory and surface is apparently optimum – someone has actually worked that out.

You can do this just for the pure aesthetic pleasure of the movement and watching the

skips spread across the water or there can be a challenge; try to reach the other side in as few skips as possible, or as many skips, or go for the most skips with one stone.

If you can manage 16 skips you probably consider yourself a bit of a star skipper. While most people will manage to achieve around eight skips on a good stone, the world record as currently recognised by the *Guiness Book of Records* (2011), is 51 skips, achieved by Russell Byars in 2007. If you get really professional and wish to compete against the best then there are actually skipping stones championships you can enter. The North American Stone Skipping Association (NASSA) organises the World Championships where they count the number of skips being achieved by the competitors. There is also the World Stone Skimming Championships held on a disused quarry in Easdale, Scotland. Easdale Island is the smallest inhabited island of the Inner Hebrides and once home to the local slate mining industry. The competition uses slate stones from the now disused quarries and the skimming is performed across a flooded quarry. In this contest they count the distance that the stone travels before sinking; the longest skim with at least three skips wins.

Rather than skipping the stones, try finding a long thin stone with which to perfect the single entry in stone high board diving. Balance the long thin stone on your fingers. Imagine the stone is a high board diver then toss it into the air so that it performs full twists and somersaults worthy of an Olympic diver

and before landing in the water. The ultimate goal is to achieve the best diving 'rip' entry. The smaller the splash, the higher the score will be. If you really want to expand this idea you can enlist a board of scorers to give the 'dive' marks out of ten; or even do a pairs event and try to get the stones to synchronise (one in each hand or two people!)

Just throwing stones in the water can be strangely satisfying, listening to the plop and splash as it lands. This is also much more achievable than skipping stones for small children. I remember, before I had my own children, taking my nephew as a toddler, down to the stream and dropping stones in, each stone was accompanied by a chant of 'plop' before we searched for the next stone and the ritual was repeated — ad infinitum — hours of fun.

On a lazy day lie back and grab any old collection of stones from the beach. Throw them by the handful on to quiet water. Listen to the sounds they make.... A drum symphony? Popcorn popping on the fire? Horses' hooves drumming on frozen moorland?

Why not try...

pools of flat water with a good supply of river smoothed stones: somewhere you can get down to water level and not too much danger of hitting people.

River Barle, Tarr Steps, Exmoor **(1)**

Badgeworthy Water, Above Cloud Farm, Malmsmead, Exmoor **(6)**

Cuckmere River, Cuckmere Meanders, Seaford, East Sussex **(29)**

River Thames, Buscot Weir, Oxfordshire **(43)**

River Bure, Buxton and Lammas, Norfolk **(64)**

River Wye, The Warren, Hay-on-Wye, Powys, Wales **(68)**

River Lune, under Devil's Bridge, Kirby Lonsdale, Yorkshire Dales **(88)**

Langstrath Beck, above Black Moss Pot, Lake District **(100)**

River Derwent, Grange, Lake District **(103)**

Yewdale Beck, Low Tilberthwaite, Lake District **(108)**

River Rawthey, Sedbergh, Cumbria **(111)**

(x) numbers relate to site listings in the resources section.

Virtually any river will be blessed with stones along its margin or on the river bed. There is something very compelling and elemental about stones and I can happily collect them and turn them into patterns and sculptures, skip them or just throw them in to water. If you do get to the point where you have exhausted those stone activities then here are a couple of other games we often enjoy. Both these games can be adapted for indoor entertainment in a washing up bowl in the house or inside the tent.

Sink the boat This is a game that started off at the waterside and has been enjoyed so much that we now play it anywhere.

Have an empty tin or other floating container such as a tuna tin, small sandwich box, yoghurt pot, water bottle with top chopped off to be the boat. To begin everyone collects some stones (around ten each) of varying sizes from plum- to pea-sized.

All the stones are placed in the middle of the circle in a pile and each player in turn

selects a stone (top tip: take the smallest stones first), keep going taking stones in turn until they are all gone and each player has their own small pile of stones in front of them.

The last player to pick starts the game.

Place the container in the water (a still bit of water or slow eddy works well) and the first player puts their stone in the 'boat' (tip: it is best to get rid of the biggest stones first). Play moves around the circle with each player putting a stone in the tin in turn. Very quickly the critical point of the game is reached where the water reaches the rim of the tin and the 'boat' is in danger of being sunk. The player who puts in the stone that finally sinks the boat has to take all the stones from the boat and the game continues with a new round.

The first player to run out of stones is the winner.

Once you get addicted to this game it can be played in the bath, sink, washing up bowl or even saucepan full of water.

Water boules This is the watery version of the beach game of boules. Two or more players can play, or you can just play on your own by setting your own challenge. Start by choosing a target on the river bed. This may be a distinctive stone or patch of moss.

Alternatively you can throw your own carefully chosen 'jack' (again a distinctive stone will do).

Each player then chooses their 'sinker'; any smallish item that sinks – again usually a distinctive stone.

Drop your sinker from just above the water surface and aim to get onto the 'jack'. The

movement of the water and depth of water will make this quite difficult so get ready to measure in foot lengths or finger widths for the closest 'sinker'. The closest 'sinker' wins and that person usually gets to set the 'jack' for the next game. First to five is the usual target but you can make your own end point based on time and inclination.

As an alternative use the supply of stones collected for 'Sink the boat'. Each time your sinker is closest you get to claim all the participating stones. The player with the largest number of stones at the end of the game (or all the stones if you play that long) wins.

To test out the best technique try dropping a flat stone in thin end first and compare your accuracy with dropping it wide side first. Dropping it flat side first will result in it floating and zig-zagging like a leaf floating to the ground from a tree – almost impossible to direct its fall. If you drop it sharp end first, however, it will go much more directly and you will hit the target more easily.

Why not try...

good access to the river side, small pools of slow moving water and a good supply of stones.

Horner Water, Horner, Exmoor **(5)**

River Kennet, Ramsbury Mill Lane, Ramsbury, Wiltshire **(17)**

River Wey, Tilford, Surrey **(39)**

River Thames, downstream Buscot Weir, Oxfordshire **(43)**

River Bure, Buxton and Lammas, Norfolk **(64)**

River Lugg, Lugg Meadows, Hereford, Herefordshire **(78)**

River Monnow, Skenfrith Castle, Monmouthshire, Wales **(79)**

River Aire, Newfield Bridge, Gargrave, Yorkshire Dales **(85)**

Styhead Gill, Seathwaite, Lake District **(99)**

Yewdale Beck, under Raven Crag, Tilberthwaite, Lake District **(107)**

(x) numbers relate to site listings in the resources section.

Water magic

At home, Reigate, Surrey

... It was a sparklingly hot day today so we had lunch outside, with a large plastic jug full of water on the table. Poppy held it up so we could see half her face through it. It was like the bendy mirrors at the fair. Her face through the water was stretched so that she had the most enormous wide mouth and nose. The rest of her around the jug appeared normal. We were in stitches. Then we all had a lot of fun making faces through the jug, taking pictures and telling the wide mouth frog joke ...

Wide mouth frog joke...

One day a wide mouth frog was hopping through the jungle when he came across a rabbit.

'Hello! I'm a wide mouth frog,' said the wide mouth frog, 'I eat flies. What do you eat?' 'I eat leaves and green things,' said the rabbit. The frog hopped on and before very long he met a wild boar.

'Hello! I'm a wide mouth frog. I eat flies. What do you eat?' 'I root around for juicy roots and insects', said the boar.

Just then the frog spotted a snake almost completely camouflaged in the dead leaves. 'Hello snake. What do you eat?' asked the wide mouth frog. 'I eat wide mouth frogs,' said the snake. 'Oh, that's nice', said the frog with his mouth scrunched up as small as possible. 'You don't see many of those round here do you? '

We then moved on to all sorts of other magic tricks with water and bottles and glasses that we knew between us: Thea in particular seemed to have a large supply of tricks and came up with three of the ones below.

Water magic

It is the amazing properties of water that make it so versatile and fun to play with.

The scientific reason the water in the jugs made such a great change to Poppy's face was that water has a different refractive index than air. So when the light passes from the air into the water it is bent. This explains why fishermen always think fish are bigger than they actually are and why a straw in a glass of

water is fatter and kinks sideways in the water compared to above the water.

Animals like herons, kingfishers and fish are able to allow for this change in refractive index to catch fish and insects accurately even through the surface of the water. Birds that fish underwater have a second fovea where the light is directed for accurate vision that helps them to focus in the different refractive index of water.

These are some other water tricks to stun and amaze your friends:

Does metal float? Water has very strong surface tension caused by the water molecules at the surface holding tightly onto each other. This is the reason that water forms into droplets and that insects like pond skaters and whirligig beetles can walk on the water surface. So ask your friends if they think that a solid piece of metal can float. But if you have a small enough piece of metal like a needle or pin and lie it sideways on the water surface the surface tension should hold it. Poke it end on through the surface of the water and it will indeed sink, so you need to be very careful how you lower it onto the surface.

Spin a full bucket round and stay dry Making the most of centripetal forces you can in fact spin a bucket full of water around, without the water coming out even when it is directly above your head. But you can't let the bucket stop there or it will lose its outward energy and the water will come crashing down.

Can you turn a glass upside down without the water falling out? Of course you can't... can you? Investigate air pressure and surface tension and what they can do with this next series of tricks. Fill your glass of water to the brim and place a sheet of paper or light card on top. Turn the glass upside down while holding the paper and then remove your hand from under the paper. You should be able to hold the glass upside down, without holding on to the paper while the water stays in the glass. The air pressure holds the water in the glass. Try it, it works.

Can you keep your drink in a bottle with a hole in it? Usually, you would assume that if your bottle has a hole in it, the water will come out. However, find an old plastic bottle, and stab a

When you have finished your drinks, keep the glasses, ask for a jug of tap water and use a beer mat.

The properties of water are exploited by animals and plants in the natural world which have adapted to overcome the restrictions and make the most of the opportunities the specific properties present. Throughout this book there are many examples of the ways that animals have adapted to exploit water's specific properties of surface tension, buoyancy and the refractive index of water in their everyday search for food and survival.

hole near the bottom with a sharp implement; keep the water bottle completely full, with the lid on and in spite of the hole the water will stay in. Unfortunately as soon as you open the bottle and try to drink it, the water will come out of the hole. The way to counteract this is to open the lid with the bottle upright and drink from the stream of water coming out of the hole.

Can you balance an inverted glass full of water on another glass full of water without the water coming out? The next stage of this trick is to place a second glass of the same size, also full to the brim with water, under the upside down one. Once the rims are perfectly lined up, slide the paper out. The two glasses are now both full of water and balanced on top of each other, the top one inverted.

Can you prop the glasses open without the water coming out? You can now try sliding in two pence pieces between the two glasses. See how many you can do before the gap between the glasses is too great and the water comes gushing out; we usually manage around three. These last two challenges are good pub garden tricks.

Why not try...

this wherever you can get the containers and some water, you don't even have to be by the river.

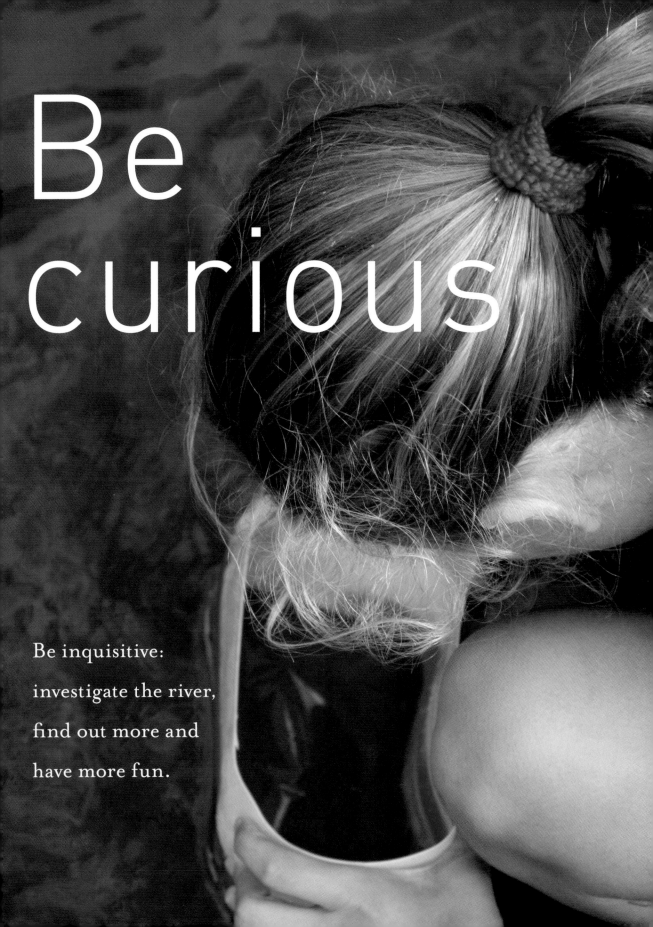

Be
curious

Be inquisitive:
investigate the river,
find out more and
have more fun.

Holmesdale School pond, Reigate, Surrey ... June

... I was helping out with Poppy's class today. They have a 'grounds day' in the summer where they do various activities outside. One of the activities is to go out to the school pond and have a good look at what lives there.

Armed with nets, white trays, magnifying glasses, ID sheets and clip boards we set out with around 12 five and six year olds. We sat them down well back from the edge and explained some safety issues and how we would look at the animals on the top of the water, then use the nets in the water and finally in the mud. Then we moved towards the pond. Immediately one small boy headed straight for the steepest bank and just kept going. A father and I both caught an arm as he dangled almost horizontally over the water surface. Within seconds the water was churned up as the pond nets were dug straight into the soft silty bottom. The kids had a great time and found an amazing amount of little beasts: they screamed at the leeches and oohed at the snails and wowed at the dragonfly larvae, but it was the newts that really stole the day. As soon as the first newt was netted that was it. Everyone wanted one. We had about 24 in the tanks by the end.

The real star of the day was the little boy who spotted a crusty brown thing on one of the long, bright green iris leaves. Tugging at my shirt he asked me what it was. I was so excited I nearly fell in the water. He had spotted the empty case of a dragonfly larva that had climbed up the grass stem before the adult winged dragonfly emerged from the larval exoskeleton. The papery remains left behind are a perfect replica of the dragon fly larva but completely empty. The children watched transfixed, and finally silent, as I performed a complicated manoeuvre, balancing on one foot, leaning over the little wooden bridge and, at full stretch, scooping it off the leaf with two pond nets. They all had a good look, amazed at the intricacy and lightness of the exoskeleton. It is a testament to nature that a relatively small pond that is regularly terrorised by large groups of over-enthusiastic mini-beasters can still support such a good range of delicate and intriguing creatures ...

Even a relatively small pond
that is regularly investigated
by over-enthusiastic minibeast
hunters will yield a surprising
range of complex and
intriguing creatures.

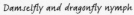

Damselfly and dragonfly nymph

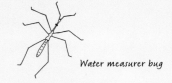

Water measurer bug

HOW TO HUNT FOR MINIBEASTS

Seeking out the tiny creatures that inhabit rivers, ponds and puddles is easy. All you need for minibeast hunting is a pond net with which to collect the animals and a container or tray in which to view them (shallow trays, picnic boxes and buckets are all useful for looking at minibeasts, but a shallow white plastic tray is best). A magnifying glass will help you look in more detail but you can see all the animals so don't worry if you don't have one.

❶ Approach the river slowly and have a look at the surface of the water, particularly along the edges, where it is flowing slowly. You will probably see the pond skaters scooting over the surface of the water, making the most of the water tension, and the water boatmen — beetles that swim upside down — with their water bubble air supply and buoyancy aid sparkling. If it is very still and the water quality poor, you may see mosquito larvae snorkelling for oxygen rich air at the surface; scoop them up in your net and deposit them in your container with a little water.

❷ Next quietly and gently step into the water. Be aware of the speed of the water, it needs to be flowing but not so fast that you get swept off your feet.

❸ Pick up a few stones and pick off any animals or put the stone with animals attached into your container. There may be freshwater limpets: the more chalky the river geology the greater the number of shelled animals there will be; caddis fly larvae in their stone or leaf built cases, they will use which ever materials are available and just merge into the background. Cased caddis that live in faster flowing streams tend to have smaller, stony cases while those in slower water can have quite cumbersome cases dominated by leaf and twig remains. In clear water streams you may find the more flattened mayfly larvae that can cling on to the rock even in the faster flowing water.

Once you have looked at any stones in the river sweep the net through the pond weed or give it a gentle shake, both in the main flow of the river and in the margins. Amongst the plants in the main flow there is likely to be an abundance of black fly larvae (*Simulium*), the freshwater shrimp (*Gammarus*) or water hog louse (*Assellus*) as well as some leeches. Plants in the margins are more likely to be home to beetle larvae as well as the voracious and alien looking dragonfly and damselfly larvae.

The next step is to move into the main flow and sample the river bottom. Place the edge of the net on the bottom just a foot length downstream of your foot and kick gently, don't dig a great big hole, just ruffle up the bottom a bit so the sediment is disturbed; this is known as 'kick sampling'. The flow of water will carry the small animals downstream to be caught in the net while most of the debris, being heavier, should drop out before it reaches the net. Pick up the net and have a look, tip it gently upside down and wash the contents out in to your

Water boatman

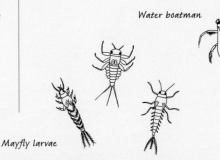

Water hog louse

Mayfly larvae

Mosquito larva

Blackfly larva

Freshwater shrimp

Caddisfly larva

container. Have a good look at what you've found. In the sediments you will find leeches, flatworms, and many of the fly larvae such as mayfly and stonefly as well as the rather maggoty true fly larvae.

Repeat this kick sampling in all the habitats you can see — under plants, amongst tree roots, in the main flow and along the edges, in shallow, gravel, riffly areas and in deeper, more silty pools. If you want to get an idea of where different animals live, either put your catch in different containers, or return each net load before you sample the next habitat.

Once you have collected a few animals have a good look at them. While you are looking at what you've caught try to work out which animals you have found. Many of the animals will be the larvae of flying insects — try to work out who their parents are. If you have a dragonfly larva you may find that it is the only thing left at the end of your investigations as it may eat everything else!

If you want to identify the animals you have found, some of these pictures may help and there are some suggestions for other books and publications in the links section on page 222.

When you have finished looking at your animals always return them carefully to their homes. Replace all turned over stones and logs where you found them to minimise disturbance. All these creatures have chosen their homes to meet their specific needs and some of the limpets and cased caddis fly, for example, can't relocate themselves very easily to find the right flow conditions if their home is disturbed or returned the wrong way up in the main flow of the river.

Why not try...

water less than knee deep, moderate flow with good access is ideal for minibeast hunting.

River Barle, Landacre Bridge, Withypool, Exmoor (3)

Badgeworthy Water, Malmsmead and Cloud Farm, Exmoor (6)

Latchmore Brook, Ogdens, New Forest (14)

River Kennet, Ramsbury Mill Lane, Ramsbury, Wiltshire (17)

River Mole, Norbury Park, Leatherhead, Surrey (35)

River Bure, Little Hautbois, Norfolk (63)

River Evenlode, Stonesfield, Oxfordshire (75)

Goredale Beck, Malham, Yorkshire Dales (84)

Easedale Beck, Grassmere, Lake District (104)

(x) numbers relate to site listings in the resources section.

The mayfly are an important element of any river or stream as they are a major food source for many of the fish, particularly trout. Fishermen will judge the quality of a stream by its mayfly and will look out for the emergence of the mayfly in their brief flying form.

There are many species of mayfly and their larvae have evolved differentially to make the most of every habitat available in the river. Mayfly larvae can be found digging into the sediments, clinging on to the rocks in the fast flow or swimming freely. The larvae live in the water for up to two years, growing and developing until they emerge in their short-lived adult flying form. The adult mayflies have no mouthparts or digestive system and live for one or two days in which they use their energy reserves to mate and then exhausted they die.

The timing of the emergence of the adult mayfly from the water is of particular interest to fishermen. Trout and salmon will feed heartily at the surface of the water as the nymphs struggle to emerge, the flies used in fly fishing are elaborate copies of the mayfly that fishermen put on their lines, the fly fishing techniques then mimic the movements of the mayfly on the water surface to attract these trophy fish.

The mayfly of each species hatch out in response to an environmental cue so that great clouds of one species of mayfly will emerge at the same time on a summer's evening. Fishermen will know and mark the timing of the emergence of each individual species of mayfly on their river.

The adult mayflies emerge from the water as drab coloured 'dun' and within hours undergo a second moult into a more colourful and sexually mature 'spinner'. They then perform a dance in which they fly up and down almost as if on a yoyo, to attract the females.

Once mating is complete and the eggs deposited below the water surface, the adults collapse, exhausted, onto the water surface, their stored energy all used up and the reproductive job complete. The mayfly life cycle has now returned under the water surface and continues unseen for another year.

* Notebook · Leeches (Hirudinea)

The leeches are generally low on anyone's list of must-see animals. Their blood-sucking reputation and the fact that they live in most murky rivers means that they don't even register on the 'aaah' scale. Nevertheless they are fascinating creatures.

In UK waters you will be hard pressed to find a leech with mouthparts that can penetrate the human skin. Only two exist and these are both very rare; the medicinal leech which features highly in historical novels as a blood-letting remedy is actually endangered in the wild. Medicinal leeches are seeing a revival in medicine today but the ones they use are all farmed – not harvested from the wild. The leeches commonly found in our rivers are all carnivores which either suck the blood of mammals, birds, fish, reptiles, amphibians, molluscs and invertebrates or live on small invertebrates which they can swallow whole.

The movement of the leeches is quite beautiful to watch as they loop themselves along and I love to watch the way they reach out from a leaf sensing and feeling with their primitive heads towards the warmth of a fish or mammal as it passes by.

I came across a wonderfully gory leech story in the *QI Book of Animal Ignorance*. During the Napoleonic wars Napoleon's troops were marching through the Sinai desert. In their thirst they unknowingly drank water contaminated with small leeches. The leeches attached themselves to their nasal passages, mouths and throats. Leeches tend to be binge eaters and can double in size after a big meal. This caused havoc in the soldiers narrow nasal passages and throats where the leeches' increased size caused such an obstruction that many of the men died of suffocation.

River Itchen, St Cross and College Natural Area, Winchester ... July (21)

... I set off early this morning and reached Winchester at about 8am. As I parked the car in a woody glade, the sun was filtering through the trees and I disturbed a female fallow deer. Her ears pricked up as she noticed me and she stepped delicately away into the shadows and within moments had dissolved into the trees. Across the road through the park railings the mist was just beginning to rise from the neatly cropped grass and shafts of morning sunlight cut through a majestic oak tree and sparkled off a spider's web hanging from the wrought iron.

I headed up a loop of the river that runs through the St Cross and College Natural Area. There is a small conservation area in one of the branches of the river with mown paths winding between the waterways. The banks are a riot of grasses, irises, reeds, rushes and all manner of marginal plants. The waterways are full of crowsfoot, starwort, milfoils and lilies. It is a real miniature Eden and all around the birds were singing their morning songs with great industry while the damselflies and dragonflies were coming to life as the sunlight reached the dewy leaves. I was transfixed and spent several hours in this small area just absorbed by the richness of the wildlife. I stalked the damselflies, entranced by their iridescent colours and managed to get a few wonderful pictures as they sunned themselves ...

Why not try...

rivers with plenty of marginal vegetation and good water quality are good places to see dragonflies. Typically these include southern and midlands lowland floodplains, but increasingly spreading northwards with greater diversity now seen in lowland Lake District.

River Dart Country Park, Ashburton, Dartmoor **(9)**

Beaulieu River, Beaulieu, New Forest **(15)**

River Frome, Farleigh Hungerford, Somerset **(18)**

Pevensey Levels NNR, East Sussex **(30)**

River Thames, Chimney Meadows, Oxfordshire **(44)**

River Stour, Flatford Mill to Dedham, Essex **(56)**

River Ant, How Hill, Ludham, Norfolk **(65)**

River Ant, Weyford Bridge, Wroxham, Norfolk **(66)**

River Cherwell, Park Town, Oxford, Oxfordshire **(74)**

Grizedale Beck, Grizedale Forest, Lake District **(109)**

(x) numbers relate to site listings in the resources section.

Dragons have long been associated with water. In the church of St Mary the Virgin on the River Stour in Suffolk there is a picture of the Wissington Dragon. The Dragon, depicted as a bright red monster, bat winged and curled tail, which roamed the land, devouring villagers. Eventually it dived into the river and swam to hide in Wormingford Mere (Dragon's Ford Pool). Dragons are often called worms from the old Norse 'ormr' as in the Worms Head at Rhossilli in Wales and the Worms Den at Linton Hill in the north-east. Have a look at the map and try to spot any dragon links in your local area.

Happily the only dragons you will find by a modern river are dragonflies. There is fossil evidence that these voracious carnivores have been around since the late Palaeozoic – over 300 million years ago – long before humans and around 100 million years before dinosaurs.

Prehistoric dragonflies were huge, with the wingspan of a mallard duck. These days, dragonflies are no bigger than 8cm but they can fly at 30mph. With their bright colours and rapid whirring flight, dragonflies are one of the largest, most conspicuous and easily identifiable insects alongside any British river.

DAMSELFLIES Damselflies are often grouped together with dragonflies and although superficially similar they are easily differentiated. Damselflies are generally smaller (up to 4cm) with a more delicate cylindrical shape. They are generally more colourful than dragonflies (particularly the males) with metallic colours on their bodies and wings. They do not fly as strongly as dragonflies and are rarely seen far from the water. The best distinguishing feature is their wings. Dragonflies are able to hover while damselflies are not and at rest the dragonfly holds its wings wide open while damselflies fold their wings together over their backs.

The life cycle of both insects, involves a long juvenile (nymph) stage that lives in the river for up to two years. They hang out deep in the marginal grasses and mud where they are easily captured with a pond net.

The nymphs are ferocious and well worth a look at with a magnifying glass. They have been the inspiration of many Hollywood aliens with their powerful, extendible jaws. The bottom lip-like jaw shoots out to catch young fish, tadpoles and newt larvae faster than the eye can see.

THE EMERGING ADULT When ready to emerge the nymph climbs up a reed or grass stem and cracks open its outer skin (exoskeleton) and out climbs the dragonfly adult. If you look carefully

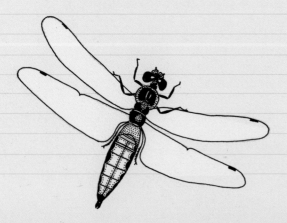

at the grasses on a river bank you may see the papery remains of a nymph, looking exactly like the living nymph but completely empty. The bright colour of the adult normally takes a week or two to develop at which time they also become sexually mature. This adult stage is short lived; damselflies live for two to four weeks while dragonflies may survive for up to two months.

Mating dragonflies and damselflies can be seen carrying out the most dramatic courtship flights attached together, with the male clasping the female. You may see them releasing their eggs either mid flight, as they dip down piercing the water with the tip of their abdomen or settling on plants and carefully gluing the individual eggs onto the plant.

DRAGONFLY MYTHS AND LEGENDS These beautiful insects have often been perceived as sinister in their associated myths and legends. In fact, they are non-biting, require clean water and feed extensively on insects such as midges and mosquitoes, so they deserve a positive reputation.

Dragonflies have been known as 'horse stingers' and the 'devil's darning needle' in England. The 'horse stinger' name came from the fact that dragonflies were seen flying around panicking horses which people believed the dragonflies were biting. In reality the dragonflies were probably feasting on the insects that were biting the horses. The 'devil's darning needle' moniker came from the

dragonflies zig-zagging 'sewing' motion as they hover, the story developed that the devil used dragonflies to sew shut the mouths of nagging wives and lying children.

Conversely the Japanese revere dragonflies as symbols of happiness, success, strength and courage. Japan was even temporarily named 'Isle of the Dragonfly' when, as legend has it, a dragonfly ate the horsefly that bit the emperor.

Catch crayfish

Shagbrook, Reigate Heath, Surrey ... March

... I saw something new this morning. I set off for a Sunday morning run, still scraping the sleep from my eyes as I ran. I had just about got into my stride as I headed across Reigate Heath. I headed down towards the Shagbrook and just at the bend in the path where the brook goes under the track there was a family wearing socks on their hands. As I ran down towards them the two boys were in the stream feeling around under the water between the tree roots with their socked hands. I have never seen this before so I stopped to have a chat. Apparently this is a recognised method of catching crayfish. They had a bucket of signal crayfish so they were obviously being quite successful. The crayfish ranged from 10cm to a bumper old boy of 25cm long from tip of claw to tail — all destined for the family's Sunday lunch ...

How to go about crayfishing

There are two types of crayfish in the UK and it is vitally important that you can tell them apart if you plan to catch and eat them. The White-clawed native crayfish, *Austropotamobius pallipes*, is an endangered species and as such it is illegal to catch and eat them. The invading American Signal crayfish, *Pacifastus leniusculus*, was released in to the wild in the 1970s from failed crayfish farms and has since wreaked havoc on our native wildlife: if caught these must be killed.

The Signal Crayfish is much more widespread and larger than the White-clawed species (all the better for eating), much more aggressive and feeds voraciously on fish eggs and invertebrates. They also carry a plague to which the natives are not resistant and have caused a 50 per cent decline in the native numbers since the 1970s. At any point where signal crayfish are present there will be no native crayfish in the river downstream. This means that native crayfish are largely present only in the upper reaches of the rivers where they have held on to their territory so far. The signal crayfish not only have a big impact on the White-clawed Crayfish but they can devastate salmon and trout spawning grounds and cause extensive damage to river banks as they dig their large burrows (up to 1m deep), often resulting in bank collapse.

TELLING THE SPECIES APART

The most distinctive differences in the two species are their size and claw colour. Anything more than 12cm long is a Signal Crayfish as this is the maximum size of the white-clawed species. The signal can, in theory, grow up to 30cm — although I have never found one that size; much more common are those 15 to 20cm long. The Signal also has distinctive reddish colouring on the underside

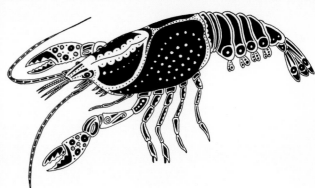

Size and claw colour are the easiest ways to differentiate crayfish. Signals are larger — more than 12cm long, with reddish colouring on the underside of their claws.

of the claws, with a turquoise blob on the upper surface of the pincer joint. The White-clawed, native crayfish is aptly named as it has a whiteish underside to its claws.

Since the white-clawed crayfish is endangered, all sites with good populations of the species are designated as Special Areas for Conservation (SAC's) and protected under the EU Habitats Directive (92/43/EEC).

To catch your crayfish

If you want to catch signal crayfish to eat you must always check that there is no chance that there may be White-clawed Crayfish in your river. Type the name of your river into the JNCC database of protected sites (SACs) and if it comes up with a designation for the white-clawed crayfish, stay away from the river and its tributaries. (*www.jncc.defra.gov.uk/protectedsites/sacselection*). Not all sites will be designated so you can also check with your local Wildlife Trust to check on their presence in your local area to be really sure.

Crayfishing is very similar to crabbing. Crayfish like to hang out in their burrows or along the margins of rivers and streams, tucked in to holes in the bank and around tree roots. They are most active around dusk so this is the best time to fish.

DIFFERENT TECHNIQUES

Any technique you would use for crabbing works with crayfish. You can use a pond net to sweep around in the margins or feel around with gloves or (now I know) socks on your hands. The classic crabbing line and net also work perfectly well. I have seen all kinds of homemade tackle: old baskets, plastic containers with string and we used to catch crayfish for monitoring with a length of downpipe closed in at one end and weighted with a bit of brick. As with crabbing, everyone has their favourite bait, but any old bit of raw meat, such as bacon or oily fish heads, works well. In prolific areas you will only have to lower your line and bait down for a few minutes and you should find supper ready and waiting for you.

Hold the crayfish firmly around the abdomen just behind the pincers to avoid being nipped by their strong claws.

GET PERMISSION

If you are considering trapping crayfish, you will require permission from the Environment Agency. This is so that they can monitor activities and alert people fully to the concerns and to eliminate the risk of further spreading of the invading signals. There is a concern that by taking the large crayfish to eat you may actually encourage more small crayfish to flourish and actually create a population boom. If you catch any Signal Crayfish, including small ones, it is illegal to return them to the water: they must be killed. Never transfer crayfish between watercourses and always clean any equipment very carefully when you move from one river to another.

To eat your crayfish

If you fancy a meal of crayfish then you are actively encouraged to gorge yourself on the signal crayfish; eat as many as you can and do your bit to preserve our natural environment.

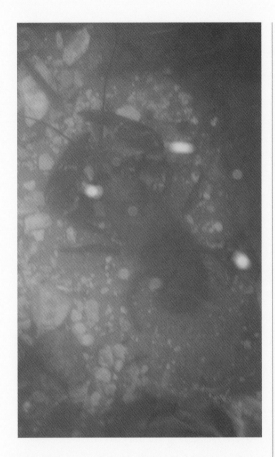

butter or wild garlic aioli with a squeeze of lemon.

If you are concerned about cooking live crayfish it is possible to put them in the freezer for an hour before cooking or kill them with a sharp knife between and behind the eyes. In fact the boiling water will kill them almost as efficiently as either of these techniques.

Be extremely careful to avoid rivers with populations of the native white-clawed crayfish. Always check the JNCC website or local wildlife trusts to be sure.

Crayfish eaten directly from the river may be somewhat bitter so it is better to let them empty their stomachs before you cook them. This can be done by keeping them in a damp cloth bag for a couple of days or by placing them in a box stuffed full of nettles and leaving them for 24 hours. Once they have been cleaned out, wash them in clean water and tip them into a large pan of fast boiling salted water. Only cook a few at a time so the temperature doesn't drop and they will die in just a few seconds; simmer them for just five minutes. Eat them like lobster or shrimps taking the meat from the tail and the claws and dip it in wild garlic

Why not try...

rivers with non-native crayfish populations.

River Dart, Deeper Marsh, Ashburton, Dartmoor **(10)**

River Rother, Fittleworth, West Sussex **(24)**

River Ouse, Barcombe Mills, East Sussex **(27)**

River Wey, Shalford, Surrey **(37)**

River Lambourne, Boxford, Berkshire **(41)**

Any of River Thames sites **(42–54)**

River Stour, Flatford Mill to Dedham **(56)**

River Cam, Grantchester Meadows, Cambridge, Cambridgeshire **(59)**

River Waveney, Outney Common, Bungay, Suffolk **(61)**

River Skirfare, Arncliffe, Yorkshire Dales **(90)**

(x) numbers relate to site listings in the resources section.

Look at the plants

Above the River Kennet, Wiltshire and Hampshire ... July

... The plant surveys I have been carrying out on the River Kennet are labour intensive and some sections of river are inaccessible, so a bright spark came up with the idea of aerial surveys. In theory these should be a quick assessment tool to survey the whole river in one day, take pictures, analyse them on the ground and decide where to go in for the detailed surveys. So, today I set off with a newly-qualified microlight pilot.

I was a little bemused when we drove up to what appeared to be a corrugated iron cowshed in a grazing field at the bottom of a valley. The 'cowshed' was a hangar housing about six aircraft: microlights really are micro. To my eye our plane resembled a motorcycle sidecar under wings. Then I was told to climb the hill as the plane wouldn't take off from the grass airstrip at the bottom with my weight in it: I only weigh 55kg so I wasn't reassured! So up to the top of the hill I went as the microlight took off and then joined me. The extra lift at the top was enough and after bumping across the field for some distance we were airborne. Navigation seemed to be by visual cues only and it took us a while, circling round, to orientate ourselves and find the river.

The river valley looked fantastic with the dense myriad green growths of trees, the river, shining like burnished silver, threading its way in and out of the green, collecting tributaries and splitting and reforming weaving a silver plait as the side channels came and went. The whole layout of the river in the context of its valley was amazing to see and made sense with what I knew from the ground. But taking photos was almost impossible. To get a photo looking directly down to the river I had to lean over the side of the plane, the wind buffeting me so that my eyes watered and I could hardly see. There was no chance of scientific rigour; each photo was from a different angle and height. Much of the river and its margins were obscured by tree canopy and the instream vegetation was hidden by reflections of the sun and sky, so their use for scientific analysis will be minimal. Nevertheless, what a great experience to see the river in this way and to get a feel for the river valley as a whole ...

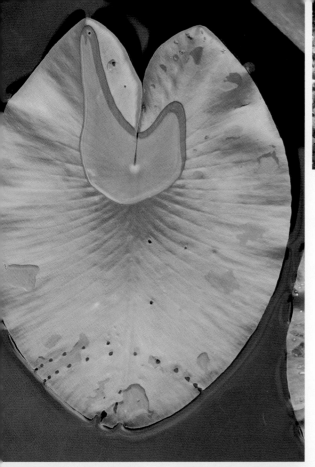

While I'm always up for an adventure, the severity of the banter from my colleagues before I set off did begin to make me wonder a little about the sanity of this exercise.

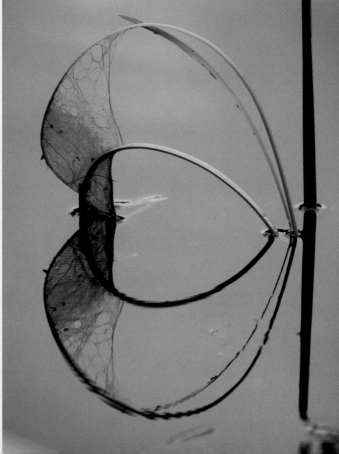

Look at the plants

If the river channel is like the walls of your house then the plants in the river landscape are rather like the soft furnishings. They give the river its soft edges and provide a habitat for the wildlife.

The plants that will grow in a section of river are dictated by the depth and speed of the water as well as the water chemistry. These parameters are influenced in turn by the plants that are growing there. A feedback system occurs between the plants and the water in the river whereby each influences the state of the other.

Different users require different conditions in the river. Too many plants slow down the movement of the water and increase the depth, causing a flood risk. Too few and salmon and trout have no refuges and the food chain suffers. There is a balance to be maintained between river keepers and their preferred mosaic of water plants and open gravels to support salmon fisheries and flood managers trying to keep the water moving smoothly.

HOW PLANTS PROVIDE OXYGEN

Plants are extremely important in maintaining the oxygen levels in rivers particularly in the

lower reaches. In the upper reaches as the river leaps over chutes and spins around rocks the water is nicely mixed and oxygen gets caught up in bubbles and then entrained in the water. As the stream slows down there is little opportunity for air to get in amongst the water and only the water surface is available to absorb oxygen. On a hot sunny day look at the plants under the water and you will see the leaves are covered in a silvery layer of air bubbles – this is oxygen produced by the plants as they photosynthesise and helps maintain oxygen levels in the water. At the end of a busy day of photosynthesis, water in well-vegetated areas can be supersaturated with oxygen – hence the release of bubbles as the water cannot take on even one more wafer thin nibble of oxygen.

The types of plants that can grow in any given stream are so influenced by the physical nature of the substrates and water that it is possible to predict the plants that should be expected in a stream based solely on its geology and size. Rivers are sometimes classified on the basis of the plants that grow there. When the expected plants are not present it is often as a result of man's activities – such as excessive water abstraction, changing the water chemistry by addition of pollutants or affecting the river structure by over engineering. We can assess the level of human impact by checking the plants that are present.

How to assess the health of your river

Take just one look at a river and the plants that are growing there can tell you so much about the river. Even if you don't really know why, a river with hardly any plants in the water or on the banks doesn't look right. Neither does a river where the water is held up by dense clumps of grasses and long-stemmed plants that go right across the river channel. You may not know why that isn't right but something in the balance of the river is not working.

As a very general measure of the quality of your river, you can look at the ratio of the cover in the river and the diversity of plants in the river. As with all environments, a good mix of species is the ideal. A diversity of plants in a river suggests a suitable physical structure which would present a good selection of microhabitats for the invertebrates and appropriate conditions for higher animals too.

The great thing about this measure is that it is not necessary to identify the different plants; you just need to be able to recognise that they are different.

COUNTING THE NUMBER OF PLANT SPECIES

❶ Find a good vantage point – a bridge or raised bank.

❷ From your lookout point and then work out and count how many different types of plants you can see in the river channel. Each species you can see counts as ONE. Note that a number of species are grouped together and only count as ONE. For example, no matter how many different mosses are present they only count as ONE. All *Ranunculus* spp. (water buttercup) are aggregated as are *Callitriche* spp. (starwort which has a small notch at the end of each leaf, which are often arranged into a rosette).

❸ Estimate how much of the river surface is covered in plant growth. Every 10 per cent of the river that is covered counts as ONE. **NOTE** If floating duckweed – *Lemna* spp. or *Azolla* spp. cover more than 10 per cent of the water surface they still only count as ONE.

❹ Add up your species and cover scores. For example, let's say you have managed to identify 10 different-looking plants and the total water surface cover of these is 50 per cent, but there is also duckweed covering about a further 30 per cent of the water surface then your cover diversity number (CoDi for short) is 11 species plus 6 for cover (remember duckweed never counts as more than one for cover), a total of 17.

• •

CoDi numbers greater than 20 are generally considered good and 15 would be acceptable. Lower numbers suggest there has been too

The reedmace is the plant with the big brown fluffy seedhead, which is also often called a bulrush. In fact officially the bulrush is the American common name of a much smaller plant of the clubrush family (Schoenolplectus spp.). The common name of bulrush for the reedmace seems to have almost taken over and become accepted now in the UK.

much human impact in one way or another.

This is a very rough guide but it can be interesting to see how the CoDi number changes as you walk along the stream. The CoDi on or below a weir may be much lower than the score upstream of the weir, concave eroded banks much lower than shelving banks etc. It is then possible to see what the impact of humans on the physical river may be having on the health of our rivers.

Useful water plants

Before the advent of synthetic drugs and medicines the only place to go for cures was nature and many of our existing medicines were originally derived from natural sources. Probably the most widely used medicine was originally derived from two riverside plants: pre-synthetic aspirin was developed originally from Meadowsweet (*Filipendula ulmaria*) and the White Willow tree (*Salix alba*) bark. It was originally known as a remedy to aid digestion, to cure headaches and provide pain relief. It was and still is used as an anti-inflammatory to provide respite for arthritis and rheumatism sufferers. Many other plants have less well celebrated and recognised medicinal properties that are no longer exploited widely.

The Yellow Flag Iris (*Iris pseudachorus*) found around the margins of slow flowing rivers has wonderful yellow flowers (flags) that are used as a yellow dye, the roots conversely provide a black dye.

The peat moss (*Sphagnum* spp.) is mildly antiseptic and has the amazing characteristic of being able to hold up to twenty times its own weight in water. This feature has led to its use in many ways including as a sponge, sanitary towel, a wound dressing and a nappy. This sponge-like character has made it useful as bedding for animals as well as man and a kind of primitive bubble wrap for precious belongings — including small children.

The Norfolk Reed (*Phragmites australis*) is the source of the whispering reeds found alongside lowland slow flowing rivers. The sound is made as the wind blows through the stems and leaves. Home to many small birds and mammals the reed was harvested extensively in the Norfolk

Duckweed

Crack Willow

Peat moss

Meadowsweet

Yellow Flag Iris

Norfolk Reed

Plants are affected by the conditions in which they are growing. The rock type in an area will strongly affect the chemistry of the river water that favours some plants above others. Human activities also affect the water chemistry of the river and will alter the types of plants that flourish there. The plants are therefore good indicators of what is going on in the river.

Pollutants enter our rivers as a result of man's activities, these include: chemicals which will be toxic to the wildlife; human and animal waste which uses dissolved oxygen from the water as it decays, suffocating the waterlife; run-off from agricultural land increasing the nutrients in the river – this fertilises the river causing the rapid increase in growth of some plants; as these die they decay, which uses up all the oxygen.

RECOGNISING POLLUTION An indicator of extreme pollution is 'sewage fungus' – the slimy brown growth on the bottom of highly polluted rivers. Sewage fungus is usually present immediately downstream of a polluting input such as raw sewage; no other plants can tolerate such polluted conditions. As the pollution is broken down downstream blanket weed will appear. The filamentous green algae grow in long, hair-like growths; with unlimited nutrients the growth can blanket the river, hence the name.

A classic problem in nutrient-enriched areas is the growth of blue green algae. These single-celled algae form huge blooms; they can turn the water green and are sometimes toxic.

At the other end of the nutrient enrichment scale, peat moss (*Sphagnum* spp.) is often seen in and around springs and small upland watercourses. Sphagnum moss is never seen in nutrient-rich waters so is a reliable indicator of low levels of nutrients. Water Mint (*Mentha aquatica*) similarly favours low nutrient waters in lowland areas.

HOW THE RIVER FLOWS Plants are also highly influenced by river flows so that the plants can be used to identify flow changes. Nearly all rivers in this country are exploited for their water; which goes to our taps as well as agriculture and industry. The flows are carefully managed to ensure that sufficient water is available for downstream users, to support the wildlife and also to ensure water quality is maintained. This is a careful balance, some plants will move in when flow conditions change and can indicate a problem.

Grasses, rushes and reeds can only root in shallow water. In a typical river they will be restricted to the shallow water at the margins of the river. If there are flow problems in the river then these groups of plants will be able to extend right across the riverbed. Once this happens sediment gets trapped and water flow can be restricted. This in turn can cause a problem in times of high flow when the channel cannot transport the water efficiently and flooding occurs.

A typical succession of dominant grasses occurs as you move downstream from the faster flowing, nutrient poor uplands to the slower flowing and more nutrient rich lowland rivers. In the highlands the dominant grass will be the reed canary grass – *Phalaris arundinacea*; moving downstream the next would be the branched bur-reed – *Sparganium erectum* and the next the reedmace – *Typha latifolia*, the sedges – *Carex* spp. and the sweet-grass – *Glyceria* spp. all of which thrive low down rivers where there is naturally more silt. The presence of any of these in the main channel suggests poor flow conditions.

RECOGNISING CHANGES IN THE RIVER Plants can indicate all kinds of changes in the river environment, sometimes quite subtle changes.

One particularly useful set of indicators is the water buttercup family – the Ranunculaceae – also known as water crowsfoot and identifiable by their white buttercup-like flower in spring.

The different members of the family favour slightly different conditions, and their common names reflect the conditions they like to inhabit. The presence or absence of each species will indicate the prevailing environmental conditions.

Stream water Crowfoot – *Ranunculus penicillatus*, is the signature plant of lowland chalk streams. In areas with flow problems the Pond water Crowfoot – *R. peltatus* may be dominant, as it is in ponds and lakes. In upland regions River water Crowfoot – *R. fluitans*, will dominate, its long fingered leaf shape perfectly adapted to the faster flowing water. When the river gets salty, close to its tidal limit, the brackish water crowfoot – *R. baudotii* takes over.

It is by monitoring the presence and changes in abundance of these kinds of species that ecologists can assess the evolving health of our rivers.

broads and Norfolk coastline where freshwater springs meet the sea marshes. The Norfolk Reed was always prized as a particularly durable thatching material, being long-lived and resistant to rotting. The thatching industry and harvesting of reed still goes on today but at much lesser levels than previously. Along with the reeds, the Great Fen Sedge (*Cladium mariscus*) is harvested for use as an edging material on thatched roofs.

A number of the riverside plants are known for their sweet smell and were much prized in the days before house-cleaning products became so dominant. The leaves were picked and spread around the floor of houses and churches to provide a pleasant aroma. Plants that were used widely include Sweet Flag (*Acorus calamus*) and Meadowsweet (*Filipendula ulmaria*).

Why not try...

any good quality river, but rivers in chalk areas are especially good for seeing water buttercups.

River Barle, Wheal Eliza, Simondsbath, Exmoor (4)

River Test, Mottisfont Abbey, Hampshire (19)

River Itchen, Martyr Worthy, Winchester, Hampshire (20/21)

River Ouse, Barcombe Mills, Lewes, East Sussex (27)

River Lambourne, Boxford, Berkshire (41)

River Thames, Duxford, Oxfordshire (45)

Little Ouse, Santon Downham, Thetford, Norfolk (58)

Waveney, Hoxne Weir, Suffolk (62)

River Ant, Broad Fen, Weyford Bridge, Norfolk (66)

River East Allen, Allendale,, County Durham (113)

(x) numbers relate to site listings in the resources section.

All rivers involve a bit of wilderness and the chances are there will be some wild plants around. So why not forage for something wild to brighten your meal? Foraging for wild foods has become an increasingly popular pastime but it need not be a burden or just a passing trend, it is extremely rewarding and can be environmentally friendly too if you catch some invading signal crayfish for example.

The best time to forage is spring when all the fresh young shoots and leaves are just getting going, or autumn when good root stock has been laid down for winter and the berries are ripening. On your walk down to the river and again when you get there, forage for food to supplement the picnic you have carried in. Some plants to avoid at all costs are given on p104.

The following is an entirely subjective list of a few favourite plants commonly found near rivers, easily identified and which make a tasty addition to food you may already have.

Wild Garlic or ramsons (*Allium ursinum*) These are common in woodland and damp ground. There are many river banks and approaches where I have been treated to a visual display of the six-starred white flower with its vibrant long, wide, strap-shaped green leaves and straight juicy stems. Contrasting beautifully with their seasonal partners, the bluebells, they make a fragrant carpet throughout spring and early summer. Often the smell will alert you to their presence. The leaves are best harvested before the flower emerges and can be used chopped up or shredded to give a mild garlic flavour to any food. They can be added to salad, slipped into a sandwich, used for garlic butter or added to mayonnaise to make a wonderful aioli or wrap fish in the leaves before you grill them. The bulbs themselves can be used as you would dried garlic.

Water Mint (*Mentha aquatica*) One of my personal favourites, this grows abundantly along the margins of rivers and in damp ground. Another highly fragrant plant, you may smell it before you see it, particularly if the leaves are crushed as you walk by. The leaves, which grow in opposing pairs, are slightly hairy, a deep green often tinged with a purple margin; the stem is hairy and square. When in flower, between July and October, they have a cluster of mauve flowers that stand up above the leaves.

The leaves make a refreshing infusion as a

mint tea. It can be bitter compared to the domestic variety so take the Moroccan approach and add sugar. It is a wonderfully restorative tea — and good for the digestion too. A few leaves shredded into a salad or added to a cheese sandwich give a bit of a zing. Chop and mix them into plain yoghurt with some wild garlic leaves and you have a lovely 'Wild England' tzatziki to dip bread into.

Watercress (*Nasturtium officinale*) Growing wild on the margins of rivers and streams, watercress is still farmed and harvested in water diverted from main rivers throughout the UK. It is a well-known peppery addition to salads which is packed with goodness and has high levels of vitamin C and zinc.

The first problem is to distinguish true watercress from Fool's Watercress, *Apium nodiflorum*. The easiest way to tell them apart is actually to crush the leaves. *Apium* smells of parsnip or carrot while the true watercress has a distinctive peppery taste and smell. The leaves of watercress are rounder, darker, smoother edged and slightly shiny while those of *Apium* are more papery with toothed edges.

Common nettle (*Urtica dioica*) A plant that gardeners wage war on, the nettle is actually very important for wildlife in the UK. Many insects and birds, as well as some of our native butterflies, rely on the nettle for food. It is best harvested, using gloves, between March and May after which is gets tough. You can cook it and eat it as you would spinach as the cooking denatures the stingers. It can also make a nice tea if used as an infusion.

Reedmace (*Typha latifolia*) These are the plants that most people know as the bulrush — which is confusing as it is actually a reed. They are common in England and Wales but rare in Scotland, growing in still or slow flowing water and ditches. They are easily identifiable once they grow their trademark dark brown and velvety flower spike, between June and July. The leaves are long and strap shaped with a bluish-green colour, wrap around each other at the base and are flat in cross section sometimes twisting round. The roots can be boiled up and used as a potato substitute. It is ideally harvested, like potatoes, in autumn. In spring they send up shoots from the base which can also be steamed or boiled as a vegetable.

Water Mint

Watercress

Nettle

Blackberry (*Rubus fruticosa*) These are the best and most prolific wild berries around. Brambles grow almost anywhere they can — and are another plant that many gardeners spend considerable time and energy in clearing. We had just managed to clear our plot when we were given a tank full of stick insects as a gift — and their favourite food was bramble leaves. I couldn't believe we were now obliged to go out on foraging trips to find brambles in the hedgerows to bring home. The blackberry is almost guaranteed in hedgerows bordering the rough grazing which runs alongside most of Britain's rivers. The berries ripen between August and October and can either be eaten on the day or warrant a dedicated foraging mission to be taken home for jams, jellies and crumbles as well as fresh fruit in its own right.

Other berries that make good foraging include bilberries, wild raspberries, rosehips and rowan berries or try sloes to make sloe gin.

Foraging rules

When you are foraging for wild food there are some rules to remember:

● Collect in areas well away from roads — for safety and because exhaust fumes and dust don't do the food any good.

● Collect sparingly and only as much as you will use. Never clear all the plants from an area, you want to be able to forage next time.

● Clean all plants well in clean water before you eat them.

● Be aware of liver flukes. These tiny flatworms live in the liver ducts of sheep and cattle. They lay up to 500,000 eggs a day which are passed out of the host animal and end up in river clinging to vegetation. They cause a condition known as fascioliasis. The symptoms are vomiting, diarrhoea, fever and abdominal pain. If there is a chance your water plants have been exposed to animals wash thoroughly or cook to kill any eggs present.

Why not try...

foraging for wild foods at any of the listed locations, they will all have something to offer.

Reedmace

Blackberry

Sloeberry

✻ Notebook: Plants to avoid

Cowbane leaf

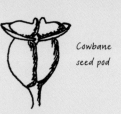
Cowbane seed pod

THE CARROT FAMILY Several plants of the carrot family live with their roots in the water or on the damp margins of rivers. The most important ones to identify are the Cowbane, Hemlock and Hemlock Water Dropwort, which are extremely poisonous and Giant Hogweed with its phototoxic sap.

Hemlock (*Conium maculatum*) is highly poisonous. It grows erect up to 2m, commonly has red streaks on the stem and has leaves divided, up to four times, into fine leaflets. The toxin is present throughout the plant and eating six to eight leaves of hemlock would be fatal to an adult. The symptoms are depression, paralysis of the respiratory system and death. Patients can be kept alive with artificial ventilation for 72 hours while the poison works its way out of the system.

Cowbane (*Cicuta virosa*) is also highly toxic. It grows erect to just over 1m and has sharply toothed almost triangular leaves divided two to three times. The toxin is concentrated in the lower stem and root. A chunk of cowbane root the size of an eating apple would kill a dog and two apples a horse. Symptoms include vomiting, tremors and seizures, all of which develop rapidly and are usually untreatable.

Hemlock Water Dropwort (*Oenanthe crocata*) is also highly toxic although it has edible leaves but poisonous roots. The upper leaves are celery or parsley like and broadly triangular, the lower leaves spread wide and can reach up to 30cm long. A chunk of Hemlock Water Dropwort root the size of an eating apple would kill a dog, and two apples a horse. Symptoms include vomiting, tremors and seizures, all of which develop rapidly and are usually untreatable.

There are less lethal, members of the carrot family on the river bank; Water Parsnip (*Berula erecta*), Water Dropwort (*Oenanthe aquatic*) and Fool's Watercress (*Apium nodiflorum*), they can all be differentiated by their growth and leaves but if you are in any doubt, avoid them all.

Giant Hogweed (*Heracleum mantegazzianum*)
This vast species can form great forests alongside lowland streams towering up to 5m tall with hollow, brittle, purplish stems, up to 8cm across and deeply incised compound leaves up to 1.5m across. In summer it has huge umbellifer flowerheads that can be 80cm across and in winter the stems remain standing, to signal where the plants are. The sap of the stem can burn the skin; sap in the eyes can lead to temporary or permanent blindness. The initial response to the sap is reddening and itching of the skin; once the sap covered skin is exposed to sunlight the skin rapidly blisters, as if the skin has been burnt severely. Once healed the blisters leave permanent purple scars.

If you see the giant hogweed don't touch it. If any sap does get on the skin wash off immediately with soap and water and keep covered from sunlight for several days.

Hemlock leaf

Hemlock seed pod

The world you observe on the surface of the water is wonderful but it is only when you venture under the water that you will begin to understand how rivers really work.

Once in the water there are really only three ways to travel: hold your breath like a Dipper, scuba dive like a water boatman or snorkel like a mosquito larva.

Hold your breath

The Dipper is unique amongst British diving birds as it actually runs along the bottom of the river, holding on to the stones and picking out insects. However, in common with other diving birds, other than nasal flaps to stop the water getting in through their beaks and high levels of haemoglobin, they have no specialised breathing tricks; they basically hold their breath. If you go under the water like a Dipper, it is quick and easy, requires little specialised equipment but there are obviously limitations to the amount of time you can stay underwater. This means that while you are investigating the rocks and plants or coming nose to nose with a brown trout, the pressure will gradually be building and you may not be able to fully enjoy the experience before you are forced to

explode to the surface scaring all the wildlife 50m upstream and downstream.

Scuba divers

At the other end of the scale, you can take your own air supply with you and scuba dive. The water beetles are the masters of this little trick. The water boatmen can be seen quite clearly from the water surface swimming upside down carrying with them their silvery ball of air. They use this air bubble for buoyancy as well as for oxygen supply. When they compress the bubble it increases its density and the beetle sinks, release it and the density decreases again and they rise up. This system is very simple for beetles that can capture air simply under their wings. For humans the process is much more complex — and pricey, requiring tanks, tubes,

regulators, buoyancy aids, fins, wetsuits and weights as an absolute minimum. While I have known people who scuba dive in rivers and have even taken part myself on the odd occasion, it is generally not necessary. Rivers in this country are typically quite shallow and the visibility not that good, so you can see and reach everything you want by swimming along the surface and on short dives. This means it is ideal snorkelling territory.

Snorkelling

The mosquito larva is the natural world's snorkeller. Renowned for living in stagnant pools in conditions with virtually no oxygen, the mosquito larva uses a breathing tube or snorkel to take in oxygen from the air above the water, so outwitting the competition and living in otherwise uninhabitable waters. I recommend that you emulate the mosquito in using a snorkel but not in the kind of waters you investigate. Stick to the flowing, well-oxygenated waters of British rivers and have a look at the abundant wildlife going about its daily tasks under the water.

Looking under the water

At the most basic level you will need some kind of goggles or mask and a snorkel. If you get more advanced you can add fins and if you feel the cold or want to stay in longer, a wetsuit. A good mask that fits well is important as it keeps the water out and makes your breathing more efficient so you can enjoy the view better and for longer. A good pair of fins also makes a big difference in a river. The flowing nature of a river means you can allow yourself to be carried downstream and get a good view on your way without having to put any effort in. If you want to stop and take a longer look you will need fins to work against the current to hold yourself still with the minimum of effort and disturbance to the wildlife. Only try this in, at most, a moderately flowing river — anything too fast and the only option is to go downstream or hold on to a tree trunk.

CHECK THE CURRENT

You can make a simple calculation to work out what speed of current you can swim against. We will assume that you just want to kick so that you can keep your hands free for exploring. At your local pool do a few lengths kicking only and calculate your speed e.g. 25m taking 60secs calculate $25/60 = 0.4$m/s so you will only be able to hold your position in virtually still waters. With fins it may be more like 25m in 20s = 1.25m/s so you will be able to hold your position in slowly flowing water.

Remember preceding weather conditions can have a big impact on river conditions so be prepared to keep an eye out for faster conditions and adapt your plans if necessary.

While you are underwater it can be great fun to take a camera and get some pictures. Although you can't take a standard camera, at little expense you can get a disposable underwater camera. With this you can take pictures of yourself and your companions as well as the wildlife. I love pictures taken at the water surface where you get a bit of the greeny murk underwater as well as some of the action above the water.

HOW TO MAKE AN UNDERWATER VIEWER

A great alternative to getting into the water is to make your own underwater viewer.

❶ Find an empty, unwanted plastic container ideally with a well fitting lid — if you have lost the lid don't worry.

❷ Cut the bottom off the container and the centre out of the lid, if you have one.

❸ Stretch cling film or, even better, a more robust plastic film — the kind used to wrap bunches of flowers is perfect — over the open top of the container.

❹ Hold it in place by putting on the cut out

Why not try...

rivers with easy access to the water and nice clear water, preferably at least knee deep.

River Dart, Deeper Marsh, Ashburton, Dartmoor (10)

River Kennet, Ramsbury Mill Lane, Ramsbury, Wiltshire (17)

Cuckmere River, Cuckmere Meanders, Seaford, East Sussex (29)

River Thames, Duxford, Oxfordshire (45)

Little Ouse, Santon Downham, Thetford, Norfolk (58)

River Ant, Broad Fen, Weyford Bridge, Norfolk (66)

Goredale Beck, Janets Foss, Malham, Yorkshire Dales (83)

Langstrath Beck, Black Moss Pot, Lake District (100)

River Derwent, near Shepherds Crag, Lake District (102)

North Tyne, Chesters Fort, Hadrian's Wall, Northumberland (115)

(x) numbers relate to site listings in the resources section.

lid. If you have no lid then just tape it into place.

❺ As a refinement, once the lid is on, tape the whole lot around with plenty of dark strong tape — black duct tape works well. The dark colour helps to cut out glare.

❻ You can then lower the plastic covered end of the box in to the water and look in — you now have your own glass-bottomed boat to go underwater wildlife spotting. Don't move around too much and the wildlife will become accustomed to you and you should get some great viewing.

River Wey at Tilford, Surrey ... April (39)

... I took Lottie off to the River Wey today. Just 15 minutes drive from Guildford, weaving through leafy country-lanes down the Wey Valley. Bounded by the North Downs to the north and the South Downs to the south, Tilford sits picturesquely on the river. There is the quintessentially English village green with pub and village stores and cluster of buildings, with a wonderful arched bridge spanning the wide and shallow River Wey. The shallow grassy bank of the Wey in the village is perfect for small people. We had taken our pond net as well as glass jars with lengths of string to make fish traps. With our picnic we were set for an afternoon of fun. The picnic soon attracted some very persistent ducks which were not to be deterred, even by Lottie's strong bellow and some gentle pushing.

As soon as we set up the fishing jars we found we had attracted some equally persistent small boys who were not put off by Lottie's favourite words 'mine' and 'no', said in equally strident terms with hand held up like a traffic warden. Eventually with settlements negotiated, we all had a great time luring tiddlers into our jars with the lunch remains while the ducks picked over the smaller debris and looked on indignantly with rather pitiful, lugubrious quacks ...

HOW TO FISH WITH A JAM JAR

One way to catch fish in the river without lines and rods is to prowl and pounce with your pond net; you may be lucky but for proper tiddler fishing what you really need is a jam jar. The equipment is simple:

❶ Tie string as tightly as possible around the neck of a jar, then leave a long loop above the jar as a handle. You may also want to tie under the base of the jar for additional security (see illustration).

❷ Put your bait, a bit of bread or other tasty morsel, in the bottom of the jam jar.

❸ Have a good look into the water and see if you can spot some small fish flitting around in the shallows. Slowly lower the jam jar slowly in to the water in their vicinity. If you do it slowly, the bait should stay in the jar and you will scare the fish less. If you have a problem with the bait floating away you could try putting it in a small mesh bag — the ones satsumas are sold in are perfect — and weighting it in to the bottom of the jar, or use a honey sandwich and place it honey side down! Before long these curious fish will come over and have a good look at the jar, bumping their noses up against it and if you are patient, it won't be long before they find their way into the jar to get at the bait.

❹ Pick your moment when they are well settled in and then act fast: quickly and carefully lift the jar out of the water with the fish inside.

Now take your time and observe your fish.

Why not try...

any river or stream where you can reach the water.

River Barle, Withypool, Exmoor **(2)**

Dockens Water, Linwood, New Forest **(13)**

River Kennet, Ramsbury Mill Lane, Ramsbury, Wiltshire **(17)**

River Thames/Isis, Port Meadow, Oxford, Oxfordshire **(46)**

River Stour, Dedham Bridge, Essex **(56)**

River Bure, Little Hautbois and Buxton and Lammas, Norfolk **(63/64)**

River Wye, Wilton Bridge, Ross on Wye, Herefordshire **(70)**

River Monnow, Skenfrith Castle, Monmouthshire, Wales **(79)**

River Wharfe, Appletreewick, Yorkshire Dales **(93)**

River Derwent, near Shepherds Crag, Lodore, Lake District **(102)**

(x) numbers relate to site listings in the resources section.

One of the loveliest fish to catch is the stickleback. They are extremely adaptable and can live anywhere from rivers to ponds and ditches. There are two main varieties in the UK – the Three-spined and Nine-spined sticklebacks. They are easily identifiable by the spines that stick up on the top of their backs; three – in the case of the three-spined or in the case of the nine-spined somewhere between seven and ten spines.

The sticklebacks have no scales but a row of bony plates along their sides and are generally a dark olive-green colour. In spring the male's front develops a red blush as he attempts to attract a mate. The male is very territorial to other males and will fight ferociously to keep them away – adult females meanwhile are welcomed with open fins! The male shows off to the females whizzing around in a zigzag dance and if he gets a positive response, he will take her down to a tunnel-like nest he has constructed in the weeds.

These are great fish to watch as you can investigate some of their unusual behaviour very simply.

If you catch a pink-bellied male stickleback in the spring you will be able to observe his territorial behaviour. Once you have the stickleback in a good sized container (e.g. a 1 litre ice cream tub) with plenty of river water, lower a mirror down one of the sides. The male stickleback, seeing his reflection in the mirror, will think that his territory has been invaded by another male and will go into attack mode. He will puff himself up, gape his gills as if flaring his nostrils and start attacking his reflection trying to drive his foe away. Since he is very persistent and will keep this up for some time it may be kindest to remove the mirror before too long.

Don't keep the fish out of the water too long, particularly on a hot day. Once you have finished looking lower the jar gently back into the water where you found the fish and tip it slightly to let the fish swim out.

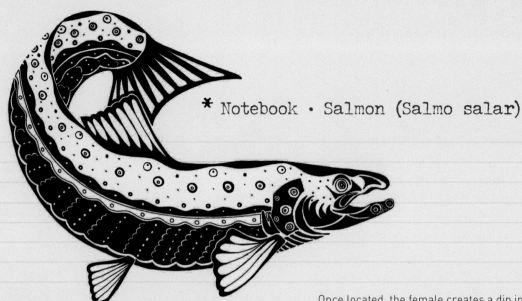

Salmon are at the top of the freshwater fish family tree. Since they require ample cool, clean freshwater, a well-functioning habitat and an open route between river and sea, the presence of the iconic salmon in a river is the ultimate acclaim and indicates a top quality river. The River Thames supports 116 different fish species, however, it was only when the salmon returned to the river in 1974, for the first time in 150 years that people took notice and the image of the Thames as a polluted river was transformed.

THE GREAT MIGRATION The salmon's complex life history accentuates their special nature. The salmon undertakes a major migration from the ocean back to the spawning grounds in the headwaters of its birth-river. It has to overcome many barriers on the way up the river and Salmon may be seen on their journey leaping up waterfalls and fish ladders between October and November. The female requires clean, well-oxygenated gravel beds to lay her eggs in.

Once located, the female creates a dip in the gravel by flexing her body and fans the gravel with her fins to clear away silt and create the 'redd'. The female deposits her eggs, as the male simultaneously ejects milt to fertilise the eggs, which the female then covers with gravel.

The egg's development rate is dependent on water temperature, but usually it is a few months before the alevins hatch. These tiny alevins live off the yolk sac as they develop, still under the gravel, for two or three months. In spring they have developed into fry which wriggle out through the gravels into the water above. Two or three months later the young change colour and develop finger-like markings along their side; they are now known as 'parr' and will stay in the river until they turn a silvery colour and begin their migration downriver and out to sea as two year old 'smolts'. The smolts congregate in shoals and wait for high flows to make this journey.

After the fish have matured for a year or more at sea they return again, to their birth river, as silvery 'grilse' to spawn. After spawning most fish return to the sea and die although a minority will return to spawn again.

The eel is probably one of the least sexy of the river animals, although fantastically interesting and mysterious.

If the salmon life cycle looks amazing then the current theory on the eel is even more so. There are still so many unproven elements of the eel life cycle that the mystery surrounding them makes them almost mythical creatures.

Aristotle believed that eels spontaneously arose from the wet soil while Pliny the Elder thought that they shed bits of skin, by rubbing against rocks, and these pieces of skin came to life to create new eels.

A MYSTERIOUS LIFE CYCLE The mystery of the eel's life cycle was apparently solved in the 1920s by the Danish oceanographer Johannes Schmidt. After 16 years trawling the sea he concluded that all eels are born in the Sargasso Sea in the North Atlantic. From here the eel larvae (virtually transparent, 'glass' eels just 5cm long) are carried by the Gulf Stream the 3000 to 4000 miles to Europe. They are carried into river mouths and on reaching the freshwater, transform into freshwater fish (elvers). These have a thick mucus covering on their skin which allows them to travel across wet grassland to reach more remote water bodies so are able to colonise the whole of the country. They live in freshwaters until they reach maturity (anything between two and 40 years). They then undergo a physical transformation, including increase in eye size, change in colour, swim bladder and

reproductive organs, to become silver eels. They then build up their fat stores before returning to the Sargasso Sea where the females spawn, the males fertilise the eggs and they all die of exhaustion.

While this is a widely accepted theory there has been little confirmation of this life cycle. While glass eels have been found in the Sargasso Sea neither live adults nor any eggs have been found. No eel has ever bred in captivity. All studies of the reproductive organs of eels have failed as they shut down immediately on capture. As a young man the founder of psychoanalysis, Sigmund Freud, was fascinated by eels and dedicated himself to studying their life cycle. He studied hundreds of eels but was so disgusted by his lack of progress that he moved on to his other, more famous, studies.

* Notebook · Pike (Esox lucius)

All fish are worthy of mention and investigation but of particular interest is the much-maligned monster of England's freshwater – the Pike.

The Pike is an ancient fish; the modern day Pike is little altered from its fossil ancestors of 20 million years ago.

There are so many stories of Pike it is hard to know where to begin. In almost any lowland water body the locals will tell you eye popping stories that allude to the grandfather of all Pike, an uncatchable beast that evades the hook or has broken rods, pulled in fishermen, killed dogs or even horses that have stopped to drink; but all these stories seem to greatly exaggerate the age and voracity of the Pike.

There is one apocryphal tale of the 'Emperor's Pike' taken from a lake near Mannheim in Germany in 1497. Measuring 19ft (6m) and weighing 350lb (160kg), it was apparently captured with a copper ring on its gills that indicated it had been in the lake for 267 years since Emperor Frederick II placed it there. The story was supported by a Pike skeleton preserved in Mannheim Cathedral. Eventually a scientist investigated the skeleton and found that it had acquired a whole section of extra vertebrae and the myth was exploded.

In spite of all the exaggerated tales there is no doubt that the Pike is a big and cantankerous predator. It can take prey up to half its own weight and has been observed picking off ducklings one by one as they follow their mother. It is easily recognised with its elongated body and long, wide, flattened snout. They generally mature at around 1m length and 8kg weight but an old fish of 30 years may reach 1.5m and over 40kg.

In the mediaeval Antiphoner at Ranworth Church on the Norfolk Broads – where many great Pike roam – the illuminated 'S' contains a picture of Jonah being swallowed by the big fish often referred to as a whale. This whale has distinctly Pike-like features. Five hundred years ago, when the local monks were illustrating their book of prayers and hymns, they would have taken the biblical reference to a big fish and modelled their illustration on the biggest fish in their waters – the Pike.

There are many fictional tales where tickling is mentioned, from Shakespeare's *Twelfth Night* where Maria greets Malvolio with the words, 'for here comes the trout that must be caught with tickling' (Act 2, Scene 5) to Roald Dahl's *Danny, Champion of the World* and Arthur Ransome's *Swallows and Amazons*.

The art of tickling is to watch where the fish are lying up and then move into the water near their hole. Trout in particular like to lie up in dark holes – this may be amongst tree roots, under overhanging banks or under flat rocks or even in little waterfall plunge pools. Push your hand, or even better, hands in a pincer like movement in to the deep, dark hole and feel with your fingers until you feel the fish. This is the tricky bit because, while tickling the fish, you need to move your hands towards the head of the fish until they are just behind the gills. The fish should be in a trance of ecstasy at this point and can be grasped and flicked rapidly out of the water.

That is the theory, but it has never worked that way for me... Finding my likely spot I move in close and start to put my arm down to the hole. In my head I have vivid pictures of large, barbaric Pike and the knowledge that they like to lurk around in dark places alongside crayfish with outsized pincers. I feel around and my hand touches something – it could be a fish, it could be a tree stump but my mind is overactive and with a scream I don't hang around to find out which way leads to the head. Floundering around in the thigh deep water, I get completely drenched and muddy and retreat from the river in disgrace. I have heard it said that it is worth the initial fifty failures when you get your first fish – but I wouldn't know.

Note: You should be aware that trout tickling is illegal in most circumstances in Britain; however this relates mainly to fishing in prohibited areas or private waters without permission

Go bird watching

Swan Upping on the Thames ... July (52-47)

... Swan Upping is a swan census ceremony that started as a means for medieval noblemen to mark valuable swans as their property. To signal a ownership of a swan, small nicks were made on the beak in a pattern unique to each nobleman. The cygnets of a swan belonging to a particular nobleman would also belong to him. The week-long census would establish ownership of all the season's cygnets on the river. Any unmarked swans and cygnets were claimed by the Crown. Swan Upping has always been held in the third week in July, when the adults are mid-moult and the cygnets still young, so that none can fly away.

Starting on the Monday of the third week in July at Sunbury in Surrey, the Royal Swan Master and the Swan Uppers travel upstream in traditional rowing skiffs, capturing and marking swans on the way, until they reach Abingdon on Friday, where they drink a toast to the Queen at Abingdon Bridge. Two livery companies – the Vintners and the Dyers – and the Crown, maintain the tradition. These two companies, along with the Ilchester family in Dorset, are the only three bodies who have retained the right to own swans in England. Swans lost their financial value when poultry took over as a cheap source of protein in the 1850s; today the ceremony is now more about conservation. The Swan Upping is a wonderful example of a royal custom although amazingly, the Queen, who is known as the 'Seigneur of the Swans' during the ceremony, only watched it for the first time in 2009.

Today there was a small crowd of us who came and went following the Swan Uppers as they travelled slowly upstream in their skiffs. A few people followed in boats, a few travelled along the towpath on cycles and a few like me travelled from bridge to bridge by car, intercepting the Swan Uppers from time to time. I ran along the towpath for a couple of miles at each stop before going back to retrieve my car and move on to the next convenient crossing.

The whole event has a rather carnival day feel to it. The whole cavalcade looked wonderful. The skiffs carry the embroidered livery flags and everyone

is dressed in their 'uniform'. The Swan Marker wore his captain's hat with swan feather adornment, the Dyers were dapper in their blazers while the Vintners were more homely wearing rustic naval jumpers which showed off their generous proportions.

Whenever swans are sighted the Uppers call out 'all up' and the boats converge on the family, the oars are upended in the boats and the swans are surrounded and captured. Although largely a symbolic process these days it still provides a useful census of swan populations. The swans are taken ashore for a health check by the Queen's Swan Warden. The Queen's Swan Marker then establishes ownership of the parents and the cygnets are marked. No beak notching is done these days but each company has its own ring which is fitted around the swan's leg, while those belonging to The Crown remain unmarked. All swans that are healthy are then returned to the river; those needing treatment are taken to one of the swan rescue centres in the area.

At Abingdon there was a small crowd on the bridge as the Swan Uppers lined up their skiffs, handed round the glasses and finally all stood to toast the Queen – the culmination of a week travelling a large length of the Thames ...

Why not try...

All of the rivers listed here have a particularly rich birdlife.

River Barle, Wheal Eliza, Simondsbath, Exmoor **(4)**

River Arun, WWT reserve, Arundel, West Sussex **(23)**

Pevensey Levels NNR, Pevensey, East Sussex **(30)**

River Stour, Grove Ferry, Canterbury, Kent **(32)**

River Thames, Abingdon, Oxfordshire **(47)**

River Thames, Chertsey Meads, Surrey **(52)**

River Cherwell, Park Town, Oxford, Oxfordshire **(74)**

Goredale Beck and Scar, Malham, Yorkshire Dales **(84)**

River Derwent, near Shepherds Crag, Lodore, Lake District **(102)**

River East Allen, Allendale, Yorkshire Dales **(113)**

(x) numbers relate to site listings in the resources section.

* Notebook • Mute Swans (Cygnus olor)

Mute Swans (the male is a cob, the female, a pen) are the royalty of British lowland waterways with their large size, rich white plumage and long, sinuous necks. A cob may have a wingspan of 2 to 3m and reach 15kg – the weight of a five-year-old child. The impressive neck comes courtesy of the 25 vertebrae, as compared to all mammals (even the giraffe) that have only seven. Swans can be aggressive if they feel their nest or young are threatened, so it is wise to be wary.

In some areas you may see the yellow and black billed Whooper and Bewick's swans as they breeze in to overwinter from Iceland and Siberia but the Mute Swan with its orangey-red bill is resident year round throughout the UK.

Swans usually live around ten years having mated for life at three to four years old. The pen lays around six eggs in nests – messy structures of assorted vegetation on banks or islands, which hatch out as cygnets in late spring. The cygnets learn to fly in around September and their grey plumage transforms over winter so that by one year they are almost indistinguishable from their parents. The following 'teenage' years are spent in the flock until they pair off.

THE SWAN AS A SYMBOL In many cultures, the swan has a symbolic status. At Vaedbaek in Denmark a Mesolithic burial site was uncovered which contained a mother and child; the child had been buried nestled on a swan's wing. It may have been a symbol of good eating to nourish the child in the afterlife or maybe the purity of the swan's plumage reflected the untainted life of the child, and provided the perfect burial shroud.

The swan's metamorphosis from the ugly duckling of Hans Anderson's fairytale to the beautiful swan has made swans a symbol for transformation. Folklore, Arthurian legend, opera, dream interpretation and Greek mythology all contain tales of the swan and people changing roles.

In contrast to their physical beauty their lack of singing voice is notable and Aristotle, Plato and Socrates all believed that the swan would sing a beautiful song when they were close to death which gave rise to the idea of the 'swan song' a final, and most stunning, performance.

A Bewick's Swan

A Mute Swan

The Grey Heron is the biggest bird native to England, standing up to 1m tall with a wingspan of up to 2m. They are often seen flying with their distinctive slow wing beat and concertinaed, u-bend neck. They come from the same family as the egrets and very rare Bittern. Heron prefer sloping shores into shallow water and will wade to 50cm deep. Although rarely seen at high altitudes they are resident and breed throughout lowland Britain. They dislike disturbance and nest in large trees in heronries up to 30km from their feeding grounds.

KEEPING A LOOKOUT Heron are precision hunters and can stand motionless for long periods just waiting for their unsuspecting prey to wander into range. They sometimes stalk their prey, looking very much like Ron Moody's Fagin in the film of *Oliver*, with hunched up shoulders, placing each foot carefully down, never for a second taking their beady eyes from the water. When they spot their prey they dart forwards and catch or spear them on their perfectly adapted dagger-like beak. Herons need half a kilo of fish a day, eating fish up to 16cm long as well as amphibians, invertebrates, small mammals and birds. Herons are sensitive to disturbance and will often fly off if they sense company, often before you have realised they are there. They can be very well camouflaged; with their long lines of colour and linear body they blend in perfectly to the riverside grasses and branches, particularly in winter.

'Old Nog' was the name of the heron in Henry Williamson's *Tarka the Otter*. My father would often point out 'Old Nog' as we disturbed herons when we were out on Exmoor. It has been suggested that the name comes from a fisherman in Norse mythology which would be very apt; however, I have found no references to a Nordic Nog other than Noggin the Nog, the fictional creation of Oliver Postgate. *Tarka the Otter* predates Noggin by some 25 years so can't have been inspired by that.

* Notebook · Coot (Fulica atra) and Moorhen (Gallinula chloropus)

The Coot and the Moorhen are widespread residents throughout the lowlands of Britain and are often misidentified. Although they look superficially similar and occupy similar habitats, the Coot andMoorhen are easily separated. Aside from their generally dark plumage the Coot has a white bill and forehead, while the Moorhen has a yellow tipped red bill and red forehead.

The Coot and the Moorhen are usually seen on slow flowing rivers with good bank-side plant growth. They both feed on plants and invertebrates. Moorhens can tolerate conditions in higher areas in the summer but move to lower ground in winter – the Coot is rarely seen above 250m.

Coots nest on floating mats of vegetation anchored in the plants, which means they are fairly resilient to flooding as the nest will rise with the water level. These nests are often quite out in the open. I have seen Coots choose some very dubious nesting sites; perhaps the most unusual was the nest on a small pile of debris caught by the bridge upright in the middle of the River Thames right in the centre of Abingdon. Moorhens nest on emergent plants or in the branches of trees that overhang the water and can therefore be susceptible to flooding.

Coots have long, strong legs and can walk and run strongly while their wings are short and rounded and result in fairly weak flying. Their feet are very distinctive and differ completely from the moorhen. The Coot has long toes with lobes or flaps on either side, almost like webbed feet that have not quite joined in the middle. The Moorhen's toes are long and bony with no webs or lobes at all.

The Moorhen seems quite a nervous bird; they tend to stay in the margins of the water, nest out of sight and have jerky twitchy movements and for this reason they are sometimes known as 'skitty coots'. Like the Coot, the Moorhen has long strong legs and reasonably weak flight. You will rarely see them flying, but when you do, you will be struck by the way their legs dangle down.

I have always enjoyed the antics of ducks. Almost everyone's first encounter with water birds is with the mallard duck at the local pond or river, where they go to feed them with stale bread and watch the goings on.

Ducks are social animals with a comical waddle and a comical quack. It seems that there is a quantifiable scientific reason why a duck's quack is funny. When you say the word, quack, you are forced to end in a smile and so this automatically makes you and your audience laugh. Remember this if you want to make someone laugh – ducks are funnier than cows – so quack, don't moo.

THE QUACK There is a scientific myth that a duck's quack has no echo. In spring 2003, this scientific myth was perpetuated on BBC Radio 4's *Home Truths* and again on *Shooting Stars* on BBC 2. As a result of this, Professor Cox of the acoustic research centre at Salford University decided to investigate the theory as part of the British Association Festival of Science. He took Daisy the duck into an anechoic chamber to test how the quack sounded with no echoes and then into a specialised reverberation chamber. The quack performed as expected and Professor Cox can now confirm that a duck's quack does in fact echo.

A RUSH FOR A MATE By far the most common duck in this country is the Mallard and most people will have no problem identifying the different sexes: the male with its iridescent green head and neck and the female a generally dull mottled-brown. Both have the distinctive indigo blue and white patch on the trailing edge of the inner wing (the speculum). The differing apparel of the sexes is quite typical of sexual dimorphism in the animal kingdom.

The male Mallard wants to mate with as many females as he can to pass on his genetic material. To attract the females he therefore needs something to show off and that accounts

the blue-billed Ruddy duck from the USA (Defra started a five-year eradication programme in 2005 so they are rarely seen now). Other regular breeders include the Goosander and Red-breasted Merganser, which are most commonly seen in the north of the country, the Gadwall in East Anglia and the familiar and distinctive Tufted duck with its yellow eye, dark tufted head and tail and white wings and tummy.

All other freshwater ducks breed very rarely but can overwinter (or in the case of the Garganey oversummer) in significant numbers on still waters. These include the Wigeon, Gadwall, Teal, Shoveler, Pintail, Scaup, Pochard and Goldeneye.

for his vibrant green head. The female is hotly pursued by the male and really has no desire to encourage him further, consequently her tweedy brown outfit is quite sufficient. In the breeding season, between September and June – it is quite common to see a female Mallard being mobbed by a group of males all trying to mate with her. This can sometimes get quite aggressive and females have been known to be drowned in the crush.

Mallard ducks are so familiar that it is easy to forget that they have to undergo the rigours of life in a wild environment along with other birds and mammals. They, their eggs and their young are as susceptible to predation by foxes and mink as any other bird and are particularly vulnerable to human interference and pollution as they live alongside us in so many areas.

OTHER DUCKS There are around 15 other species of freshwater ducks that are either fully resident or overwinter in this country. There are only a few which regularly breed here, including a couple of introduced species: the locally common, exotic looking Mandarin duck which were originally introduced from East Asia and

The Great Crested Grebe is a distinctive and distinguished bird. They swim low in the water, hold their dagger-like beaks high and peer down them, with their dark beady eyes, in a haughty fashion. As they swim you will see theß long pale neck and face with its rusty orange ruff and dark cap terminating in the distinctive crest which both sexes develop in summer. The feathers of this crest were once in great demand for decorating ladies' hats for which the birds were nearly hunted to extinction.

Great Crested Grebes are usually found on lowland, slow-flowing rivers and lakes throughout England (less commonly in Scotland and Wales), moving to tidal waters in winter.

They are strong swimmers and divers feeding on fish, molluscs, invertebrates and plants. As they dive they make an upward jump, before breaking the surface of the water and disappearing with barely a ripple. They can hold their breath and swim strongly underwater, so it is a guessing game as to where they will reappear – often up to 100m away. Because they are strong swimmers Great Crested Grebes prefer to dive rather than fly away from danger.

EXTRAORDINARY DISPLAYS Great Crested Grebes have the most spectacular mating ritual which, if you are lucky, you may see in spring. The ritual starts when the male and female bird come together face to face and mirror each other in performing symmetrical head shaking, neck bending and beak touching movements. This is an elaborate bonding procedure and can be repeated for several days before the ritual progresses. At some point one of the birds will retreat and return with a beak full of weed as a gift. The ritual climaxes as the birds dance: they rise chest to chest, beaks together full of weeds as they tread water with their bodies almost completely out of the water.

They then make their nest on mounds of emergent vegetation anchored to tree branches, in the water. The male and female share the egg and young tending duties between them.

Family groups are very endearing. The flamboyant adults accessorise nicely with their chicks – balls of grey down with distinctive black and white striped heads, necks and beaks. The young grebes often ride on their parents' backs.

* Notebook · Cormorant (Phalacrocorax carbo)

The Cormorant is a wonderfully characterful bird with a slightly prehistoric appearance of ragged black wings and long hook-tipped bill. Although more commonly thought of as a seabird, the Cormorant regularly comes inland in winter to escape the harsh coastal conditions and can be seen fishing on rivers and lakes all over the country. They have a very distinctive profile and behaviour which makes them easy to identify and fun to watch. Like the Great Crested Grebe they almost jump out of the water as they dive, often reappearing a long way from their point of submergence. Probably the most distinctive behaviour is their stance, either singly or in groups, standing on posts and prominent rocks with wings outstretched. The reason they take on this pose is that their wings have incomplete waterproofing so they need to be dried out after the bird leaves the water.

FISHERMEN'S ALLIES Cormorants are extremely proficient fishermen. In the past their fishing prowess has led to their exploitation. In Japan and China, fishermen capture the birds and tie a ligature around their throats. The Cormorants fish from their boats and then regurgitate their catch, which the ligature prevents them from swallowing, for the fishermen. This practice still takes place today but largely to entertain tourists rather than to supply communities with fish.

Because of their slightly sinister appearance, Cormorants have often been taken as symbols and harbingers of bad fortune. In Ireland, a cormorant perched on a church steeple is a sign of bad luck to follow. John Milton uses this negative image in his epic poem *Paradise Lost*: Satan takes the form of the cormorant as a disguise to enable him to enter Eden, so that he can tempt Eve.

Conversely, their presence suggests good fishing and prosperity so they became symbols of good fortune in other areas. In northern Norway when Cormorants gather in a village, it is seen as a symbol of good luck.

In this country the Cormorant is the official symbol of the city of Liverpool. The two birds on the Liver Building look in opposite directions: one looks over the city – the people – while the other looks over the sea – the city's prosperity.

River Bure, Little Hautbois, Norfolk ... July (65)

... There's a great place on the Bure called Little Hautbois. When I say great, it is very small and the thing I like about it is its name. Our family has a house just three miles from Hautbois which my grandfather built for my grandmother and where they lived and farmed all their married lives. My mother was born and brought up there, I spent a lot of my childhood in the area and we visit regularly these days. I have known the area well all my life. It was only today that I realised the place I have always known as 'Hobbis', a very earthy, Norfolk-sounding place, is actually the Hautbois that I had seen on the road signs and marked on the map and that had conjured quite a different impression in my mind.

Today I made my way to 'Hobbis' and launched the old wooden kayak, still going strong after nearly 40 years. In fact an old Norfolk boy asked me if it was an antique as I loaded it onto the car and was most surprised when I said I was actually contemplating paddling it.

Despite it being the middle of the summer holidays I paddled down one of the most beautiful stretches of river in Norfolk and didn't see a soul until I moored up at the pub in Coltishall. The Bure here runs between unmanicured banks, thick with marginal vegetation and trees. With the gentle current carrying me on, I was able to float almost silently down-stream and it wasn't long before I realised I was following a Kingfisher. Every time I came within about five metres he would take off and fly 20 metres downstream and perch on a branch. This happened several times until he finally settled on a low branch that reached out over the water. This time he stayed, presumably at the limit of his territory and watched me as I floated right past his beak. He was barely a metre away and I could see every shining feather on him. Just after I went past, I dipped one paddle in the water so I could turn to keep watching him; this minute movement alerted him and disturbed, he took off and flew low over the water, letting out his piercing whistling call as he went. I could hear him for some time after he was out of sight ...

It was only today that I realised the place I have always known as 'Hobbis', a very earthy, Norfolk-sounding place is actually the Hautbois I had seen on the road signs …

How to map a bird territory

Making maps of a river corridor is a satisfyingly achievable activity. The fact that you start with one good strong feature – the river – gives a really good point of reference on which to build your map.

MAKE A MAP

To map a bird territory you first need to start with a map of a stretch of river with some good features marked on it. You could use a large-scale Ordnance Survey map or even trace one but it is more fun to draw your own map.

Decide whether you are going to draw to scale or not.

If you want to draw to scale you can measure out the distance with your natural stride. You need to keep your walk natural – strictly no striding out, as it will be less accurate. Count each time your right heel strikes the ground as one complete stride. Then you can mark the distances between each feature in paces rather than metres. At a later date you can calibrate this to a known distance by working out how many of your natural strides it takes to walk a known distance e.g. 100m (details of how to calculate your pace are on page 194).

❶ Start with the basic shape of the river.

❷ Put in major features e.g. bridges or fords, large trees, field boundaries and fences.

❸ Fill in whichever features take your fancy: cattle drinks, clumps of riverside plants, picnic spots, rope swings etc.

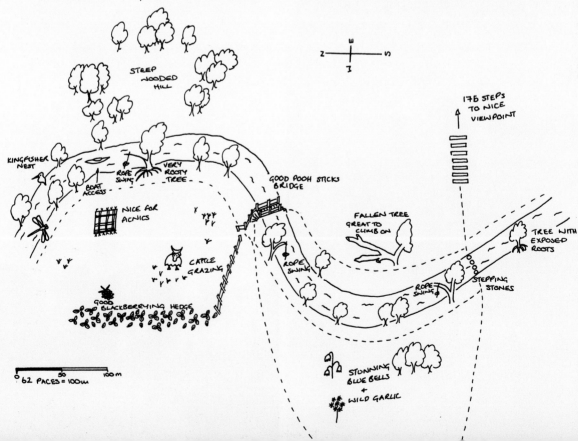

If you need a vantage point, get on to a bridge or hone your tree climbing skills. Remember you will need a good stopping point where you can balance to do your map drawing.

MAP THE TERRITORY

❶ Choose your bird. Two of the best river birds for territory mapping are Kingfishers, if you are in Southern England or Dippers, if you are in the north or south-west. They are also highly entertaining and interesting birds to spend some time watching – if you can find them in the first place.

❷ Find the bird. The easiest time to map a territory is when birds are nesting, as they tend to be out and about a lot more and base themselves more clearly around one location. If you can find their nest then this is a good starting point.

❸ Find the limits of their territory. It is quite easy to work out where the territories start and finish. Being quite timid birds, both Dippers and Kingfishers will try to stay away from you. As you walk along the river bank or travel up the river in a boat, the birds will fly ahead of you to maintain a safe distance. Eventually, when you reach the bird's territorial limit, he will turn and fly back downstream; that will be the edge of its territory in one direction. Repeat the process going in the other direction and you have its territorial limits. Once you have identified the edge of a bird's territory this can be a great place to sit quietly and watch, particularly in spring around mating and nesting time. It is at the edge of territories that displays of territorial bravado are most often seen when territorial conflicts arise.

Why not try...

rivers with Kingfishers and Dippers, details can be found from the local wildlife trusts.

Horner Water, Horner, Exmoor **(5)**

River Itchen, Winchester St Cross and College, Hampshire **(21)**

River Mole, Norbury Park, Leatherhead, Surrey **(35)**

River Wey, Shalford, Surrey **(37)**

River Thames, Chimney Meadows, Oxfordshire **(44)**

River Ant, Broad Fen, Weyford Bridge, Norfolk **(66)**

Wellow Brook, Wellow, Bath, Somerset **(76)**

River Lune, Devils Bridge, Kirby Lonsdale **(88)**

Grizedale Beck, Grizedale Forest, Lake District **(109)**

River Coquet, Linshiels, Northumberland **(114)**

(x) numbers relate to site listings in the resources section.

* Notebook · Dippers (Cinclus cinclus)

Dippers are decidedly unflashy birds, blackbird-sized with a dumpy body shape and uniformly brown plumage with a distinctive white bib. In the human world the dipper would be a maitre d', bowing in a self-deprecating manner. They usually nest in bridges or walls, always over or close to water and can be seen all year round in turbulent, stony rivers, mostly in the north and southwest of Britain.

Dippers are easily spotted, even though they don't stay still for long. It is most likely you will see one perched on a rock mid-stream bobbing up and down and cocking its tail. If you suspect Dippers are present look out for a mid-stream rock liberally covered with white droppings; this may well be a dipper's favourite haunt.

When they fish, Dippers are able to stay and hunt underwater and it is here that its daredevil alter ego is released. Once in the water it takes on the guise of a 007 rather than a maitre d'. Diving into the water from a rock perch and re-emerging some way along the stream, it can either fly under the water using its wings as flippers, like a penguin's, or, using its unique ability to actually walk along the bottom, it grips with its toes and claws, turning over stones with its beaks to find the insects and small fish on which it feeds. Dippers' eyes have clear protective eyelids that work a bit like swimming goggles.

* Notebook · Kingfisher (Alcedo atthis)

The Common Kingfisher is one of the UK's most exotic resident birds. They live by and feed in slow-flowing, clear watercourses, largely in aouthern England and Wales.

Often all that you will see of a Kingfisher is a flash of blue and orange as one whizzes by low over the water, accompanied by their shrill, whistling call. This striking plumage is the most distinctive feature, however, it is worth noting that, if looked at in the shade, their feathers are surprisingly dull. The sunlight shining on and reflecting off the different semi-transparent layers of the feather gives the bird its beautiful colours – a phenomenon that is known as irridescence.

SEEING KINGFISHERS If you can identify their favourite perch or nest you will dramatically increase your chances of seeing a Kingfisher. A likely fishing perch would be a branch extending low over the water, no more than a couple of feet off the water, where the Kingfisher has a good view into a shallow pool. A typical nesting place would be in a muddy or sandy bank or cliff. Look for holes in the bank 1–2 m above normal water level and around 50cm from the top of the bank. Kingfishers are monogamous and the couples work together for up to two weeks to excavate their nest hole, scooping the mud out with their beaks. They create an upward sloping tunnel (to avoid flooding) with a chamber at the end of it, in which the female lays up to 17 eggs each year.

Kingfishers fish from a perch, diving to a maximum depth of around 1m, folding their wings back into a 'V' for streamlining and return to the perch with their catch. They feed primarily on fish, as well as insects and tadpoles. Fish are nearly always carried across their middle then knocked against the perch to kill them, tossed in the air and swallowed head first. There are reasons... The spines on fish such as sticklebacks will only relax once the fish is dead and breaking the bones softens the fish, while head first works with the scales and spines; making for easier swallowing.

Kingfishers are very territorial birds and disputes are not uncommon in the nesting and breeding season when young males are out

Ovid identifies this mythical bird as the origin of the phrase 'halcyon days'. Now used as a term to describe a peaceful, happy and prosperous time, it was originally specifically used to describe the seven days in winter, either side of the winter solstice, when storms rarely occur in the Mediterranean. The myths tell us that these were the fourteen days during which Alcyone (now transformed into a Kingfisher) laid her eggs and launched her nest on to the sea while her father Aeolus, god of the winds, forbade the winds from blowing, therefore calming the waves and allowing her chicks to hatch in safety.

looking for fishing and nesting sites as well as females to poach. These territorial battles are serious business for the Kingfishers and if no-one backs down, individuals have been known to fight to the death.

THE HALCYON BIRD The Kingfisher is known as the halcyon bird; the name originates from Greek mythology and is also related to the origin of the phrase 'halcyon days'. Ovid tells of Alcyone, daughter of the god of wind, Aeoleus. Alcyone is happily married to Ceyx (son of the morning star). They are so happy together that they often refer to themselves as the gods Zeus and Hera. This so angers the gods, that when Ceyx travels by boat to consult with an oracle, they throw up a storm and he is drowned. When Alcyone hears of her husband's death she also throws herself into the sea and drowns. The gods, in a rare moment of compassion, transform them both into Kingfishers or 'halcyon birds', named after her and which now gives the name to two of the Kingfisher families – Alicidinidae and Halcyonidae.

So you can tell the weather by the birds feeding on insects but are you confident that you can tell the difference between swifts, swallows and martins?

All of these birds feed over rivers making the most of the rich insect life and they all take part in an annual migration between Africa, where they hang out over our winter, and Britain and Ireland, where we see them during our summer.

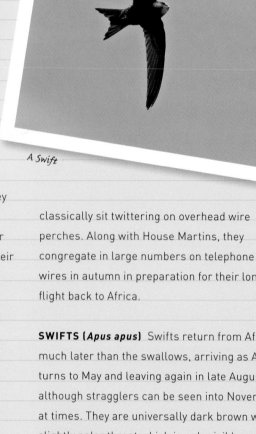

A Swift

SWALLOWS (*Hirundo rustica*) The first swallows arrive from Africa on the south coast around mid-March and are eagerly awaited as the first sign of spring. In flight they are identifiable by the pointed wing tips and strongly forked tail with long streamers. Their upperparts are a dark, inky blue-black and their fronts are white. They have a red throat and small flick of red on their forehead, although from any distance these are hard to see. They build their half-cup nests in barns and sheds. They utter a rather clipped chirp in flight but classically sit twittering on overhead wire perches. Along with House Martins, they congregate in large numbers on telephone wires in autumn in preparation for their long flight back to Africa.

SWIFTS (*Apus apus*) Swifts return from Africa much later than the swallows, arriving as April turns to May and leaving again in late August, although stragglers can be seen into November at times. They are universally dark brown with a slightly paler throat which is only visible very close up. They have distinctive, long, scythe-shaped wings and a slightly forked tail – often not visible in flight. They are significantly larger than the swallows and martins and have a slower flight pattern, incorporating more gliding, which shows off their long scythe shaped wings. On a hot summer's day they can be seen at great height – almost out of sight.

A Swallow

A House Martin

Their distinctive screaming call is often heard as they chase each other around buildings and is a sign that summer has fully arrived.

The scythe shaped wings and the screaming call have given rise to some ghoulish myths. They are often seen in old English mythology as harbingers of doom. They are distinctive birds with unusual habits. They remain on the wing throughout their entire life – so will never be seen on telephone wires, landing only to nest and lay their eggs. They typically nest in buildings – often church towers and sheds – very unobtrusively and always out of sight. They have specially developed claws to help them grip vertical walls but otherwise their legs are rather short and undeveloped so that, if they land on the ground, they are unable to relaunch without some help. In fact the family name 'Apodidae' comes from the Greek, meaning 'no feet'.

HOUSE MARTINS (*Delichon urbica*) House
Martins, in general, return back to Britain from mid-April; you may occasionally see a few in late March but they are in the minority. House Martins are usually found where they can stick on their mud cup nests under the eaves of houses or sometimes on cliffs. They can be seen collecting the mud from puddles which they mix with saliva and then use to build their

nest. House Martins have white underparts, blue-black upperparts and the distinctive white rumps with a short, forked tail. They have two distinctive calls; you will often hear their twittering call as they perch near the nest but while in the air they have a rather unusual call as if practising rolling their r's – almost blowing a raspberry.

SAND MARTINS (*Riparia riparia*) Sand Martins
are one of the first migratory birds to return to British shores, the earliest arriving in March and the last leaving in October. They have a sandy brown upper body and chest band with a white chin and underneath. The tail is short and forked. They are regularly seen with their rapid jerky flight along rivers or in sand and gravel quarries, nesting in large colonies and feeding in acrobatic displays low over the water. Due to the unstable nature of their nesting grounds they frequently have to relocate. A typical nesting area would be a sandy river cut cliff around 1–1.5m high, dotted with holes dug out by the birds. There is usually plenty of activity to and from the nests when the birds are feeding.

A Sand Martin

River Stour, Dedham Vale, Suffolk ... 6th September (56)

... I went for a memorial walk in Dedham Vale along the River Stour with Ruth and Mum today. It is a year since Dad died. My father was an art and water loving walker so this bit of Constable country is particularly evocative for the whole family.

Walking around Flatford and down the Stour the whole landscape could come straight off a Constable canvas — even without the specific locations of Willy Lotts' cottage and the 'Haywain' river crossing. As you head towards Dedham, the scenery of pollarded willows with the cattle grazing under them in the water meadows is timeless; the only notable change, even on this midweek day, is the number and style of the people, no longer the occasional rustic farm hand but numerous Gore-Tex-clad visitors with binoculars.

As we walked after lunch we were entertained by the flying acrobatics of feeding Swallows, House Martins and Sand Martins. There were a huge number of them. They were wheeling and dive bombing all around us, making dramatic dives right down to the surface of the river, skimming along just above the ripples, pulling up, soaring and swooping, before circling round for another attack. They were making the most of the insect life. The racket they made was quite something as well, shrieking and calling as they tied themselves in ever more dramatic knots, feasting and fattening themselves up before their mammoth migrations to warmer southern lands. How they manage not to collide is astounding.

Driving home we went through a woodland tunnel, the tree branches met and wove together over our heads until we felt as though we were swimming underwater through the green depths of a kelp forest. As the trees thinned we could see the flickering, vivid oranges and reds of a forest fire in the undergrowth, spreading across the horizon. Leaving the trees behind us, the fire was revealed as the setting sun bouncing off the low boiling clouds and giving the illusion of flames above the blackened cauldron of the hillside in silhouette and the promise of a fine day tomorrow ...

How to predict the weather

Swallows high, staying dry;
Swallows low, wet will blow...

There are many old sayings about the behaviour of plants and animals that can help you to predict the weather. Some are more accurate than others; swallows and in fact, all the birds that feed on insects on the wing, are quite reliable predictors. The birds that feed on insects will fly where the insects are plentiful. In fine weather the insects are carried up on warm thermal currents and the birds, also affected by the low pressure and finding it easier to get up high too, will follow for a feast.

Many other examples of wildlife and country lore which profess to help you predict the weather can be highly misleading, particularly anything to do with cows. Many animals and plants are very good weathervanes because they are hardwired to respond to certain environmental cues in very specific ways; their response to certain environmental conditions will always be the same. If you can interpret what that environmental cue means in terms of the coming weather then you can predict the weather. If not then it gets you no further. For example, dandelion clocks and pine cones both close up in damp conditions to protect their seeds and open up wide in the dry, but does that actually allow you to predict the coming weather? I'm not sure.

A great weather reflector with which you can stun and amaze your friends is the cricket.

Crickets chirp more in dry weather than in wet, they also increase their chirping as the temperature increases. Being cold-blooded insects they actually require the warmth to enable them to be active; not only this but they become more active in direct relation to air temperature. On a warm day listen out for the crickets chirping, they won't chirp at all below about 45°F (7°C) or above 100°F (38°C). Count the number of chirps a cricket makes in 15 seconds, add 37 (although some sources say 40); the total will be the air temperature in Fahrenheit.

WILDLIFE AND THE WEATHER

There are many other wildlife cues that can help to predict the weather but they vary greatly in their efficacy. Keep your eyes open for some of these signs and see if the resultant weather ties in or not:

Flowers smell best just before rain

This is because smells are stronger in moist air as the odorous chemicals dissolve in the water vapour; high humidity tends to precede rain.

Red sky at night, shepherds' delight,
red sky in the morning shepherds' warning

Weather patterns in this country tend to come from the west with the prevailing winds. Dry weather in the west creates dust in the atmosphere that reflects the setting sun, so a red sunset suggests dry weather on its way. Conversely, redness in the morning sky indicates dry weather that has gone past and in this country, if it has been dry, it is probably going to be rainy before too long.

The smoke from a campfire should head straight up.

Smoke swirling and falling at a campfire suggests low pressure and bad weather on the way.

Mares' tails and mackerel scale,
tall ships carry short sails.

Mares' tails are high-level cirrus clouds and mackerel skies are altocumulus that look like mackerel scales, both are common in the early stages of a front developing. If the weather pattern continues to develop then there will be bad weather within 36 hours and ships should keep their sails low to minimise damage.

Why not try...

Most rivers in spring and early summer are alive with insect feeders feasting.

River Barle, Withypool, Exmoor (2)

River Frome, Farleigh Hungerford, Somerset (18)

River Arun, Pulborough Brooks, West Sussex (22)

Elmley Marshes, Isle of Sheppey, Kent (33)

River Thames, Lechlade, Gloucestershire (42)

River Ant, How Hill, Ludham, Norfolk (65)

River Wye, Bycross, Herefordshire (69)

River Wharfe, Loup Scar, Yorkshire Dales (94)

River Rawthey, Sedbergh, Cumbria (111)

North Tyne Chesters Fort, Hadrian's Wall, Northumberland (115)

(x) numbers relate to site listings in the resources section.

Becka Brook and Hay Tor, Dartmoor ... November

... It was the first day of our holidays on Dartmoor today and as usual Dunc and I took our chances to get out for a long run either side of exploring the area with the kids. By the time I went out for a run Dunc had already been. Itwas a sparkling October day, crisp and clear but it had rained overnight so there were extensive mud patches along the paths. As I made my way down to the stream at the bottom of the valley I became aware that I was following his route. I decided to dispense with the map and see how far I could track him.

Dunc has quite distinctive trail shoes so by looking out for damp areas of ground and trying to spot bits of his shoe prints I could see where he had gone. With the low autumn sun, the shadows showed up the marks even better. Using this technique, I managed to follow him for 5km, including a section off paths, where he ran through a primeval swamp alongside the river. The jumble of fallen birches with their silvery white bark looked like the skeletal remains of a Victorian gentleman's club, lying where they had fallen, still cloaked in their velvety smoking jackets of lush mosses. I may have been able to follow him further but I started to worry about how long and how far he had run so I left his tracks and headed for home ...

How to track animals

Humans are not the only mammals that leave evidence of their passing and are attracted to the river bank. All mammals need to find water to drink, so, if you look carefully enough along any river, you will be able to find evidence that animals have been around.

Many British mammals are shy, nocturnal, or, crepuscular, one of my favourite words, (which means they are active at dawn and dusk). Some are also very rare so they can be hard to see in the daytime. However, like humans, most animals leave some evidence of

their presence and once you know the signs they can be easy to spot. The most likely signs are feeding remains, burrows and nests, droppings and footprints or tracks. A combination of evidence will help you confirm the presence of a particular animal.

Finding a clear footprint of a wild animal is an exciting way to get an idea of what is out there on the river bank.

For the best footprints:
● Find a clear, damp, sandy or muddy patch down by the water's edge.

fresh soil or sand. Then, the next morning you can have a look to see who has been visiting. If you are able to, it can be really interesting to rake over this layer each night and check it each morning over an extended period to build up a picture of the animal's comings and goings.

If you find yourself becoming even more interested in one particular animal and want to know more about the individuals present it is possible to take careful measurements or even make plaster casts of the footprints you find. Individuals can be identified by the size and shape of the footprints, then you will know if it is just one individual you have been tracking, more than that, or even a whole family group.

● Investigate after a dusting of snow or after a very heavy frost when you can often follow tracks for some distance and learn quite a lot about the behaviour of the animal you are tracking. In these conditions the animal's footprints stand out quite clearly.

● Look early in the day before dog walkers and other people are out and about as their movements will start to mix with those of the wildlife and the picture will become obscured.

Once you have established that there are animals using a particular access point to the river, it is possible to lay down a footprint trap. On the clear ground scatter a thin layer of

Why not try...

this at any of the listed sites, you will always find a patch of mud or sand to sample. If you don't have any luck visit one of these centres to see the animals:

British Wildlife Centre, Lingfield, Surrey (121)

New Forest Wildlife Park, New Forest (122)

Butterfly and Otter Sanctuary, Buckfastleigh, Devon (123)

Tamar Otter and Wildlife Centre, Launceston, Cornwall (124)

Wildwood Trust, Canterbury, Kent (125)

(x) numbers relate to site listings in the resources section.

HOW TO MAKE A SIMPLE PLASTER OF PARIS CAST

⑥ Mix up some plaster of Paris.

⑥ Cut a circle of plastic out of an old water bottle and fit it around the print.

⑥ Pour the plaster of Paris into the section of bottle and in to the print.

⑥ Leave it to set.

⑥ Once fully set, lift the cast out of the bottle section.

⑥ Leave the cast a bit longer to allow it to become really solid before you give it a brush to clear away any excess mud you may have picked up.

Compare casts in size and shape to identify individual animals.

Some prints you may see

IN THE UK YOU ARE MOST LIKELY TO SEE THE PRINTS OF FOXES, BADGERS, MINK, OTTER, STOAT, WEASEL, RABBIT, HARE, SHREW, HEDGEHOG, RAT, SQUIRREL, PIG/WILD BOAR, SHEEP AND DEER. MIXED IN WITH THESE MAY ALSO BE HUMAN, CAT, DOG AND NUMEROUS BIRD TRACKS.

is better than it has been for over 150 years and otter hunting was outlawed in 1978. The Otter Trust breeding and release programmes have also helped boost populations. Environment Agency surveys show a 500 per cent increase in sites with otter signs between the end of the 1970s and 2002. Otters are now present in all regions of England and Wales and their range is constantly increasing.

WATCHING OTTERS In spite of their recovery otters are still incredibly hard to observe. The best way of finding out about Otters on a river is to look for the signs they leave behind. The tracks are one good sign but another particularly distinctive feature is their poo – spraint. Otters 'spraint' to mark their territory. Look out for low tree stumps, rocks sticking out of the water and clearings. The spraint will be smaller than those of your average cat; they are tarry black when fresh and white and crumbly when dry. The tell-tale signs are the presence of many white fish bones and scales and the strong, sweet, fishy smell.

The Otter is no longer as rare as it used to be on English rivers. But because they are so elusive it is still a rare treat to see one.

Otter populations went into serious decline between the 1950s and 1970s as a result of the release of pesticides into the environment. The chemicals concentrated up the food chain and had a devastating effect on the otters as top end predators. At the same time, there was pressure from hunting, loss of habitat and human disturbance; the generally poor state of our rivers at the time meant food was in short supply.

Happily things have been changing. The release of pesticides in the environment has been severely restricted, the state of our rivers

Otters are perfectly adapted to their environment and way of life. They have fantastically sharp teeth and flexible hands to manipulate their food. They are powerful and fluid swimmers, hunting by sight, with especially adapted vision, as well as by sensing the movement of fish with their whiskers. They will feed on eels, fish, frogs, waterbirds and even chickens. An adult otter eats around 20 per cent of its body weight – up to 11 kilograms – of fish a day.

ADAPTATIONS Otters always fish just below the water surface so that their prey is reflected back off the surface. Try it out when you are swimming; test out at which angle and depth you see through the surface of the water and at which angle the underwater world is reflected back. This is the otter's hunting angle.

Another adaptation is the fur: a dedicated Canadian scientist once counted 40,000 hairs in one square inch; this provides a superbly dense and waterproof protective layer.

Mature Otters are solitary animals, travelling, feeding and sleeping alone throughout most of their lives. They have large overlapping territories with many fishing grounds and a network of holts. Males will have a larger territory than females, sometimes spanning 40miles of river or more. They stay in contact with others in their territory by marking, with their spraint, and with their whistling call. Otters travel and feed primarily at night, and then settle into a holt for the day, always alone but in holts that other otters will share on consecutive nights. A holt may be anywhere dry and enclosed – a hollowed-out tree stump, a section of dry pipe, a disused badger or fox hole.

A female Otter will usually team up with a mate in spring, often while she is still tending her last brood, so that she can have her cubs in late winter or spring the following year. The male and female may stay together and travel together for a short while. A litter is typically two or three cubs, or kits, which stay with the mother to be fed and learn their fishing and hunting skills over a period of six months. They finally set off into the world on their own at around a year old, often being chased off by their mother, just in time for the birth of her next litter.

* Notebook • Mink (Mustela vison)

Mink are much maligned because they are non-native – though there is a European species, most of those on British rivers and waterways are American Mink. They were farmed for their pelts and as a result of releases from fur farms, set up their own wild population. The Mink adapted very well to the British countryside, flourishing and increasing dramatically in numbers to the point where they were a danger to the native wildlife. They tend to feed prolifically on the eggs of water birds and small mammals as well as frogs, the numbers of which have all declined since the Mink became bedded in.

At one point Mink were blamed for the decline in otters but it seems unlikely that they were at fault. A Mink is considerably smaller than an Otter, roughly half the size and a tenth of the weight – it would almost certainly lose in a straight fight. Neither do they compete for the same food, Mink tend to concentrate on terrestrial food, while otters prefer to hunt for fish, for which they are much better adapted than the mink. There is in fact anecdotal, although hard to corroborate, evidence that otters are actually excluding Mink rather than the other way round.

If you want to be sure whether you have a mink or an Otter on your river check out the spraint. Mink droppings are greenish-brown or black and a truly foul, distinctive musky smell, there will be no evidence of fish bones.

* Notebook · Water Voles (Arvicola terrestris)

'Ratty', star of the children's classic *The Wind in the Willows* was a Water Vole. In contrast to the Brown Rat, with which it is often confused, the Water Vole has a rather blunt nose (a bit like a beaver) the ears are small and tucked, almost invisibly, into the side of the head and the tail is shorter, thicker and hairy.

Water Voles have had a tough time and have disappeared from 90 per cent of their previously known sites and they are not showing a great recovery. Mink are a real problem and Water Vole habitats have been under pressure from river dredging and intensification of farming over the last 50 years leading to insensitive clearing of river banks and water courses. Ironically the Water Voles appear to be doing well in urban areas as they are more tolerant of human disturbance than mink.

WATCHING RATTY Water Voles are very rarely seen but you may hear them drop into the water with their distinctive plop, spot a hole or find some droppings. The plop that the water voles makes is quite distinctive and is actually thought to be a warning sign to other water voles. Water voles swim high in the water so that the whole length of the body is visible with a distinctive bow wave.

Water vole holes are typically 4 to 8cm in diameter, with internal tunnels and nest chambers on many levels to counteract flooding, there are also underwater entrances for predator evasion. The holes are often visible just above the water level with a lovingly tended 'lawn' around their front door. They crop this grass with their teeth.

Another good identifier are the droppings: the green, cigar-shaped droppings are comparable to, but larger than, mouse droppings (8–12mm long and 4–5mm thick). When broken open you can see concentric rings of plant matter. Water Voles feed on virtually any plant; surveys have identified over 200 food plants for water voles. They use the droppings to mark their territory – anything from 20m to 100m depending on the quality of the vegetation.

Becka Brook, Dartmoor ... October (12)

... We were down at the babbling Becka Brook this afternoon, relaxing after some complex boat making. While munching on biscuits and watching the ripples and reflections on the water surface, we noticed that the branches of an alder tree were dipping into the water as it fell over a small rock chute. Each one had a different pattern of ripples forming around it depending on whether it was in the slow flow at the top or bottom of the drop or in the fast flow as it went over the rock lip. I realised that we had a perfect demonstration of how the pattern of the flow of water round an object changes as the speed of the water changes.

From my studies I remembered that this phenomenon had been investigated by a man called William Froude, who began by working on the railways with Brunel before moving on to naval architecture, looking at the way boats move through water. His work led to the development of the Froude Number that is used in many different areas of hydrodynamics. Froude originally devised the number so that he could look at the resistance of boats to the water as they moved through the sea. He did this by studying the shape of the waves against the hull of the boat ...

Why not try...

this at any of the listed sites, it is always possible to dip your finger or a stick into the water

✱ Notebook • Froude numbers

Froude's observations can tell us about the speed of the water by looking at the pattern of waves around a stationary object – a Froude Indicator. Your Froude indicator may be a twig, a post or even your finger.

Froude numbers are either greater than 1 – supercritical, torrential flow; or less than 1 – subcritical, slow flow. Put your indicator in the water, if waves appear upstream of the indicator then flow is subcritical; if waves only appear downstream, then flow is supercritical.

Supercritical conditions can be seen where the flow has to squeeze between boulders and other obstacles, as well as over weirs and chutes. The water surface can often look very smooth, almost metallic.

Filter feeding animals like the greater concentrations of food in the fast flow but they have to adapt to resist being washed downstream. Some animals, like the Cased Caddis-fly larvae (Glossosomatidae), stick themselves to the rock surface in mini flow shadows while others rely on the boundary layer and have adapted a flattened shape, like the Mayfly larvae Ecdyonuridae.

A flow shadow develops where the water is deflected around a solid object; a boulder at the macro-scale or bump on the bounder at the micro-scale. At the micro-scale insects can live on rocks in rapids while at the macro-scale salmon glide from flow shadow to flow shadow on their journey upstream; much more energy efficient than battling directly against the flow.

The boundary layer forms at the point where the water hits the rock surface, you can see this when you try to clean the last layer of grime off your car, a pressure hose won't touch it – you need a sponge. The flattened insects can cling on in this layer in-spite of the apparent speed of the water.

Canoeists are often interested in supercritical flow where it occurs over the top of weirs and chutes. The rapid return to subcritical flow at the bottom of the chute, known as a hydraulic jump, causes the development of a breaking wave, or in canoeing terms, a 'stopper'. Stoppers make great surfing for experienced kayakers but it is possible to get trapped in a stopper and churned round and round as if you are in the spin cycle of a washing machine.

Juniper Hill, North Downs, Surrey ... June

… I gave Dunc some water diviners as a present and they hadn't made it out of the packet so I persuaded him to let me take them on a walk today and Lottie and I decided to try out our divining skills. The valley is in an area of chalk hills, part of the North Downs. In keeping with many chalk downland valleys there is no visible water course. The valleys appear dry but there is water deep down. As I walked along the side of the valley the rods lay still in my hands. Every time I crossed over the lowest point of the valley the diviners started to cross over and at the lowest point they were 90° from their starting position.

Now, being a watery person, I know that even though there is no surface water, a valley in chalk geology suggests the water is there but underground. So maybe I was having a subconscious effect on the rods. I tried hard to stop them crossing, but still they crossed. Next I gave them to Lottie. At four she has little understanding of valleys and underground water. I showed her how to hold the diviners and set her off across the valley. They crossed in exactly the same way as they had for me. We continued on our walk up the valley and the diviners pointed straight ahead apart from a couple of times we went over muddy areas.

Now I realise this is completely unscientific and not enough to earn the £30,000 that the sceptic, James Randi, pledged to anyone who could demonstrate the paranormal; but why and how did it happen? I really don't know but there are still many who are happy to use the outcomes either as a last line of hope or to start off further investigations. As a non-invasive and cheap technique there is little to be lost and potentially much to be gained. Have a go yourself and see if you can feel the force …

HOW TO DIVINE FOR WATER

❶ Select some diving rods:

● A branched twig. The best trees to use for dowsing are those that grow alongside water, so willow or alder, although hazel is traditionally used as well.

● Two L shaped metal rods. The metal rods can be made of anything (although some diviners swear by copper alone). A short length of bamboo to slip the rod into in your hand will allow you to hold the rod firmly without preventing it from spinning round.

❷ Hold your elbows to your sides and the dowsing rods in your hands.

❸ Bend your elbows so that the rods point directly forward and slightly down.

❹ Relax and focus on what you are trying to find. Walk over the area of interest and the metal rods may start to move or the twig to twist and dip.

❺ Check your results by marking the spot and walking over it from another direction. Keep doing this until you can pinpoint the source.

❻ Once you have perfected the art of finding water, try divining for other materials and other objects. Supposedly, if you have lost a gold ring you need to hold a gold ring in your hand as you search. If you are searching for a person, holding an item of their clothing or a treasured possession will help to lead the rods to them.

Don't forget you may find this exhausting, so make sure you have access to a little sit down with a cup of tea and cake to revive yourself afterwards!

* Notebook • Dowsing

Dowsing is an ancient art also known as divining or rhabdomancy. Rhabdomancy refers specifically to the use of rods.

Rhabdomancy became an accepted skill, rather than a whitchcraft, in the early 16th century, when the Germans became proficient in the locating of metallic mineral lodes. Queen Elizabeth I was concerned that Britain was lagging behind the rest of Europe in mapping mineral resources so the merchants in charge of the Cornish mines acquired the help of the German dowsers to map the minerals there.

In spite of scepticism there are still many modern day users of dowsing. The police have used them to locate bodies and objects. In the Vietnam War, the army used dowsers to locate tunnels, booby traps and land mines. Engineers have used dowsers to search for hidden power lines and archaeologists have used them to locate burial grounds and sites of buried ruins. American dowsers still use the art to locate oil and minerals. A dowser discovered uranium deposits and the first platinum bearing ore in the USA.

There is evidence for high levels of success in the use of water divining rods but the reason it works is still elusive. Scientists have put forward all kinds of theories, none of which have any evidence to support them.

Possibly the most famous of English dowsers was John Mullins, in the mid-nineteenth century. Mullins was a stone mason working on a house for Sir John Ould in Gloucestershire when a water diviner was called in. The diviner found a good well and Ould was so taken by the art that he asked all the 150 workers on the construction site to have a go. When Mullins took hold of the rods they twisted so hard that, legend has it, they broke in two. At this first attempt he located a water source that yielded 200 gallons of water an hour. From that moment Mullins became a renowned diviner and well sinker, even gaining royal patronage. He was so confident in his art that he would not charge his client the expensive drilling fees if his divining prediction did not result in a productive well. Mullins is credited with locating over 5000 sources of water.

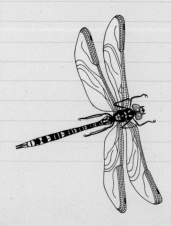

Be adventurous

Be bold and embrace the unknown.

Experience something new and challenge yourself.

River Mole, Surrey ... May

... I was so grouchy today. So, I decided to ignore all my responsibilities and work and head down to the river. It was a murky day and the water appeared flat and grey. Emerald green, saw-edged spears pierced the surface like an army of Excaliburs gathered along the edges and emerging from the mysterious depths. I shuffled my way along an exposed tree root to reach the deepest water. My feet moulded to the gnarled contours of the wood as I paused momentarily before jumping in, feet first. The water washed up my body like a tidal wave, taking with it all the pent-up tension which was released from the tips of my hair exploding as a mass of spray on the water's surface. I twisted and turned staying under the water as long as my breath lasted before I emerged to enjoy the water from a new angle.

It didn't take much, just a few seconds submerged in real water and I am shocked back to my senses: it is like hitting the reset button. What was it I was so het up about? I'm all smoothed out and balanced again ...

River swimming

At some point, if you really want to get close to your river, you need to get into the water.

There is quite a strong body of scientific evidence that backs up those who extol the virtues of cold water immersion, however, the physical, emotional and spiritual well-being induced by immersion in water are beyond scientific measure. It is no coincidence that many religions and cultures involve water in their rituals of birth, cleansing, renewal, rites of passage and death. However you feel when you go into the water, when you come out all your worries will have been washed away – you will feel cleansed and reborn!

Swimming in wild waters has been around as long as people and rivers have co-existed.

While it is currently undergoing a revival and is increasing in popularity again, it has developed a reputation as a subversive activity. Ever since water was tamed, captured and held in bright blue tiled tanks, heated to germ breeding temperatures and then suffused with chemicals, swimming pools have become the norm, the sanitised version of swimming that we all adhere to.

Swimming in wild waters is nothing like swimming in a swimming pool. Very often you can't see the bottom and there certainly won't be a handy black line or lane ropes to guide your way. The water feels and tastes different and is nearly always much colder. But break free from your expectations, be confident and overcome the unfamiliar sensations and cold

The water washed up my body like a tidal wave, taking with it all my pent up tension which was released from the tips of my hair, exploding as a mass of spray on the water's surface.

of wild, free, real, living water and swimming becomes a new adventure, a feast for the senses, providing a whole new perspective. Your inner fish will really be in its element.

GETTING STARTED

There are some access and safety implications in wild swimming, have a look at the resources sections at the end of the book before you go. If you want to find your own swimming site then there are some tips in the first section.

Alternatively, have a look at Google maps; in conjunction with *www.wildswimming.co.uk* they have a site where you can select your area and see a photo and brief description of some possible swimming sites.

As you stand peering into the water, ready to launch yourself, don't worry if you feel apprehensive; this is normal, all wild swimmers suffer from edge of the water jitters. Once you've been swimming in the wild a few times you will know that the buzz you get overrides the first few seconds of shock. Don't take too long getting in: mental blocks will get harder to break the longer you let them develop. Get in quickly, but don't jump in as cold water shooting up your nose can give you a real headache. Let your body recover from the first shock and jump about a bit to warm up, then push off, savour the feel of the water on your skin, enjoy this wonderful, living sensation and start to warm up.

JUST A DIP

The best thing to do if you are new to wild swimming is to just get in for a dip. Find a nice deep pool or stretch of water, strip off and get in for a quick swim around. Almost any river in the UK will have suitable places to get right in and have a quick dip; this may be to feel the wild water on your skin or just to cool down. Even in quite a shallow river there will be deeper holes caused by the river's flow or possibly human activities. Look upstream and downstream of bridges and weirs where the river has been held up by the structure, forming a deeper section of river and where it has then scoured out a pool downstream. If the river is meandering, the flow will be slower on the inside of the bends which make nice beaches for paddling and getting in to the water slowly, while the outside of the bend will have been deepened by the faster current. There can often be good dip spots there. These same patterns are seen in both shallow and deeper rivers. Upland rivers will have more rocky sections with waterfall sequences; each drop is followed by a deeper pool which may only be enough for a wallow but could be big enough for a dip.

SWIM UPSTREAM

If there is only a short length of swimmable river and you want some good training, swim upstream against the current – it is like being on a treadmill. Depending on the speed of the current, you may only need a reasonably short stretch of river to have a really good workout. You may be surprised that, even in apparently slow flowing lowland rivers, you can have a great workout against the current. Work hard

to swim upstream and then take a break as you relax on the downstream lap; the difference between upstream and downstream speeds is dramatic and as you tire, this effect will become more accentuated so bear this in mind for safety's sake.

You can work out the ideal speed of river for your swimming speed. If you usually complete a 25m length at the swimming pool in around 20 seconds then you are swimming at 1.25m/s (25 divided by 20). By looking at the surface of the water you can have some idea of the speed of the water in your stretch of river. On page 194 we used a calculation to work out the speed of the water, so get measuring if you are uncertain whether you will be able to swim upstream against your river's flow.

SWIM LIKE TARZAN

It can be really exciting to swim with the current. Just be careful that you are still in control and look out for hazards downstream. If you want to feel like a motor boat or an Olympic swimmer, swim with the current as fast as you can; maybe even put on some flippers. Get someone to race you along the riverbank either on foot or on a bike. Some dogs love to race alongside people in the water, but watch out as they usually get very excited and leap on your head when you least expect it.

SWIM BREASTSTROKE

So often when we swim, we put our heads down and power up and down. In the swimming pool this is understandable as there is not much of any interest to see. In the outdoors there are so many more interesting things to look at, plus it gets really cold if your head is in the water for too long. Swim breaststroke with your head up and have a good look around. Take in the surroundings and enjoy meeting

some of the residents — they will be much less wary of you in the water than they are at any other time. Roger Deakin in his book *Waterlog*, the wild swimmer's bible, talks about having 'a frog's eye view' when you are in the water. It is true that you see the river's wildlife very differently when you are in the water. Not only do you see it from a new angle but it tends to look at you differently; fish, birds and amphibians will all come up to have a look if you float around gently for a while.

To increase your chances of seeing some wildlife it is best to slink into the water slowly and have a look around before your fast swimming scatters the wildlife far and wide. However, for warmth, you may want to get going a bit quicker. The best solution is probably to go for a blast downstream and then return further upstream, slide into the water quietly and merge with the wildlife — it is up to you to find the balance.

GO FOR A SKINNY DIP

Going for a swim in wild waters without any clothes on refreshes the parts that other swims can only dream about. It is an amazing sensation and many celebrated wild swimmers refuse to swim with their clothes on, or at the very most will only ever don a bikini. Kate Rew, the founder of the Outdoor Swimming Society, is one such wild swimmer. Iris Murdoch and her husband John Bailey were renowned wild swimmers. They would sneak off to hidden sections of the Thames or Isis and strip off for an illicit swim. Even as her health declined in later years John recalled, in her biography, how Iris would be refreshed,

shedding off the shackles of her Alzheimer's and return to her old self when he smuggled her down to the river.

When you are finding a spot for a skinny dip just remember that while it can be romantic or fun you need make sure it is a quiet spot: once you are past the age of about five the sight of your bare flesh may not be everyone else's idea of a great day out.

Why not try...

anywhere you can get to the water's edge with deep enough water for a dip.

River Barle, Wheal Eliza, Simonsbath, Exmoor (4)

River Dart, Deeper Marsh, Ashburton, Dartmoor (10)

River Frome, Farleigh Hungerford, Somerset (18)

Cuckmere River, Cuckmere Meanders, Seaford, East Sussex (29)

Little Ouse, Santon Downham, Thetford, Norfolk (58)

River Waveney, Outney Common, Bungay, Suffolk (61)

River Teme, Leintwardine, Herefordshire (77)

Goredale Beck, Janets Foss, Malham, Yorkshire Dales (83)

River Wharfe, Loup Scar Yorkshire Dales (94)

River Derwent, near Shepherds Crag, Lodore, Lake District (102)

(x) numbers relate to site listings in the resources section.

A journey down a river can feel like a real adventure. The linear nature of the river means you can never get lost — and if you travel downstream you don't necessarily have to expend much energy as the flow will carry you over greater distances than you could travel on still water. The hardest challenge is sorting out the logistics of getting there and back when you end up a long way from where you started.

The simplest options for making a journey downstream on the river are to swim, float or take a boat ...

River Thames ... July (42,43,44,45)

... Swim I: Today is the first day of my solo adventures and I've decided to go for a swim safari. I seem to be dogged by heavy rainfall whenever I attempt long river swims. The last time I planned a safari on the Thames it rained solidly for two weeks and the river burst its banks for long sections and was not safe to swim in. This time things are looking up. I'm doing a solo safari today so I'm actually planning to swim sections then return to the car. I used to work along the length of the Thames so I'm pretty happy I can pick some of the best bits and have a great day.

Having parked the car at Buscot, I walked to where I wanted to start swimming, upstream of Lechlade. It was just a 2km walk which gave me about a 3km swim once the meanders were accounted for. It was a really warm day so I got away with wearing just a t-shirt and old trainers on top of my swimming things for walking so I stashed them in a plastic bag under a hedge. I teetered on the edge for a moment, then slithered and slid in for my swim. The water was not particularly cold and felt smooth to the touch, but my whole body tingled and sang as I set off. I slipped swiftly downstream between bright green grazing fields; the cows seemed mildly interested often pausing mid-chew to observe my progress. Being mid-week there were not too many walkers or fishermen out, so I didn't have many spectators to start with. As I swam in to Lechlade it was strange to see the church and other buildings from my new perspective below ground level. All the boats seemed to be moored up so I didn't have any dodging to do. I couldn't resist testing out the echo as I went under Ha'penny Bridge and when I came through the other side I did find I had a few spectators so I just gave a cheery wave and swam on.

I kept going and just moved sto the side and stood up when boats were passing, so they could see me and weren't worrying about a collision. Everyone was very friendly and would call a few comments as they went by. Swimming downstream, even in the relatively slow-flowing Thames, you make good progress. A lot of the time I swam breaststroke, with my head up, to see the

sights and watch the wildlife. I almost got past a heron without him moving but I was spotted at the last moment and he took off with his barking call, leisurely whomping his wings as he went. It seemed not time at all before I was back at Buscot and had to get out to avoid the weir. I tried out a few rope swings in the weir pool and then headed back to the car. I did get a few strange looks at that point, walking barefoot in my swimming things. Dried off and covered up, I stopped at the rather nice tearooms for some lunch before going to retrieve my clothes and find another dip ...

... Swim 2: The next section I decided to try was from Tadpole Bridge. This time I reversed my system, so I drove to Tadpole Bridge via Duxford (the end of the swim), where I left my shoes and t-shirt under a log by the ford. Back at the bridge, I leapt straight into the river and started swimming downstream. I swam fast for a bit, setting up a bow wave like a small speedboat, with the current behind me. I attracted the attention of a family of swans with their cygnets. The female burst out of the rushes hissing and then stopped abruptly as she tried to work out what I was; the look of confusion was palpable. She clearly couldn't work me out so settled for a superior, malevolent air, peering down her beak. I floated a bit and the mother swan, nonplussed, rejoined her cygnets and they all floated along the margins, heads down, dabbling for weed and sneaking the occasional peek at this strange passerby. Willows dangle the tips of their branches into the water and the margins were a profusion of nettles, hemlocks and Rosebay Willowherb growing around and through a matrix of dropped branches. Life was going along quietly in this section of river. I only saw one boat, a London lead company barge with an old boy at the helm. We exchanged nods and he seemed unconcerned at my presence, standing in the shallows at the side of the river as he went about his business.

I was enjoying myself so much that I missed the turning down the weir towards Duxford. So I had to keep going to the arched, wooden bridge where I climbed out and walked across the wetlands, mud oozing between my toes, to reclaim my shoes at Duxford ford. For a bit of variety I cut across the fields to find my way back to the car.

It was a great way to spend a day on a mini-adventure — and I was back in time for tea! ...

Why not try...

a good stretch of deep, safe water with regular public right of way access and navigation rights.

River Ouse, East Sussex **(27/28)**

River Thames Lechlade to Teddington **(42-54)**

River Stour Flatford Mill to Dedham **(56)**

River Cam, Grantchester Meadows, Cambridge, Cambridgeshire **(59)**

River Stort, Sawbridgeworth, Hertfordshire **(60)**

River Wye, Hay on Wye to Monmouth **(68-71)**

(x) numbers relate to site listings in the resources section.

River Mole ... August

... It was a rare, free summer's day and we finally managed to do what we have been talking about for months: a float down the River Mole. Armed with large, rubber ring and boogie boards we headed down to a quiet section of the Mole. We walked to the upstream section in our sun tops and swimming things, river shoes on. The access was quite tricky; the river is some two metres below the surface of the bank at this point so we had to slither down the bank holding on

to branches and standing on stumps sticking out of the clay. There was plenty of screaming and screeching. Dunc and the big girls got themselves into the surprisingly fresh – not to say cold – water and onto their trusty steeds. Next it was my turn with Lottie. I carried her on my hip as I lowered myself into the water, but the second her foot made contact with the cold she started scrabbling for safety. Safety, it turned out was anywhere up and out of the water and as I was carrying her, that meant up on top of me. As hard as I tried to calm her, while trying to keep my balance on very muddy ground and in increasingly deep water, she scrabbled her way up my body until I was standing chin deep, with Lottie perched precariously on top of my head, squawking and flapping.

I strategically accepted defeat, so while the others floated down amidst joyful screeching and splashing, I walked to the end point and headed upstream to meet them. In the river's meanders that the footpaths don't reach there were little, virtual islands – secret gardens. Lottie was temporarily subdued and in the silences the sunlight glanced through the leaves of the alders and lit up the vibrant green of the riverside grasses where there was a multitude, possibly even a host, of deep indigo dragonflies; a combination of Beautiful and Banded Demoiselles. In each sunny patch they had congregated, sunning themselves and flittering in amongst the tall, lime green strap leaves of the grasses …

Why not try…

rivers with a moderate flow and good access over some distance.

River Mole, Box Hill Stepping Stones, Surrey **(34)**

River Bure, Buxton and Lammas, Norfolk **(64)**

River Evenlode, Stonesfield, Oxfordshire **(75)**

Wellow Brook, Wellow, bath, Somerset **(76)**

River Teme, Leintwardine, Herefordshire **(77)**

River Usk, Crickhowell, Wales **(80)**

River Skirfare, Arncliffe Church, Yorkshire Dales **(90)**

River Wharfe, Bolton Abbey, Yorkshire Dales **(91)**

River Derwent, Near Shepherd's Crag, Lodore, Lake District **(102)**

(x) numbers relate to site listings in the resources section.

Three days on the River Wye ... end of May (68-69)

... Day 1: It takes a logistical genius to organise my siblings and our families. Luckily my brother Chris is up to the task. So here we are, three and a half of the four families, setting up camp on the banks of the River Wye, ready for our canoeing adventure. The weather is great, the campsite is amazing and the river we are beside looks perfect. We have managed to commandeer one end of the campsite in the orchard, away from all the other canoeists and kayakers and we have set up our seven tents along with hammocks, shelters, campfire and volleyball net among the handily positioned apple trees. The kids are having a riot with all their cousins while the tea is on permanent brew for the adults.

Just down the bank from our tents are some narrow rapids which we shall have to run in the canoes tomorrow, which may be a challenge; but for today they look very inviting for the rubber rings and boogie boards ...

... Day 2: The day didn't dawn quite so fair and we all got togged up in our waterproofs, trying to work out what we needed to carry in our bags and on our persons for a day of paddling. We jumped in the cars and headed up river to Hay-on-Wye, our launch point. The river was invisible through the drizzle so we didn't get much of a preview for the day, but the forecast was good so we were hopeful.

The rain had slowed to a mizzle as we organised ourselves into four rafted-up boats with all their kit. Then we were off. Within seconds we were floundering in the shallows. The river levels were very low and immediately we launched we were confronted by broken water of shallows reaching diagonally across the river. We headed for the deepest section and with a minor scraping we made it through and paddled off; looking back there was carnage as the other more heavily loaded boats floundered in the shallows and bare legs and feet reached tentatively over the side feeling for the rocks to push themselves off. This was to be the theme of the day; heading for shallow rapids, trying to identify the fastest and deepest water to increase our chances of getting through without stopping; and for the most part it was possible. Then we were off again. With four boats we spent some time traveling together, racing, having water-fights and sharing snacks and some time apart enjoying a bit more peace and quiet but with our camp already set up we were under no time pressure and we could travel at our own speed. When we saw a rope swing, we could stop for a play; a good picnic spot, stop and eat; interesting wildlife, slow down to watch. When we got hot and tired from paddling we were able to jump in and have a swim.

We reached camp, with aching palms and shoulders but elated after our day on the river, to be greeted by the remaining half of the fourth family and Granny, who had taken over the evening catering for us weary travellers,

provided a much appreciated welcome back to camp. The weather had been clearing up throughout the day so we had beautiful sunshine in which to relax in the hammocks, with plenty of sausages sizzling on the fire and marshmallows to look forward to …

… Day 3: It dawned bright and clear and after a quick breakfast we headed off to do battle with the rapids at Monnington Falls just down from the campsite. From the bank they looked very narrow and we weren't sure how easy it would be to run them in our rafted up Canadian canoes. One by one we lined ourselves up and headed into the wild water hoping the current would carry us on a good line and preparing ourselves for some hard paddling. In the event we had no problem: a few moments of excitement, shouted instructions and uncertainty and we were through it bobbing our way downstream. Now old hands we were more relaxed on this second day, confident in our paddling teams and happier to take what we found on the river, consequently we saw more wildlife. In addition to the rich bird life that we saw yesterday, today we saw Kingfishers and, briefly, an Otter. This section of river was particularly abundant in swans, standing on the banks in great groups, presumably mostly 'teenagers' and by lunch we had counted over 60 individuals.

As the day drew on we came under pressure to get down to Hereford as we had a rendezvous with the boat hire company who would meet us and return us to our camp. Time was getting a bit tight and we needed all the help from our tired crew to get us along the never-ending last straight leading into Hereford. A long headwind blowing down the rather dull final few kilometres meant we had to lean to our paddles to make our final goal.

Back at the camp we were able to relax and enjoy the river, taking on Monnington Falls in our own time. As predicted, the rubber rings and boogie boards we'd brought proved to be the perfect equipment and in fact simple body surfing was also a lot of fun …

A day on the River Ant, Norfolk Broads ... August (66)

… We just made a day trip on the river today. Our group's age range is five to 75 and we have four adults and seven children. We have hired three Canadian canoes and brought two of our own wooden kayaks. We set off from Wayford Bridge and headed up the Ant towards Broad Fen. It took a while for the paddlers to settle in and we weaved our way, zig-zagging up the waterways which soon become narrow and tree lined. The water was lovely and clear until we passed by and churned it up, but, as an outrider in one of the kayaks, I was in a privileged position and got to see it first. I could see fish darting between the torpedo leaves of the Potamogeton.

There were masses of water lilies and the submerged leaves waved around in slow motion a little like drowned lettuce leaves; the seed pods stood out of the water on their robust stems appearing quite beautiful and somehow oriental, reminiscent of lotus flowers in Buddhist paintings. Dragonflies of almost prehistoric scale buzzed past and settled on the kayak for a ride, sunning themselves before heading off again – I managed to identify the bronze colouring of a Norfolk Hawker as well as the broad blue body of a female Blue-bodied Chaser. In the margins, flitting between the grasses, I caught

glimpses of clusters of damselflies. Several had the banded blue and black body of the Southern Damselfly and many the distinctive iridescent petrol wing and wing bands of the Beautiful and Banded demoiselles. I have seen kingfishers on this route before and there are several hopeful looking branches, close to the water's surface, which would make ideal perches, but I we were making too much noise today and were not the only boats around.

We found a lovely open grazing meadow alongside the river to stop for lunch and Dunc, being first ashore, went to help my mother land her crew. For some reason he decided to lift the bows of the boat; in the process the stern dipped down and began to fill with water. Poppy, at the front, got out sharpish, Mollie, in the middle, was up to her waist in water, while Mum, in the stern, abandoned ship, but found herself almost up to her shoulders in the water. Eventually everyone got to shore, the bags were unloaded and our lunch was saved.

With a handy skipping rope we rigged up an impromptu line to try and dry out some of the clothes.

On the return journey Diggory saw a snake swimming across the river in front of him. Some fishermen on the bank also spotted it and when it was followed by another, smaller one they managed to scoop it up with their keep net. We all crowded round to have a look — an aquatic Grass Snake!

Why not try...

a river where you can hire a boat and get navigation rights for at least a day's paddling.

*River Rother, Newenden Bridge, West Sussex **(25)**

*River Ouse, Anchor Inn Boat Hire, East Sussex **(28)**

River Stour, Grove Ferry, Canterbury, Kent **(32)**

River Mole, Box Hill Stepping Stones, Surrey **(34)**

*River Wey, Shalford and Guildford, Surrey **(37/38)**

*River Thames, Ham to Kingston or Richmond, London **(54)**

*River Stour, Flatford Mill to Dedham, Essex **(56)**

*River Cam, Grantchester Meadows, Cambridgeshire **(59)**

River Stort, Sawbridgeworth, Hertfordshire **(60)**

*River Cherwell, Park Town, Oxford, Oxfordshire **(74)**

(x) numbers relate to site listings in the resources section.

There are a lot of things to think about before you head off on safari:

- The river: Where are you going to go and what are the conditions going to be? Are you legally allowed on the river? Access issues are set out on page 219. Some rivers require you to buy day permits if you want to go on the water and all boats require a licence from British Waterways or the Environment Agency.
- What kind of transport do you plan to use?
- How long do you want your adventure to last? Short days or half days out on hired boats are very accessible for the skilled and unskilled alike. Rowing boats, Canadian canoes and kayaks can be hired throughout the UK. There are many places where you can stop on the riverside for a picnic or even treat yourself to a pub lunch.
- Logistics: How are you going to organise yourself, the rest of your group and your belongings?
- Start and finish points: How to get there and away and reclaim all your belongings.

Access during the day, for rest, toilet and food stops. This is particularly important for swimmers if you don't have boat accompaniment.

- How will you keep everything dry?
- How far can you go? If you are travelling by boat, who will be in the boat and will they actually paddle effectively?
- If it is a multi-day trip, where will you sleep? Camping is lovely and there are many good riverside campsites. Carrying your own camping gear and stopping off feels like a real adventure but requires careful planning and control of your equipment as it has to fit in the boats with you. Having lots of children can make this very tricky. Youth Hostels can work well if they are in the right places.
- Safety: Be responsible and think about your safety. Judge your safety based on your own and your group's abilities. Just because someone else is doing it doesn't mean you should. Always act on the side of caution and follow the golden rule: If in doubt, don't.

SWIMMING SPECIFICS

- Think about the capabilities of all swimmers and plan for the weakest swimmer.
- If possible have boat support on hand, particularly if you are unsure about access points on the river.
- Not that many rivers in the UK lend themselves to swim safaris with sufficient lengths of swimmable water. Look at the map: on a 1:25,000 map the river needs to be more than a single blue line to be worth investigating. Higher up, the river will generally have better water quality and probably nicer surroundings, but it may not be deep enough.
- Consider your legal right to access.

CONSIDER YOUR OPTIONS

- Travel light and carefree. Jump in the water with nothing but your swimming things, but be prepared to endure the long walk home, barefoot and in your swimming costume, that can be part of the adventure too.
- Tow a dry bag (available from outdoor shops) behind you with a surf leash (or length of string/tape/cord). Take along some shoes as a minimum, maybe some warm clothes, a snack and some cash. You can at least have a more comfortable walk home or find a convenient bus route or a cafe.
- Be really organised: go for the gourmet swimming safari and lay out the route before you go. Leave a car and supplies at the end of the swim.
- Enlist friends and family to meet you for a slap up lunch, have kayak support boats laden with drinks and snacks and equipment, end your day at a pre-arranged camp. You could then camp out and turn the adventure into a multi-day safari — think as big or as small as you fancy.
- If you don't have the inclination to organise an elaborate swim safari for yourself but you like the idea then there are companies that run organised trips, providing company, support boats, food and accommodation. Swimtrek organise swimming and walking holidays in the UK and other countries in rivers, lakes and seas (*www.swimtrek.co.uk*).

Climb a tree

A tree that hangs over a river is the best kind of tree to climb. Sitting in the branches you get a completely different view of the world. If you are over the river, you will see down into the water and be able to observe the everyday goings on of the river without being observed. If the water is clear enough and the reflections are not too great, you will be able to watch fish and diving birds in the water from a whole new perspective. You get a true bird's eye view.

From this vantage point, find a comfortable perch; sit back and relax, take in the sights and sounds and activities of the river. If you stay still the birds will return to the trees and life will go on under you, without any notice being taken of you.

Hang upside down and make like a sloth. One of my favourite book openings is in *The Life of Pi*, where there is a description of life as a sloth. It's absolutely brilliant and tickles me every time. Read it and go and hang in a tree.

Trees beside rivers are great for more than just contemplation. The river and its surroundings are laid out beneath you like a map. Watching the wildlife, and sometimes people, going about their lives oblivious to your presence, is like having a living map beneath you, much like Harry Potter's Marauder's Map of Hogwarts Castle where all the people are identified by a dot and can be seen moving around the castle and grounds.

Check out the river beneath the tree. If the water is deep enough and clear of rocks, submerged logs and other river debris, then you can launch off and have some fun. There are numerous rope swings that hang off trees

as well as jumps directly out of the branches. What I love to do, once I have exhausted my capacity for observation and following my sloth impression, is to hang in the tree over the water, completely relaxed, then simply release my grip. As I splash into the water every cell in your body sings and I never feel more alive.

For some wonderful descriptions of tree climbing read *The Baron in the Trees* by Italo Calvino. A young boy, Cosimo, climbs a tree in a fit of umbrage and refuses to come down. He then stays up there for the rest of his days. Calvino's observations of the trees are very informative and it all makes sense once you find yourself up in the branches.

Always make sure tree branches are sound before you climb and if you plan on jumping into the water make sure there are no obstacles. The water depth must be at least your own height with your arms stretched above your head to be safe.

Why not try...

rivers with good bankside trees.

Horner Water, Horner, Exmoor **(5)**

Badgeworthy Water, Malmsmead and Cloud Farm, Exmoor **(6)**

Becka Brook, Becky Falls, Bovey Tracey, Dartmoor **(12)**

Beaulieu River, Beaulieu, New Forest **(15)**

Trib of River Adur, Woods Mill, Henfield, West Sussex **(26)**

River Mole, Norbury Park, Leatherhead, Surrey **(35)**

Little Ouse, Santon Downham, Thetford, Norfolk **(58)**

River Waveney, Outney Common, Bungay, Suffolk **(61)**

River Skirfare, Arncliffe, Yorkshire Dales **(90)**

Easdale Beck, Grassmere, Lake District **(104)**

(x) numbers relate to site listings in the resources section.

Black Moss Pot, Langstrath, Lake District ... April (100)

... In a country of amazing river possibilities, Black Moss Pot is one of the jewels in the crown. In the wide flat-bottomed glacial Langstrath Valley the river winds its way in front of a backdrop of majestic mountain ridges. The river is shallow and spreads out over a rock bed which, acting like solar panels, heats the water temperature from frigid to bearable. The river widens appealingly beside short cropped grassy banks ideal for picnics and playing and then ... out of nowhere the river drops off a small waterfall and enters a limestone gorge. Who would believe that such a place could exist?

The Pot is a natural playground. First there is a mini waterfall, with a rock pool jacuzzi at its base — it exits into a cauldron. Then there is a deepwater channel surrounded by steep limestone cliffs. The cliffs and boulders are perfect for jumping in to the deep pools, ranging from 2m to a heart-stopping 6m. Standing at the top, the water is so clear that you can see right down to the bottom, some 10m away, which makes the jump seem even bigger.

It is certainly long enough to let out a good scream and wonder what you are doing on the way down. Once in the water you can swim down the gorge for around 20m before you come to the beginning of the next play area. Downstream of the gorge are some perfect chutes and pools for sliding and dipping and sunning yourself. With the right amount of water in the river there will be some water pools beside the chutes that have been left without an inflow and so heat up quite considerably on a warm day — ideal for a wallow.

The water in the Pot is fantastically clear, sparkling with blues, greens and golds in the sunlight; small fish are easily visible flitting around as you swim. When someone jumps in, you can look into the water and, along with the explosion of the water into bubbles, you will see a shoal of small fish bursting to the sides to give the jumper clear passage. We jumped and swam and climbed and stretched out in the sun for as long as we could before making the hour long gentle walk home. We didn't want to leave but at the end of the day we had to go, arms, legs and minds floppy from sheer exertion ...

Top tips if you want to jump in

Jumping into rivers is a great adrenaline buzz and is usually done from cliffs, bridges or trees. The best way to find a good river jumping place is to ask around or take a walk down the river on a warm summer's weekend and see where the action is.

If you are hoping to find for your own site then look for deep water. This will usually be upstream or downstream of some kind of obstacle, like a natural or artificial weir, in a waterfall pool or on the outside of a river bend where the flow of the river has carved out a section of deeper water. The depth of water required depends on the height of the jump and the weight of the jumper. The higher the jump and the heavier the jumper the greater the depth of water needed to prevent a collision with the river bed. As a general rule, always jump in feet first and as a minimum, the water depth must be greater than your height with arms stretched out above you. If the jump is more than your height with arms outstretched, you will need a greater depth.

Take care
Be extremely cautious when jumping. This is
the kind of activity where accidents can happen.
Always check the depth of the water.
Check out your landing zone every time you go
to the river - don't trust previous experiences.

Once you have established that the water is
deep enough, you really need to get in the
water to test it out. Some sites may be in
sparklingly clear water where you can see right
to the bottom but it is worth being cautious.
Make sure the water is clear of any obstacles

both natural, such as boulders and submerged
logs, and manmade; old fridges and bicycles
are unfortunately not uncommon in rivers.
Even if it is a spot you visit regularly, it is worth
checking every time you go to the river as
debris can be thrown into the water and
boulders and logs can relocate themselves and
move downstream during high flow.

Once you are sure the way is clear and it's
safe to go, then be brave, don't teeter on the
edge getting scared; the longer you wait, the
harder it gets. Take a deep breath and step off
the edge — feel the adrenaline buzz and the
zing of the water, revel in the warm glow of
success — then climb out and have a another
go; you won't be able to resist it.

Make a rope swing

River Mole ... October

... It was a sunny October Saturday on the suburban River Mole. My sister and I took our seven kids for a picnic by the river. There has been a lot of rain and the river was high, murky and sediment laden: the stepping stones were invisible under six inches of water. We urged the children to be careful and stay near the edge of the river but the temptation was too great and gradually, the water and the challenge, as always, got their way. Before long the bigger kids were teetering over the submerged stepping stones, falling off into waist-deep water, shrieking and having fun. Eventually we prised them away. We dried off, moved on and found a good picnic spot under a huge aspen with twisted roots emerging from the bank. As we munched, two lads come along and, with a long stick, pulled to the bank the multi-knotted, tangled blue rope which was dangling out into midstream.

Within minutes we were all taking turns to swing out over the water and back to the gnarled cage of tree roots, which the smaller members of the family had turned in to a den. There was a lot of hilarity, shrieks and squeals and near misses, slithering on the muddy bank and clinging precariously on to the tree roots, until inevitably, with a look of shock and astonishment, a hand slipped and in a rush the party fell into the water. Outer layers were shed and before the afternoon was out, we had found crayfish, seen kingfishers, made miniature pots drawn from handfuls of the clay river bed and perfected the rope swing, drawing in many passers-by to join in the fun ...

How to make a rope swing

If you are looking for a bit of adventure at the river then rope swings are a great place to start. With the banks of the river always on hand and trees frequently on the bank, all the ingredients are there.

If you are searching for the ideal spot for a rope swing then just ask the local youth or go for a walk along the river. Take a walk along any river and you will see numerous, mangled, knotted pieces of nylon blue rope dangling from the branches of the trees. Many accessible places with a suitable tree and suitable water depth will already have a blue rope in place.

While some rope swings are designed to take you right out over the water and then return to

Within minutes we were taking turns to swing out over the water and back to the gnarled cage of tree roots, which the smaller members of the family had turned into a den.

Overhand knot

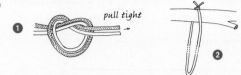

pull tight

Long loop

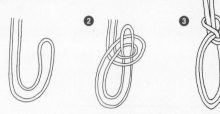

the river bank so you can attempt to stay dry, it is still worth checking on the state of the water; many planned dry days end up wet in the end!

MAKE YOUR OWN

I am always wary of ropes that other people have put up. You never know how long they have been up there and they are often alarmingly furred and display a whole host of ragged ends and knots which suggest they have broken and been mended on many occasions already. In reality, ropes already in situ are generally fairly safe and many times I have used them on the basis that, if they do break, the worst that will happen is I get wet. If you want to be really sure, take your own healthy rope and make your own rope swing. Ideally take it away with you again to reduce litter and damage to the trees.

SETTING UP THE SWING

To make a rope swing you just need a good strong rope; this may be the ubiquitous blue polypropylene waterproof rope, a more natural sisal or, if you want to be really smart, a multi-coloured rock climbing rope. The diameter of the rope should be around 6–10mm for strength but the thicker ropes make for a more comfortable hold.

If you can climb the tree to tie on the rope then that is the easiest solution for hanging your swing. However, even if you can't climb up to the branch, it is still a straightforward job to set up the swing.

To get the rope over the branch remotely, you need to throw your rope over the branch. This may be possible directly with your rope

but if it is a heavy rope, you may need to throw over a finer string first and then pull the thicker rope after it.

To start with, tie a weighted object to the end of your string or rope. This may be a plastic bag weighted with stones, a heavy shoe, a tennis or cricket ball or a chunk of wood. Unravel a long length of the string or rope into a pile at your feet to prevent it getting tangled and then throw the missile over the branch that you want to hang your rope swing from. Obviously you need to make sure you can reach the point where your missile will fall and also make sure there are no people in the way before you throw.

To get the missile over the branch is easier said than done. To get the trajectory right you usually have to aim much higher and further than you think to get over the branch. Remember you only have to get it right once.

Once you have the missile back in your hand you need to pull the rope through. If you are using a thinner rope, check that it is in roughly the right position on the branch, remove the missile and tie the rope to the end of the string; an overhand knot is the best as it is the least likely to get stuck when you are pulling the rope back – this is the knot that climbers use when they want to retrieve their rope from an abseil.

Next, pull the string with the rope attached back over the branch until you have the leading end of the rope back in your hand.

WHAT KIND OF SWING?

You can now decide what kind of swing you want to make.

Marlin spike hitch

 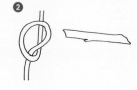

*pull branch
down firmly*

The simplest swing is just to tie the ends of the rope together into a long loop that you can sit in or put your foot in to swing out. The downside of this swing is that it is quite uncomfortable and has a tendency to twist and trap your foot or bottom. The advantage is that it is easy to remove it at the end of the day.

A very simple and very satisfying seat is to find a good solid branch. Tie this on to either a single length of rope or the double using a marlin spike hitch to make it into a simple seat. Starting with a simple loop, twist the loop around on itself then feed the branch through the upright rope and pull down firmly. This is traditionally used to give purchase on a rope when you are pulling it, but works well as a very secure, but easy to dismantle, temporary seat.

If you only have enough rope for a single length rope swing then it is possible to tie the rope around the branch using lots of string. It can be a bit of a fiddle and you will not be able to retrieve the rope easily at the end of the day but as a more permanent swing it is more satisfactory. Before you start, tie a loop into the back end of the rope, then proceed as before. Throw your missile over the branch, tie on the leading end of the rope and start to pull the string back. As the string comes down,

feed it through the loop in the back end of the rope. As you pull the string, the loop will head up and the leading end of the rope will come down and follow the string; passing through the loop. You can then pull the rope tight around the branch and the rope is hung.

On this single hanging rope you can use the marlin spike knot to make a T-bar swing or you could hang two ropes side by side and tie on a solid branch making a really smart swing.

Now you are all set up for some fun, so go ahead and swing safely.

Check the strength of the rope swing before you trust your weight to it.

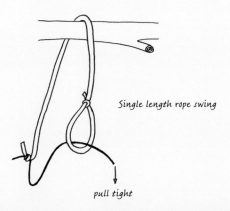

Single length rope swing

pull tight

> ## Why not try...
>
> rivers lined by trees with accessible overhanging branches.
>
> Becka Brook, upstream of Becky Falls, Bovey Tracey, Dartmoor **(12)**
>
> River Wey, Hankley Common, Tilford, Surrey **(40)**
>
> River Thames, Buscot Weir, Oxfordshire **(43)**
>
> River Thames/Isis, Portmeadow, Oxford **(46)**
>
> River Waveney, Outney Common, Bungay, Suffolk **(61)**
>
> River Teme, Leintwardine, Herefordshire **(77)**
>
> River Monnow, Skenfrith Castle, Monmouthshire, Wales **(79)**
>
> River Wharfe, Appletreewick, Yorkshire Dales **(93)**
>
> **(x)** numbers relate to site listings in the resources section.

Riuferrer, Arles-sur-Tech, Pyrenees Orientale, France ... August

... Today was the perfect day for some river fun. Just a couple of hundred metres along the river bank from our place is the most idyllic setting. The river bounces its way between boulders and between big rock walls all down its length but in this particular section of 50m or so it is the perfect playground. At the upstream end the river bends round a large boulder which tilts at about a 75° angle into a deep channel. Once wetted down it makes a great slide into the clear deep water. Just downstream the stream splits with half of it going over a waterfall of about 1m drop and the other half squeezing between several small gaps in the boulders. It is then channelled round another longer boulder and between a mini gorge just a metre or two above the water level which makes a perfect viewing platform in the sun. The exit from this mini gorge is a 2m waterfall or chute into a large round pool which has a boulder beach on one side and buddleia bushes on the far bank with their fluttering, dancing butterfly residents. From the pool the stream makes a gentle exit, babbling over cobbles, before regrouping and bounding off again through a jumble of boulders, fallen branches and overhanging vegetation.

The water chute was just the right width for the river rat (our heavy duty rubber ring) and everyone was able to have a go heading through the gorge and over the chute into the pool below. The challenge was to make it over the fall and land in the pool still attached to the ring. There were some spectacular acrobatics and some body surfing was attempted as well but that proved to be a bit painful, bruising elbows and ankles, so we mostly stuck to the rubber ring. The rock slide into the water was also popular and various techniques were trialled, from sitting to crouching to full surf skill, standing entry. The water was pretty fresh and being deep in the river valley the sun went early, so, nicely chilled we eventually headed back to the house, collecting plums and blackberries on the way back to bake in a crumble ...

There were some spectacular acrobatics and body surfing was attempted as well — but this was a bit painful so we stuck to the rubber ring.

Conditions at chutes and rapids can change rapidly depending on preceding weather conditions. Make sure you are happy with the conditions before you get in to the water.

How to shoot rapids

Lots of rivers and streams have rocky sections that provide good rock chutes to ride down on rubber rings. While shooting down on a rubber ring or boogie board is the easiest and probably safest technique, you may also want to consider being in full contact with the water and body surfing. There is something liberating about leaving the equipment behind and if you are able to relax and get the technique right it need not be too painful.

TIPS FOR BODY SURFING

There are a number of options for how to approach body surfing.

Use the same technique as you would employ if you get into trouble in fast moving water. Lie on your back, with your feet going first. Keep your head up so you can see where you are going, your feet will take the brunt of upcoming hazards and your hands are free to steer with a bit of sculling.

Alternatively, on your front, head first, hands out in front to ward off rocks; relax and let the water bend you around hazards as they appear. If you can relax and let your body move with the water you will have the best chance of success. Obviously this only works up to a certain speed; in really fast water you will be bashed onto the rocks and can be sucked under the water, so don't try it.

Personally I feel much happier body surfing in surf shorts and rash vest or in my wetsuit, where the minor scrapes that are inevitable don't cause a problem. I also tend to wear water shoes of some description so I can stand comfortably on sharp rocks when I want to.

While gentle white water provides the best fun for body surfing; even quite small streams will harbour slides and chutes. We used to slide down the muddy bank into the small stream at the bottom of our friend's garden. The bank was all of 2m high and the stream just 1m wide but we sat on bin bags and trays or our bottoms and spend ages sliding the short distance into the water having a riot. We would return home, muddy head to toe and my mother would just raise her eyebrows and hand out bin bags for the clothes and attach the hosepipe to wash us down. It's just one of the reasons I love her.

Why not try...

rivers with chutes and rapids.

Badgeworthy Water, Cloud Farm, Malmsmead, Exmoor **(6)**

River Wye, Bycross, Monnington Falls, Herefordshire **(69)**

River Monnow, Skenfrith Castle, Monmouthshire, Wales **(79)**

Stainforth Beck, Catrigg Force, Yorkshire Dales **(87)**

River Wharfe, Appletreewick, Yorkshire Dales **(93)**

River Wharfe, Ghaistrills Strid, Grassington, Yorkshire Dales **(95)**

Langstrath Beck, downstream of Black Moss Pot, Lake District **(100)**

Stonethwaite Beck, Galleny Force, Lake District **(101)**

(x) numbers relate to site listings in the resources section.

Bivvying on the River Barle ... Midsummer's Eve, June (4)

... I had fallen asleep under the darkening sky, looking down on the River Barle, cocooned in my bivvy bag. It had been a simple, summer sunset — no fuss or drama. The melting orange sun slid quietly behind the hillside out of the star studded, deepening blue sky. The river below, a silver winding ribbon reflecting the action above, turned the world upside down. The sheep, holding on to the last warmth of the setting sun, huddled together on the north-western slope, chewing lazily on their mouthfuls of grass.

Now, with the lightening of the horizon, I crawl out of my cosy dream world to salute the sun as the sheep stir and look on with tentative curiosity. The river at this time in the morning is mystical and magical. Ethereal mist rises from the surface of the water which itself takes on the colours of the morning — cold steel becomes fiery gold and cerulean blue as the river leaves the shadows. Every blade of riverside grass is bowed, laden, with its own sparkling orb of water quivering at its tip. The heron stands alone, silent, poised on one leg, sharp eyes searching, alert, ready to dart and spear a fish with unerring precision.

I have the river all to myself and will do for the next four hours until I return to my car and civilisation ...

A night on the river

If you are able to stay by the river into the evening and even better, be there at dawn, you will be treated to a river that people rarely see. In the UK's wilderness areas, beyond about 4pm and before 6am, you will see very few people and the river will take on an entirely new persona.

As it goes to sleep the river changes its character completely. Sounds that you hear in the daytime seem magnified as all the other daytime sounds settle down. The sound of the river increases and the night animals start scurrying and rustling. The daytime feeding antics of the swallows and martins are replaced by the dramatic swooping flights of bats as they scoop their prey from the water surface. I had a wonderful experience once while taking a dip just after dusk. I was floating low in the water, with just my nose and eyes emerging, enjoying the silvery darkness of the moonlit river, when a missile flew past my nose seemingly inches away.

Seconds later there came another and another. It was a while before I was able to identify the flying missiles as bats, feeding on the surface of the water. What a spectacle and

what a position to be in to watch it. I flinched every time they went past, skimming over the water at speeds of up to 25km/h; it felt as though they must collide with me. However, their amazing echolocation navigation meant that of course they never did.

One classic David Attenborough anecdote does put some doubt in my mind. Crouching in a cave full of bats, Attenborough was expounding, in his restrained, husky voice, on the amazing flight skills of bats and the accuracy they have at high speed in crowded air space and how they never collide when, thump, one flew straight into the back of his head. It was a moment of perfect natural history timing. So maybe I was right to be nervous.

One of the joys of staying out at night is that many of the shyest mammals — both small and large — become bolder. At night you may see Otters, deer and voles as well as Foxes and rats making the most of the quiet river, feeding and drinking at the water's edge.

Depending on the state of the setting sun and the moon, the river itself changes colour and texture dramatically as the sun falls and the moon lights up. On a bright moonlit night the water becomes a thread of molten mercury, lit by a thousand fairy lights of dancing silver. If you get the treat of a good sunset the river can be set alight flowing with the reds and golds of the dying sun. Once you have fallen asleep to dream of river madness you will have a treat when you wake.

If you thought the nighttime river was magical then dawn is even better. Dawn at the start of a blue-skied summer's day really takes you into the realms of unicorns and magical lands. As the day starts the cold of the night seems to lift off the river with bands of mist rising. The river takes on the colours of the morning, changing from its nighttime darkness to fiery oranges and duck egg blues. If you can, use your tent or bivvy bag as a hide, stay in your sleeping bag and peep out to see the wildlife waking up. You may be treated to heron fishing or otters passing by on their way back to their holts.

Where to camp?

There are many good campsites alongside rivers which will give you a great time right by the river's edge so you can fall asleep to the sound of the water spilling over stones and, unfortunately increasingly in this country, the midges biting. There are some excellent guides recommending good campsites and the Internet lists many too.

Many farmers supplement their income with a bit of basic camping on unused fields so it is always worth asking around and keeping your eyes open for small campsites.

Or you may want to wild camp. There is nothing to beat the feeling of freedom and at oneness with nature that can be derived from a wild camp. The law on wild camping varies from country to country. In most of England, wild camping is illegal without the prior permission of the landowner although many landowners are happy to let you camp in an empty field for a few days. There is an exception in Dartmoor National Park where there is an amendment to the standard National Parks legislation and wild camping is tolerated throughout the UK in most other remote or wild areas as long as campers are discreet and responsible. In Scotland the laws are different and wild camping is legal on open access land.

Although contrary to the strict letter of the law, if you follow this advice put out by Scottish Natural Heritage you should be fine:

❶ Wild camping should be lightweight, done in small numbers and only for two or three nights in any one place. Don't camp in enclosed fields of crops or farm animals.

❷ Keep well away from buildings, roads or historic structures. If you wish to camp close to a house or building, seek the owner's permission.

❸ Avoid disturbing deer stalking or grouse shooting.

❹ Avoid overcrowding by moving on to another location.

❺ Carry a trowel to bury your human waste and urinate well away from open water, rivers and burns.

❻ Use a stove or leave no trace of any campfire. Never cut down or damage trees.

❼ Take away your rubbish and consider picking up other litter as well.

❽ If in doubt, ask the landowner. Following their advice may help you find a better camping spot.

❾ Access rights are not an excuse for anti-social or illegal behaviour.

Why not try...

many good riverside campsites including:

Badgeworthy Water, Cloud Farm, Malmsmead, Exmoor **(6)**

River Dart Country Park, Ashburton, Dartmoor **(9)**

River Frome, Farleigh Hungerford, Somerset **(18)**

River Waveney, Outney Common, Bungay, Suffolk **(61)**

River Wye, Bycross Farm, Bycross, Herefordshire **(69)**

Goredale Beck, Goredale Farm Campsite, Malham, Yorkshire Dales **(84)**

River Wharfe, Appletreewick, Yorkshire Dales **(93)**

Styhead Gill, Seathwaite, Lake District **(99)**

Stonethwaite, Beck, Stonethwaite, Lake District **(101)**

(x) numbers relate to site listings in the resources section.

* Notebook · Bats (Chiroptera)

Several of the British bat species feed along rivers and streams making the most of their rich insect life; however there is one which feeds exclusively over water and is therefore particularly known for its low, fast flight over water. Daubenton's bat (just 4–5cm long) has large feet that are perfectly designed for plucking insects from the surface of the water. Bats have poor eyesight and at night, when they feed, rely on producing ultrasonic sounds and echolocation to find their insect prey. They need to eat a lot of insects to power their active flying lifestyle and can eat up to 3000 insects in one evening. The riparian zone is very important for these bats and many roost in the underside of river bridges.

Other bats that you may see along the river include Britain's most common bat, the Pipistrelle. This is a tiny bat, only 4cm long and weighing about 5 grams – less than a 2p coin! Although commonly seen in buildings they are also popular visitors to rivers and streams for foraging. Other common bats include the Noctule but this is more typically seen flying up above the trees looking for insects above the canopy.

HOW TO WATCH BATS Bats can be very hard to identify in flight and really the only way is either by their behaviour or by using a bat detector that slows their ultrasonic calls right down to a frequency that humans can hear. The pattern and frequency of the bat sounds will identify the bats that are flying around you. It is amazing to think that all this noise and activity is going on but being outside our auditory range we know nothing of it. What else are we missing?

Late spring, summer and early autumn is the time to look for bats – between April and November – as they hibernate in winter. Bats will mate in autumn or winter just before they hibernate. The female then stores the sperm over winter not becoming pregnant until she can feed again in the spring. Surprisingly for their size, bats will only have one baby at a time and they can live for up to 30 years.

As the dark finally settles and the only sounds are those of the river, share some scary river stories with your companions. There are many lurid tales of unscrupulous characters lurking in the shadows and taking advantage of the dark depths in remote rivers.

Wheal Eliza

In 1857 at Wheal Eliza, an abandoned tin mine on the banks of the River Barle, the body of little Anna Maria Burgess was found, several months after she had been murdered by her father and her body dumped down one of the shafts. Legend has it that mysterious blue lights hovering over the shaft guided the searchers to her resting place. A truly heartless individual, William Burgess was was brought to justice by the curate of Simonsbath at the time, who took it upon himself to investigate the murder. The nearest high-ranking police officer in those days was 35 miles away, beyond Taunton.

Eventually the father was caught, tried and hanged. The reason he gave for killing his daughter was chilling, 'The child was in the way, sir – in my way and in everybody else's way – and I thought she'd be better out of the way.' In fact it turned out that Burgess, a widower, had wanted to remarry and the woman he loved hated his daughter so he decided to do away with her.

Tommy Lee

Another tale of bloodthirsty murder is the tale of Tom Lee. A blacksmith and landlord in Grassington, Yorkshire, Tom Lee was also a part-time highwayman. One evening, as the result of a bungled heist, he ended up getting himself shot, but not fatally. The doctor who treated him, Dr Petty, did not turn him in for his illegal activities. Unfortunately, Tom did not trust the doctor's integrity and on his recovery decided to ensure his silence. He ambushed Dr Petty on his rounds and cudgelled him to death, leaving the body temporarily concealed in the undergrowth.

Returning later with his assistant to move the body he found the doctor was not dead but crawling around in agony. Tom Lee finished him off in front of his shocked assistant and they then buried the body in a shallow peat grave. Hearing later about the preservative properties of peat, Tom persuaded his wife to help him move the body again. This time they weighted the body and dropped it into the River Wharfe at Loup Scar. Unfortunately for Tom this act was witnessed, the body was retrieved and his apprentice, turning against him, confessed all. Tom Lee was hung on July 25 1768. His body was left to hang in chains from a tree in Grass Wood, the very wood where he had maimed the unfortunate doctor.

Hard Apple

A story that is easier to romanticise is the story of a smuggler who operated on the River Roach. Known as Hard Apple, William Blyth was a church warden and shopkeeper, possibly even a magistrate; but also a character and a showman. At the beginning of the 19th century the River Roach was a smuggler's heaven, with few revenue officers on the Essex coast and a network of muddy creeks through the marshes. Boats could cross over to Dunkirk and return with a booty of tobacco, alcohol and tea. Approaching the marshes they would transfer the goods to flat-bottomed boats which could evade the customs men, navigate the shallow creeks and make their way up the river for distribution.

The tales of William Blyth's hard drinking and extravagant exploits as Hard Apple have lasted into posterity. On one occasion he apparently tricked the excise men who had him imprisoned on their boat having been caught with an illegal cargo of brandy kegs. Aboard the revenue boat the captain drank with Hard Apple in his cabin, while the men were drinking below decks. The smugglers out-drank the king's men, overpowered them and retrieved all their boty and sailed off chortling to smuggle another day. Other tales recount how he wrestled a bull to its death when it interrupted a cricket match; on another he apparently drank two glasses of wine and then promptly ate the glasses.

Some
questions
answered

Phone in the study ... August

... I've just come off the phone with a friend and had a very typical conversation. It went something like this:

Me: We had a lovely day at the weekend; we went for a float down the river.

Friend: Really? Is the water clean enough?

Well, a friend of mine is lucky to get away in under an hour making comments like that ...

So can you tell how clean your river is?

Historically rivers in the UK have been both used and abused. At times they have been little more than glorified sewers and this, coupled with the fact that many lowland rivers contain high levels of sediment, which makes them opaque, often leads to the incorrect conclusion that they are not clean.

In fact the rivers in the UK are currently in better condition than they have been for the last century. Nevertheless all rivers are still at risk from pollutants and poor quality water reaching them and some of them are still far from pristine. If you plan to go into the water and want to reassure yourself about the water quality there are three different ways to find out more.

CHECK IT OUT ONLINE

Check out the water quality before you go by looking online at the Environment Agency website. Go to *www.environment-agency.gov.uk/maps* and look for the river you are heading for. All rivers are monitored throughout the year and based on this are given a water quality grading. Any river graded between A and C should be fine to swim in. If you want to find out more information on your river then the Environment Agency produce comprehensive River Basin Management Plans; start with the summary as they can be quite lengthy. The river grade only takes account of the water quality at the time the monitoring is undertaken so you may also want to:

LOOK AT THE RIVER ITSELF

Have a look at the river and surroundings to get an idea of how the river is feeling on the day of your visit.

If there are dead fish floating on the water surface, then don't get in. Phone the Environment Agency on their emergency line (0800 807060) as there has almost certainly been a pollution incident.

Be wary of those sites where there is brown slime covering the rocks on the bottom of the stream or blanket weed covering the surface of the water. These are clear indicators of water quality problems. Find another place to play in the water.

If, however, there are damselflies fluttering around, fish visible swimming happily about and heron fishing in the margins, then feel free to get in. If it is fine for these animals, it will also be fine for you: they, and their food supply, are much more sensitive to most pollutants than you would be and they have been in there day in, day out.

This is a very cursory look, so if you want to be a bit more incisive in your investigations then try this third option.

CHECK WHAT LIVES IN YOUR RIVER

At a more detailed level you can take the detailed results from your minibeast hunt (page 80) and actually work out how clean a particular stretch of water is by identifying the animals you have found and looking at a simple index of their tolerance to pollution. This is actually one of the most useful tools the Environment Agency has at its disposal for assessing the quality of water throughout the country. I spent the first three years of my working life conducting these surveys throughout the south and east of England.

The great thing about using animals to assess the quality of the water is that they will have been living in the water for some time so their presence reflects the water quality status over their life cycle. Any periods of poor water quality will affect the health and numbers of the animals living there and it will take some time for repopulation to occur.

When you turn up with your water sampling kit you may miss some of the intermittent pollutants that can cause a serious problem for the water course, such as a discharge of slurry from the farm upstream or engine oil tipped down a road drain that has been washed into the river, and still get a reasonable water quality reading.

How to score minibeasts

Minibeasts vary in their tolerance of oxygen levels in the water and since many polluting substances (particularly organic wastes e.g. sewage and slurry) tend to cause the oxygen levels to drop, the animals you find can be good indicators of pollution. A scoring system has been devised (by the Biological Monitoring Working Party) whereby each group of animals has been given a score between 0 for the most tolerant to pollution (animals that can live in water of quite poor quality) up to 10 for the most pollution sensitive (creatures that need good water quality to survive). The simplest version of this scoring system is presented here where the animals only need to be identified to their group level. The scoring system is also available up to species level which offers a greater distinction between the different species and their tolerance to pollution. This simplified version has no groups scoring 9 on the pollution tolerance scale which explains the empty box in the table below.

❶ Collect (using the technique described on page 80) and identify your animals

❷ Write out a list of the different types of animal you have found

❸ From the list below assign each one its score from 0–10

❹ Add up the scores to produce the total score for the sample

❺ Divide the total score by the number of different types of animal you found (ignore any that are not on the list)

This is the biotic index and will be somewhere between 0 and 10

BMWP POLLUTION TOLERANCE SCORES

1   True worms

2   Non-biting midge larvae

3   Rat tailed maggot, Snails, Leeches,
Pea Mussels, Water Hoglouse

4   Flatworms, Water mites, Alderfly larvae

5   Water Measurer, Pond Skaters, Water
Scorpion, Greater water boatmen, Lesser
Water Boatmen, Caseless Caddis, Water
beetles, Cranefly, Blackfly

6   Swan Mussel, Freshwater Shrimps,
Swimming Mayfly nymphs, other
damselfly nymphs

7   Cased Caddis

8   Freshwater Limpet, Demoiselle nymphs,
Dragonfly nymphs

9   (No group scores 9)

10   White clawed Crayfish, Burrowing
Mayfly, Flattened Mayfly, Stonefly nymph

If you find these animals:

True worm 1, non-biting midge 2, leeches 3,
Water Hoglouse 3, Freshwater Shrimp 6,
Blackfly 5, Water Boatmen 5, Caseless Caddis
5, Freshwater Limpet 8, Swimming Mayfly
nymph 6, dragonfly nymph 8, demoiselle
nymph 8.

Total score = 60, divided by number of species
= 12 = biotic index of 5

A score of 0 indicates grossly polluted water
while 10 is a pristine upland stream. In slower
flowing lowland rivers there is less mixing of
the water, it is warmer and human activities
have a greater impact. Even in the cleanest
lowland rivers substrates are silty and oxygen
levels tend to be lower, you can expect a
different group of animals to live here and you
are unlikely to achieve a score higher than 8.

Why not try...

if you can get into the water to
collect minibeasts you can make an
assessment.

River Barle, Landacre Bridge, Withypool,
Exmoor **(3)**

Badgeworthy Water, Malmsmead and Cloud
Farm, Exmoor **(6)**

River Beaulieu, Longwater Lawn, New
Forest **(14)**

River Kennet, Ramsbury Mill Lane, Ramsbury,
Wiltshire **(17)**

River Mole, Norbury Park, Leatherhead,
Surrey **(35)**

River Bure, Little Hautbois, Norfolk **(63)**

River Evenlode, Stonesfield, Oxfordshire **(75)**

Goredale Beck, Malham, Yorkshire Dales **(84)**

Easedale Beck, Grassmere, Lake District **(104)**

(x) numbers relate to site listings in
the resources section.

How fast does the water move?

Badgeworthy Water, Exmoor ... July (6)

... Dunc and I were just putting the finishing touches to our camp when the girls screeched from the edge of the river where they were exploring, just 5m away. One of them had already managed to drop her flip flop into the water and it was bobbing off downstream. I instantly leapt into action; making a rapid mental calculation of the rough speed of the water I hared off downstream to the bridge which I was sure the flip flop wouldn't have had time to get past and waded out into the river, ready to rescue it. I waited some time and there was no sign; surely it would have floated past by now, so I started wading upstream. As I neared our camping spot the stream went through some boulders and there was a tree half hanging in the water. Some 3m downstream of our camp I found the flip flop, trapped in an eddy behind a tree branch, along with an assortment of other debris ...

How to calculate the speed of the water

The defining feature of rivers, as opposed to other bodies of water, is that they flow. Possibly as a result of this, I have an insatiable fascination for how fast rivers move. Aside from pure curiosity there are practical reasons why you may want to work out how fast the water is moving.

From bitter experience I know that it is only a matter of time before something is dropped in the water. I need to know how long I have before this object disappears over the waterfall, weir, impenetrable greenery or fence 100m downstream.

Measure the fastest flowing water so that you have the worst-case scenario. Any kind of floating object can be used for the measurement — a stick or small branch, orange, half filled bottle, even a Croc or a flipflop. Obviously, if it is something important to you, make sure you have someone stationed to hook it out of the flow when the measurement is complete.

Pace out and mark (with stones, jumpers or whatever you have to hand) a known distance

Why not try...

a regular river channel with path that runs alongside the bank is best for taking measurements.

Hoar Oak Water, Brendan Two Gates, Exmoor **(7)**

River Teign, Dogmarsh Bridge, Dartmoor **(11)**

River Rother, Fittleworth, West Sussex **(24)**

River Wey, Shalford, Surrey **(37)**

River Lambourne, Boxford, Berkshire **(41)**

River Stour, Flatford Mill, Flatford to Dedham, Essex **(56)**

River Stort, Sawbridgeworth, Hertfordshire **(60)**

River Waveney, Outney Common, Suffolk **(61)**

River Windrush, Wash Meadow, Minster Lovell, Oxfordshire **(72)**

Easdale Beck, Grassmere, Lake District **(104)**

(x) numbers relate to site listings in the resources section.

on the bank, along a section of river with fairly regular flow. Ideally it should take at least 20 seconds for the object to travel the measured distance to minimise timing errors! Then throw in or place the object before the measured section, in the centre of the flow — you want it to reach the speed of the water before you start timing. An object that is neutrally buoyant, such as a half-filled water bottle or orange that floats deeper in the water, will give the most accurate measure of water speed as it won't just respond to the surface current or be affected by wind which may not be representative of the flow of the bulk of the water. However, if it is your Crocs vanishing that concerns you, they are positively buoyant and will sit right on top of the water and so in this case the surface flow is important.

Using a watch, time how long it takes the object to travel along the paced out distance. The distance divided by the number of seconds will give you the speed of travel in metres per second (m/s).

For example, if it takes 20 seconds for your object to travel 30 metres, then 30 divided by 20 means the water is traveling at 1.5m/s. This means that from the time that your daughter shrieks that her Croc has fallen in the water you have 100/1.5secs which equals 67 seconds or 1 minute 7 seconds to jump up, run 100 metres down the bank hurdling picnickers, grazing cattle, hedgesand inflatable canoes — all the while grappling with dogs and small children who think this is a game and catch the Croc before it heads over the waterfall.

Another reason to know how fast the water is flowing is its value from a safety point of view. A water speed of 3.0m/s is about the fastest water that I can comfortably stand up in knee deep. So if the velocity is heading towards that, or exceeds it, I know to be cautious.

Finally, the geek in me just quite likes to know these things. If you fit into this category, it may interest you to know that a flow of 0.1m/s is barely perceptible, while in a waterfall, velocities of up to 8.1m/s have been recorded (Hynes 1970).

This measurement will, at best, give you a rough idea of the velocity of the water in the stream. Because of friction at stream beds and banks and at the water surface, the velocity will vary across the channel and due, to eddies and turbulence, velocity at one point may change quite rapidly over time. For really accurate studies you would need to measure velocity across the river and at several depths to get detailed and accurate velocity profiles.

How much water is in the river?

River Mole, Surrey ... August

... We went for a little adventure on our local river today. A stonkingly hot day, it was ideal for a bit of fun with inflatable rings and boogie boards. The river looked its usual, slightly murky, lowland self but the bank was beautiful with lime green, lance-like grasses decorated with their attendant damselflies, looking like conveniently placed jewels. Sitting down for a little snack before launching ourselves off, Thea made the tactical error of wondering out loud how much water there was in the river. That was it, I was away ...

Calculate how much water will flow past while you picnic

There are two simple ways that you could work this out. You can either use the bucket method for very small streams or build on your previous measurement and calculation of the speed of the water.

❶ If the stream is small and flows over a weir or small waterfall then the bucket technique can be used to measure the flow. Hold a bucket under the flow or a percentage of the flow and time how long it takes to fill up. Assuming you have a 5l (0.005m³) bucket with you, we will use that for our example. If you capture only half the flow, you can then multiply back up. If it takes two seconds to fill a 0.005m³ bucket, then the flow is 0.005/2 = 0.0025m³/s; if this was only half the flow then x 2 = 0.005m³/s. This small stream would equate to 9m³ over lunchtime, or around 18 baths.

❷ Assuming that you have already calculated the speed of the water, all that is required is to measure the depth and width of the river or stream. For the depth, if you are very lucky, there will be a black and white measuring board in the stream; these are common near bridges and fords. Alternatively, get in to the water and estimate with a stick or your legs the depth of the water. For the width use a tape measure or estimate. Choose the most regular, square edged section for accuracy or, if you want to be really flash, measure the depth at several points across the river. Multiply the width by the depth to give the cross sectional area of the river. If you took more than one depth, multiply the depth by the width of river bed the depth relates to and then add all the bits together for your cross sectional area.

Now multiply the cross sectional area (m²) by the velocity that you calculated above (m/s) to reach the volume of flow per second m³/s — also known to hydrologists as discharge.

So, a stream 3m wide and 0.5m deep with a velocity of 1.5m/s will discharge:
3 x 0.5 = 1.5m² x1.5m/s = 2.25m³/sec.

Assuming it takes you half an hour to eat your picnic, that is 4050m³ of water flowing past, which is enough water to fill your average sitting room over 50 times, or a 25m swimming pool 10 times — in just one lunch break. That is a lot of water.

How much more after it rains?

We were just taking this in when Poppy pointed out that on the banks every upright stem had a little shawl of dead grasses and leaves wrapped around it from the upstream side. The banks are high here so this was 2m above the height of the river. The tree branches were also hung with desiccated straw-like material, plastic bags and other debris, often more than 3m above the water surface. We often come down here when the river breaks its banks so it should be no surprise, but it is still really hard to believe that these tree branches so far above the water surface are where the river really reaches. Next Poppy wondered 'How much more water comes down this river when it is right up in the trees?'

Well ... Once the river has broken its banks all the parameters change, so we will do the calculation for bank full. Assume the debris is just 1m above the current water surface and the shape of the channel is still squareish at that depth. We have a stream 3m wide but 1.5m deep and we will assume the velocity stayed constant at 1.5m/s. The discharge is now (3 x 1.5) x 1.5 = 6.75m³/s which would mean 12,150m³ over a picnic lunch. So, in bank full conditions, this small stream would fill your sitting room 162 times or a swimming pool 30 times in the time it takes to eat a quick lunch.

The peak river flow is very important for water supply in the UK. The main challenge for the water companies is to capture this excess flow and store it so it is available in times of low rainfall. This is why we need reservoirs to ensure that the water does not just flow out to sea but is available year round.

These peak river flows are also an important part of the natural river's cycle. The peak flows clear the river of sediments and debris and perform a critical job in keeping the water moving and maintaining a good habitat for the instream plants and animals. Without the high flows, rivers would fill with silt and stagnate, gradually filling with vegetation and no longer supporting the diversity of river plants and animals, rainfall would cause instant flooding and water quality would suffer too.

Why not try...

a river where you can see how high the levels rise after rain.

River Frome, Farleigh Hungerford, Somerset **(18)**

River Mole, Norbury Park, Leatherhead, Surrey **(35)**

River Wey, Hankley Common, Surrey **(40)**

River Thames, Chimney Meadows, Oxfordshire **(44)**

River Lugg, Lugg Meadows, Hereford, Herefordshire **(78)**

River Usk, Crickhowell, Wales **(80)**

Goredale Beck, Goredale Farm Campsite, Malham **(84)**

River Derwent, near Shepherd's Crag, Lodore, Lake District **(103)**

Scandal Beck, Smardale Bridge, Kirby Stephen, Cumbria **(110)**

River Coquet, Linshiels, Northumberland **(114)**

(x) numbers relate to site listings in the resources section.

Riuferrer, Arles-sur-Tech, Pyrenees Orientale, France ... August

... After I had been lying on my sun-warmed rock for a while, listening to the music of the river, I decided to investigate further. I had heard the rhythmic booming of what I took to be a rock being churned around in the waterfall plunge pool. So I went to see what was really happening.

There, under the clattering of the waterfall, on the river's surface, I saw a boulder the size of my head being driven round and round the scooped out depths of the plunge pool. Like a never-ending spin cycle, the force of the water landing in the pool was driving a strong circular current which was pushing the boulder into its perpetual motion. As it went on its orbit around the pool, it continued to bounce and rebound vigorously off the bedrock and cliff at the back of the pool.

Judging by the size of the crater that the boulder was circumnavigating, this process had been going on for some time with this and other similar boulders. Presumably they arrive having been washed downstream during high flow and become caught in the pool, revolving interminably, until either another high flow creates a stronger current to wash them out again, or the wear and tear of revolutions erodes them until they are light enough to be lifted out by the regular current ...

How powerful is that waterfall?

Even quite a small waterfall will have a significant plunge pool and can give you a good massage, or even a headache; so how much power is in that water?

Power is the amount of work done over a given time, measured in Watts. For a waterfall this can be calculated from:

Water velocity x height of the waterfall x (density of water x acceleration due to gravity)

The second half of the equation are both constants, the density of water is 1000kg/m^3 while acceleration due to gravity is 9.8m/s^2. We will round this up to 10 for ease of calculation.

We have just worked out the flow of the water in our river, which came to 1.5m^3/s. Going downstream we have come across the waterfall described above which is roughly 1.5m high.

The calculation is therefore:

(water speed) 1.5m^3/s x *(waterfall height)* 1.5m x *(water density)* 1000 x *(acceleration due to gravity)* 10
= *(power)* 22,500W (22.5kW)

So in a waterfall that is 1.5m high and flows at $1.5m^3/s$ the power of the falling water is 22,500W. If this was diverted to a small hydroelectric plant with common efficiencies of 70 per cent, then roughly 16,000W of energy could be produced.

That is enough to power 160 100W light bulbs or 1455 low energy light bulbs (11W each), or you could power your whole household including washing machine (400W), fridge (750W), dishwasher (2000W), TV (120W) and water heater (5000W) and lots of light bulbs, or maybe heating for one of the pools upstream of the waterfall?

That is a lot of power, produced in an entirely natural way, so why don't we just harness it and use it as a clean , alternative source of energy? Unfortunately, it's probably because the view from your heated, outdoor pool will be far less appealing once you have diverted the flow from your waterfall and have a brand-new hydroelectric plant to look out over instead.

Why not try...

rivers with good waterfalls.

East Lyn River and Hoar Oak Water, Watersmeet, Exmoor **(8)**

Becka Brook, Becky Falls, Dartmoor **(12)**

River Conwy, Fairy Glen and Conwy Falls, Betws-y-coed, Wales **(81)**

River Llugwy, Swallow Falls, Betws-y-coed, Wales **(82)**

Goredale Beck, Goredale Scar, Yorkshire Dales **(84)**

Stainforth Beck, Catrigg Foss, Stainforth, Yorkshire Dales **(87)**

Cald Beck, The Howk, Fairy Kettle, Cumbria **(96)**

Stonethwaite Beck, Galleny Force, Lake District **(101)**

River Brathay, Skelwith Force, Ambleside, Lake District **(105)**

River Tees, High Force, Barnard Castle, County Durham **(112)**

(x) numbers relate to site listings in the resources section.

Is water really blue?

As children we invariably represent water as
blue when drawing or painting and we talk of
sparkling blue water but what colour is water
really? I have seen a whole range of colours in
natural water bodies and I would say green is
much more common than blue while browns
or greys are even more predominant.

Water takes on the characteristics of its
surroundings so that it can appear turquoise,
black, green, red and many colours in between
depending on the state of the sky, the substrate
and even what is living in it.

Many rivers are named for the apparent
colour of the water. The water at Blackburn

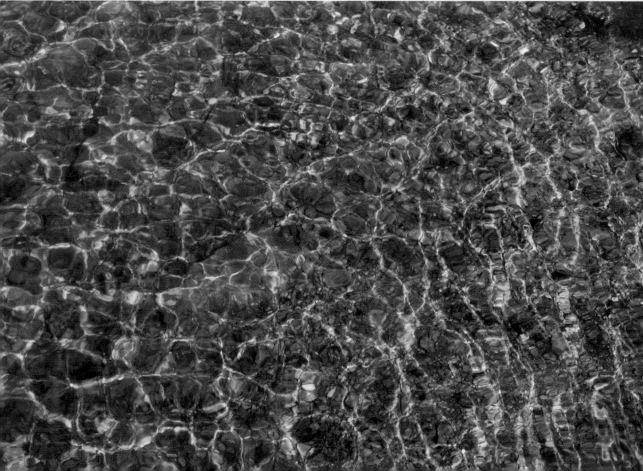

Why not try...

this anywhere you see a body of natural water.

and Blackwater is, or was when they were named, dark or black. Glazebrook would have been blue/green/grey, Radford and Retford – red and Whitford – white. None of these names mention blue but maybe that was seen as the norm so all those places with bright and clear waters such as Brightwell and Fairford were so named because of the sparkling blue nature of their waters and could just as well have been named Blueford or Azurewell.

Even when we talk to other people about water and colour we can end up in confusion. Many languages do not actually distinguish between blue and green. In Ancient Greek, surprisingly there was no word for blue and in Welsh the word for grass is, literally, 'blue straw'. In addition, just to confuse the matter further, people find it difficult to distinguish between the colours of blue and green. I have had many arguments with my daughter over whether something was blue or green and eventually we agree to disagree.

There is actually a physiological reason why people who live near the equator or up mountains find it particularly hard to differentiate between these colours. It seems that stronger, ultraviolet radiation in these locations causes yellowing of the eye lens making it harder to distinguish the shorter wavelengths of blue and green, so maybe I have just been up too many mountains in my time. Where you are and where you live and the language you speak may influence either how you see the colour of the water or how you express what it is you are seeing.

It does seem that water is actually very slightly blue. Water has a tendency to selectively absorb red light and reflect the blue, so will appear blue. However, being a universal solvent the nature of water changes the minute it comes into contact with anything. Throughout its journey to and down the river channel it will come into contact with different geologies and plants and other chemical influences and will change its chemical nature many times. As a result of this, the greater influence on the colour of the water will be the physical nature of the ground that the water has run over and man's influence on that. Not only will the sediment and chemical make up of the water change its colour but also whatever the river is reflecting – the colour of the sky, overhead vegetation, and where it is clear enough, whatever is underneath the water – the colour of the rock or the substrate at the bottom of the river as well as plants and animals in the water.

How to look at the colour of water

To have a look at the colour of your river water with as little influence as possible from the substrate and the sky, lower a mirror into the water. Hold it at an angle so that you are not seeing the river bed or the sky and see what colour the water appears to be – are you in Blackburn or Brightwell?

Try looking at the water colour in a number of different rivers in different locations and notice the how much it changes between them. You could even take a colour match card and try to record the closest match to get an idea of the range and variety of colours that are visible in natural waters.

At work ... Epsom

... My working life is quite a techie one. I work with computer modellers and scientists, surrounded by computers and conversations entailing lots of technical jargon and scientific words. I slightly revel in the fact that people will talk about delta T rather than the change in temperature as they leave the air-conditioned office.

A colleague came back from holiday today and while regaling us with holiday snippets described how, while sitting on a sand dune, he had felt compelled to calculate how many grains of sand there were in it. While we publicly derided him for this 'holiday' activity I don't think I was alone in being secretly fascinated that they had actually worked out that there were the Avogadro Constant of grains in the sand dune he was sitting on. The Avogadro Constant is a very large number, it rounds down to 6×10^{23} mol^{-1} and is actually the number of molecules in a mole of an element, a mole is equal to a substances molecular weight in grams e.g. for oxygen it is the number of molecules in 32g O$_2$. As with much of science these vast numbers are pretty mind blowing and virtually inconceivable.

William Blake famously wrote of seeing a world in a grain of sand but how many grains of sand are there in the world? ...

How to calculate the number of pebbles or grains of sand on a beach

Later that day I found myself on a patch of sand and instantly started doing a bit of mental arithmetic. Since then it has become a kind of strange addiction; whenever I am on gravelly riverside beach I find myself trying to calculate the number of stones there. Depending on the grain size of your beach, try to estimate or even count the number of grains or pebbles in a given volume — small grains think about 1cm^3 (a small grape), larger ones may be 10cm^3 (a Rubik's cube). Then multiply that up for the estimated size and depth of the beach or bank. I never quite know what to do with that information but it is somehow fascinating — although I find people look at me pityingly when I pass on the information — maybe some things should just be kept to oneself.

Look at river sediments

There is a surprising amount you can tell about the river and what kind of animals you

are likely to find just by picking up a handful of mud/sediment from the bottom. Feel the texture of sediment in your hand. The sediment is different in areas of different rock types and the amount that ends up being carried down the river depends on rainfall patterns and land-use as well as the presence of structures like bridges, weirs and sluices in the river. The amount of sediment in the water and the type of substrate in the river bed are both very important for the wildlife of the river. Very different animals will live in rivers with fine, silty river beds compared to gravelly, rocky river beds.

Pick up a handful of sediment from the bottom of the stream. You may be able to squeeze it into a ball and then rub between thumb and forefinger into a thin string — the length of the string you can produce is determined by the nature of the sediments. The more you do this, the more you will have a 'feel' for the different types of substrate and how different they can be. A sandy soil will crumble and can't be moulded. Loamy soils which are richer in organic matter will be spongy and possibly greasy; you may be able to form a short ribbon. Silt will be smooth and silky and the ball it produces can be squidged around without breaking. Clay soils produce a ball, like plasticine, which can be rolled into a long ribbon of 5cm or more. Mixtures of the main soil types produce intermediate results.

If you are interested, you can have a look at the sediment carried in the river water which is also very important for the plants and animals; too much and they will be smothered, too little and there is no food supply. Take a litre of

river water, filter it through a wet wipe/kitchen roll/muslin/fine woven t-shirt/sock and see how much silt is there and the grain size.

The river and the amount of sediment it carries varies greatly throughout the year. Just think of the water in times of high flow: a dense, boiling brown. A great quantity of sediment is carried downstream after high rainfall and sometimes, from a good vantage point on a cliff, you can clearly see, where the river enters the sea or at the confluence of two rivers, a plume of sediment billowing out into the salt water. After high rainfall this plume is more distinct and reaches further.

Why not try...

any pebbly or sandy river beach.

River Thames/Isis, Port Meadow, Oxford (46)

River Thames, Abingdon, Oxfordshire (47)

River Stour, by Dedham Bridge, Essex (56)

River Bure, Buxton and Lammas, Norfolk (64)

River Wye, The Warren, Hay-on-Wye, Powys, Wales (68)

River Lugg, Lugg Meadows, Hereford, Herefordshire (78)

River Monnow, Skenfrith Castle, Monmouthshire, Wales (79)

River Aire, Newfiled Bridge, Gargrave, Yorkshire Dales (85)

River Skirfare, Littondale, Yorkshire Dales (89)

River Derwent, Grange, Lake District (103)

(x) numbers relate to site listings in the resources section.

River Thames, London ... April

... Collecting samples through the centre of London is a logistical challenge. To get the intertidal samples you have to be able to get down to the foreshore at a neap low tide; this is the only time that the intertidal area is exposed for long enough to get all the samples. The low tide then has to fall at the right time of day. If you try to drive from site to site through the London traffic at any time after about 7am you will only manage about two sites before the tide comes in. So a low tide, at about 6am is what we aim for. At this time in the morning all is peaceful and quiet and by the river you are invariably alone. The river seems ageless; images from Dickens, Shakespeare and Sherlock Holmes are all appropriate. I feel as though I see an ancient unchanging side of London.

From Greenwich all the way up to Teddington Lock I stop off and go down to the muddy and cobbly water's edge and take a look at the animals and collect my samples. The barges on the river, moored at their bows, signal the change of tide. They start off pointing down river but as the tide turns they slowly swing round until they point upstream. Gradually the sky lightens, the street lights turn off, the bridges across the river fill with dark suited, briefcase-swinging office workers striding out and I feel a bit like an unseen stalker down by the river's edge – a mudlarker.

As I work my way upstream I'm moving from almost full salinity to freshwater and the animals reflect this change. In the salty end I get juvenile flounders and marine shells and brown shrimps; in the freshwater end it is Freshwater Limpets and Freshwater Shrimps ...

How old is your river?

We often think of rivers in terms of how far they have travelled on their journey to the sea and equate this to our own journey through life. An upland river therefore relates to a young river and a lowland river, just before it reaches the sea, an old river.

A river changes in its character as it travels downstream on its journey to the sea. There is a succession of typical animal and plant communities that would be expected at each stage of the river's 'maturity'. This age metaphor was developed many moons ago by Davis (1899) and is much frowned upon in

these days of science. I still quite like to anthropomorphise rivers and rivers are still often divided into three stages; headwaters or 'youth', middle-order or 'maturity' and lowland or 'old age'.

So what stage of life is your river in? There is a good chance you will have some idea how far away from the source or the sea you are, but even if you have no idea, have a look around; what shape is the river valley, how wide is the channel, what is the river bed like, how many plants are there in the stream?

Without going to a great level of detail there are some general characteristics of a river which are easily seen and give some idea of where you are on the river as it goes on its journey from 'youth' to 'old age'.

Headwater zone – youth

Young rivers have a lot of energy and bound around in their river channel, collecting rocks and gravel, swirling them vigorously and eroding the channel away. These youthful rivers are therefore typically set in V-shaped valleys, with steep slopes. Being close to their source and often near to tops of slopes there are relatively few tributaries and those that are present are short. The channel bed is constantly scoured by the fast flowing water and being near the rivers start has not accumulated too much small sediment. Consequently river beds usually consist of coarse gravels, boulders and rock outcrops. Water sources are not far from the sky or groundwater, any run-off water, will have travelled only short distances, so water temperatures are cool and stable. Large

quantities of water have not yet accumulated so river channels are generally narrow. This can mean that marginal vegetation can be shading and leaves and logs enter the water. Shading from riverside trees and scour from fast moving water carrying coarse, nutrient poor sediment reduce growth of algae and other plants. Organic matter from outside the stream provides the only available food for instream invertebrates and fish. Plants and animals that flourish will be those that like clean sediments, low nutrient environments with lots of oxygen.

Middle order zone – 'maturity'

As the water flows downstream and the river reaches middle age the stream slopes lessen.

Water reaches the river from greater distances of run-off, over increasingly nutrient-rich soils. Sediment from bank erosion and land use can give very variable physical conditions. Increasingly flatter land and floodplain development starts so erosion to the banks is increased leading to widening of the channels rather than the downward cutting of the channels seen in the youthful, upland river.

The middle-aged river suffers, like humans, from middle-aged spread – there should be evidence of wider channels. The increased levels of nutrients carried in from the surrounding soils and the slower flowing waters encourage more plants in the stream. These increase the oxygen available in the water that counteracts the effects of less mixing, and more nutrients to the water. The channel contains more bends as well as areas of fast, riffly water mixed in with slower glides and pools further affected by beds and turns in the channel. The river bed often changes from silty at the margins to rocks and gravels in the main channel of the river. The diversity in the channel structure, the increase in nutrient sources, the slightly warmer temperatures and greater flow all suit a greater range of species, potentially leading to a much greater diversity of plants and animals and a rich river environment.

Lowland zone – 'old age'

The river is beginning to slow down now. All the exuberance of youth is gone and water velocities tend to be low. Sediments that have been carried down from the middle aged river settle out into the channel. River bed materials are typically fine sediment – silt, sand or clay based. It takes longer for the source water to reach this area and peaks of flow are usually evened out by the time delay and the mix achieved from head waters, local land run-off and tributaries. Flow is consequently relatively stable and temperature also. Valleys are wide and flat and evidence of channel changes are present – meanders, ox bow lakes, sand and boggy/marshy areas. There are regular patterns of flooding and sediment deposition when the river tries to change its course, if left to its own devices. There is evidence of sediment deposition in the flood plain. There may be natural levées alongside the river so that the stream is higher than the surrounding floodplain. Deeper and siltier water may

prevent plant growth in the main channel so oxygen levels can also be low. Animal diversity is generally lower, although fish diversity may increase with the presence of larger fish feeding on the small fish.

These patterns of river age are very general and can be much influenced by human activities and interventions. Even in reasonably highly managed environments many of these patterns can still be observed to provide some clues as to the age of the river.

> ## Why not try...
> working out the age of the river when you are in any river valley.

The Howk, Caldbeck, Lake District (96)

… We went for a gentle walk up the Howk today — one of our favourite short walks when we are visiting friends in Caldbeck. We have a plethora of kids between us and it is achievable even for a two-year-old. We were lured on this walk today by the promise of the wild raspberries that grow along the stream here, as well as a look at the Fairy Kettle and the Fairy Kirk. Through the village the stream is quite tranquil but up at the Howk it is squeezed through a narrow limestone gorge and drops down some churning waterfalls. The narrowness of the gorge and the entangled branches of the ash and hazel that meet overhead mean that these waterfalls are in a permanent damp gloom and in these conditions the rocks have developed a thick blanket of deep green mosses and bright green ferns.

The power this stream generates has been used in the past to power a bobbin works; you can still see the vast old mill wheel — apparently once the biggest in the country — and large buildings that made up the mill. It is quite amazing to come across such evidence of past industry when you start off alongside the gentle stream in the village. On further, past the Howk and the waterfalls, the stream settles down and flows quite innocently through fields of grazing cattle, with no suggestion of the drama downstream.

There are places like this along many rivers and streams, hidden and unexpected. Building remnants to remind you of the historic links we have had with our rivers in a way we don't today …

From above ground a great deal still remains to indicate what has been going on at the river over the past century, at least. Keep your eyes peeled for remaining structures and man's modifications that will give you a glimpse into the past of your river.

Many place names reflect the lost heritage and industry of a locality, which would often have centred round the local waterways.

In Devon there are a whole cluster of place names that include Nymet, Nemet or Nimet which were derived from the local rivers: the River Mole, which was known to the ancient Celts as the Nemet and the River Yeo, the Nymet. These lead to such place names as Nymet Tracey, Broadnymet, Nichols Nimet

Why not try...

Virtually all watercourses have a visible history that can be explored and interpreted.

River Test, Mottisfont Abbey, Romsey, Hampshire **(19)**

River Wey, Guildford, Surrey **(38)**

River Thames, Runnymede and Hampton Court **(51/53)**

River Stour, Flatford Mill, Essex **(56)**

River Glaven, Letheringset Mill, Holt, Norfolk **(67)**

River Windrush, Minster Lovell Hall, Minster Lovell, Oxfordshire **(73)**

River Monnow, Skenfrith Castle, Monmouthshire, Wales **(79)**

River Wharfe, Bolton Abbey, Yorkshire Dales **(91)**

Scandal Beck, Smardale Gill Viaduct, Kirby Stephen, Cumbria **(110)**

North Tyne, Chesters Fort, Hadrian's Wall, Northumberland **(115)**

(x) numbers relate to site listings in the resources section.

and so on, an area that Ted Hughes the poet lived and farmed in and often referred to as Nymet country.

Many place names describe springs and river sources — Fonthill, Sadlers Wells; river crossings and weirs — North and South Ferriby, Trowbridge, Edgeware and even the quality or nature of the water — Caldbeck and Redbridge.

Past industry leaves us with: former mills at Melford and Millbeck; stock watering — Bulwell, and Oxford; fishing — Crabwell and Ely, Fishburn and Troutbeck; washing of sheep or clothes — Washbourne and Shiplake; salt trading — Salford and Salterforth,

Have a look at the map and the names on signs as you travel the country and you'll quickly see how closely our social, cultural and industrial history is tied up with the river environment.

River sites

There really are an almost infinite number of places where you can go in the UK to enjoy flowing waters. The following is a list of more than 100 sites that are easily accessible and mentioned in the activities as good places to give it a go. Look a bit further and you will find your own hidden places to enjoy the river.

THE SOUTH WEST

1 River Barle, Tarr Steps, Dulverton, Exmoor SS868322 Park at Tarr Steps car park and walk down the hill to the famous clapper bridge and the wide, shallow, gravel bedded River Barle. The Two Moors Way long distance footpath follows the river upstream for around 4km – almost as far as Withypool.

2 River Barle, Withypool, Exmoor SS844354 Park just by the bridge and enjoy the grassy bank and birds feeding over the water.

3 River Barle, Landacre Bridge, Withypool, Exmoor SS817362 Park beside the bridge, lot of space to get into the shallow river and play along the banks.

4 River Barle, Wheal Eliza, Simondsbath, Exmoor SS785381 Park in Simonsbath car park. Take the footpath opposite the Exmoor Forest Hotel, through Birchcleave Woods. The path follows the river valley, sticking close to its banks after a km or so near the disused mine – Wheal Eliza.

5 Horner Water, Horner, Exmoor SS896454 Park in the car park in Horner, then follow the well marked footpath alongside Horner Water into Horner Wood.

6 Badgeworthy Water, Malmsmead and Cloud Farm, Exmoor SS791477 Park in the car park in Malmsmead near Lorna Doone Farm. Follow the footpath south along the river valley. One km brings you to Cloud Farm and the path follows the river with all its possibilities right up into Doone Country. Camp at Cloud Farm, Oare, Lynton, Devon, EX35 6NU. Tel: 01598 741278. *www.cloudfarmcamping.com*

7 Hoar Oak Water, Brendan Two Gates, Exmoor, SS747430 Park at Brendon Two Gates and follow the boundary fence across the open moor for 2km to the point where it joins Hoar Oak Water at the Hoar Oak Tree.

8 East Lyn River and Hoar Oak Water, Watersmeet, Exmoor, SS744486 Park in the National Trust Car Park at Watersmeet on the A39 just outside Lynmouth. Footpaths will take you to the confluence of the rivers, the gorge and the waterfalls.

9 River Dart, Country Park, Ashburton, Dartmoor SX735705 There is a themed adventure park based around the river: you have to pay to go in unless you are camping on site. Away from the main park activities this is a lovely stretch of river with nice swimming options up towards Holne Bridge.

10 River Dart, Deeper Marsh / Spitchwick Common, Ashburton, Dartmoor SX713711 Coming from Ashburton cross the river on the medieval Newbridge, as the road takes a sharp left turn right down a small road, there is good parking along here on the left. Cross the road onto common land alongside the river. There are small side channels at the downstream end of the common good for playing and investigating. Upstream a bit are river cliffs and good access for swimming and rope swinging.

11 River Teign, Fingle Bridge, Castle Drogo, Dartmoor SX744900 There is plenty of parking both sides of Fingle Bridge. Footpaths lead upstream and downstream along the river. There are great banks of short cropped grass for playing, investigating and getting to the river. Limited parking at Dogmarsh Bridge but you can walk all the way upstream through the Castle Drogo Estate up to Fingle Bridge, a lovely stretch of river with many opportunities.

12 Becka Brook, Becky Falls, Bovey Tracey, Dartmoor SX761801 You can get to the falls through the Becky Falls visitor attraction and enjoy the facilities and activities, but you have to pay for the experience or, you can make your own way via the ironically named villages of Water and Freeland – walk the short distance to the riverside paths. There are some lovely, hidden riverside glades and rope swings on Becka Brook further upstream, accessible where footpaths cross.

THE SOUTH

13 River Lymington, Balmer Lawn, Brockenhurst New Forest SU031304 At the northern edge of Brockenhurst, you can park on the B3055 Balmer Lawn Road, (Forestry Commission owned Balmer Lawn car park) just off the A337 Lyndhurst Road. A perfect picnic and paddling spot – but can be busy in summer.

14 Beaulieu River, Longwater Lawn New Forest SU086331 Park at Matley Heath and walk 1km north on footpaths to a footbridge over the young river at Longwater Lawn. A lovely relaxing, playing and investigating spot in open country.

15 Beaulieu River, Beaulieu, New Forest SU387056 Park at the Kings Hat car park 2km north of Beaulieu. A 300m walk down forest tracks brings you to a footbridge over the river. A good place to stop and play.

16 River Kennet, Swallowhead Springs, Avebury, Wiltshire SU101681 Park at the Silbury Hill car park on the A4. Follow the footpath that skirts round Silbury Hill on the River Kennet. Follow the river until it takes a dogleg where the springs bubble up at the corner.

17 River Kennet, Ramsbury Mill Lane, Ramsbury, Wiltshire SU271713 From Ramsbury main street walk down Mill Lane to the river. Bridges and fords cross the two river channels. Good paddling, jam jar fishing and minibeast hunting territory.

18 River Frome, Farleigh Hungerford, Somerset ST810577 Just off the A366 between Trowbridge and Farleigh Hungerford is this campsite and river swimming club on the River Frome. Nice grass meadow for picnics and weir for playing as well as jumping in points and swimming river. Camp at Stowford Manor Farm, Wingfield, Trowbridge, Wiltshire BA14 9LH. Tel: 01225 752253; *www. stowfordmanorfarm.co.uk*. Farleigh and District Swimming Club, the last remaining river swimming club in the country, is half a mile down river from the campsite and for insurance purposes you must join to be able to swim. Membership is quite reasonable at £20 per family, £10 per adult and £5 per child for the year.

19 River Test, Mottisfont Abbey, Romsey, Hampshire SU327268 Start from the beautiful old abbey and and walk down to the river. Lovely riverside walks and picnic areas.

20 River Itchen, Martyr Worthy, Winchester, Hampshire SU515325 Just off the M3 before Winchester. Head in to Martyr Worthy on the B3074 turn right towards the church and river. Park past the church at the end of the road. There is a footpath heading downstream and a bridge which gives a good view up and downstream. A peaceful, contemplative stretch of river.

21 River Itchen, Winchester St Cross and College, Hampshire SU482281 Park in the car park where the road crosses the eastern-most of the river channels or walk out from the centre of town. You can walk downstream alongside the river or walk upstream and find your way into a beautiful conservation area bounded by the divided waterways of the Itchen.

22 River Arun, Pulborough Brooks RSPB reserve, Pulborough, West Sussex TQ053174 Park in the RSPB reserve off the A283 at Wiggonholt. You can pay and walk around the specially managed brooks to the banks of the Arun or walk on the public footpath that cuts across the reserve to the Arun. Alternatively park in Pulborough for quicker access to the river bank.

23 River Arun, WWT reserve, Arundel, West Sussex TQ020080 You have to pay for entry but there is free car parking on site, go down Mill Road following the brown duck signs past the castle. Alternatively there are footpaths alongside both banks of the river all the way from Littlehampton up to Bury and Amberley. Parking is possible at most bridges along this stretch for direct access to the river.

24 River Rother, Fittleworth, West Sussex TQ010183 Park in Lower Fottleworth 100m or so from the bridge and walk downstream through open grazing fields.

25 River Rother, Newenden Bridge, West Sussex, TQ837273 Hire boats or camp at the small campsite and eat cream teas. Rowing boat hire and camping at The Bodiam Ferry Company, Riverside Cottage, Rye Road, Newenden, Cranbrook TN18 5PP. Telephone 01797 253838, *www.bodiam-ferry.co.uk*

26 River Adur, Shermanbury to Wineham, West Sussex TQ219189 Park in the lay-by on the A281 2km north of Henfield, just before the old stone Mock Bridge. Cross over at the Bull Inn to get onto footpaths leading to the south bank of the Adur. You can walk upstream for 2km, cross over on the footbridge and return on small lanes on the north bank. Good access to the water's edge, look out for kingfishers. The rest of the river Adur is rather canalised and sterile in comparison to this section

27 River Ouse, Barcombe Mills, Lewes, East Sussex TQ433147 Parking near Pikes Bridge just off the A26. Footpaths around water systems, weirs and plenty of interest. You can follow the river on footpaths up to the Anchor Inn

28 River Ouse, Anchor Inn Boat Hire, Lewes, East Sussex TQ442160 Park at the Anchor Inn. You can hire small boats here, swim or walk up and downstream on the river for quite some way. Hire Boats at The Anchor Inn, Barcombe, Lewes, East Sussex BN8 5EA. Tel: 01273 400414. *www.anchorinnandboating.co.uk*

29 Cuckmere River, Cuckmere Meanders, Seaford, East Sussex TV520990 There's plenty of parking at Exceat; the Severn Sisters Visitors' Centre car parks. Walk down the left hand side of the valley along the South Downs Way beside the meanders and stop wherever you fancy on the wide grassy banks. The meanders are actually cut off from the main river so it is more of a lake than a river.

30 Pevensey Haven, Pevensey Levels NNR, Pevensey, East Sussex TQ 645053 From Pevensey Castle follow the 1066 country walk to, and along the Pevensey Haven. The Pevensey Levels are particularly known for their diversity of damsels and dragonflies, so keep your eyes peeled.

31 Pooh Sticks Bridge, Nr Hartfield, Edge of Ashdown Forest, East Sussex TQ470339 The spiritual home of Pooh Sticks. The closest parking is just off the B2026 at Chuck Hatch. A bridle path leads the 500m to the bridge.

32 River Stour, Grove Ferry, Canterbury, Kent TR235632 You can park in the picnic site with toilets. Walk down the banks of the Stour towards Fordwich taking in the Stodmarsh NNR on the way. Alternatively park at the Stodmarsh car park and walk down to the river through the NNR. Spot Voles and loads of bird life. You can canoe all of this stretch but there is some tidal influence so check out the tides and try to work with them rather than against them for an easier time.

33 Elmley Marshes, Isle of Sheppey, Kent TQ945675 Many small streams and waterways with an abundance of wildlife and birdlife to watch out for.

34 River Mole, Box Hill Stepping Stones, Dorking, Surrey TQ171514 Park just off the A24 heading in to Dorking. Walk 200m to the river and stepping stones. Follow the river downstream: there are shelving beaches, rope swings, a bridge and open meadows for picnicking.

35 River Mole, Norbury Park, Leatherhead, Surrey TQ164551 Park in the Norbury Park car park just off the A246, right next to the footpath. You can walk along the river on footpaths with easy access to the river for a km or so up and downstream.

36 Tillingbourne, Abinger Hammer, Surrey TQ095474 Alongside the A25 flowing through playing fields runs the Tillingbourne. A small babbling brook – perfect for picnics, duck races and minibeast hunting. You can even buy nets and buckets in the village shop across the road.

37 River Wey, Shalford, Surrey SU999473 Take the train to Shalford or park in the side roads and walk along the old river – look out for kingfishers and signal crayfish.

38 River Wey, Guildford, Surrey SU997490 Riverside walks and boating along the Wey are the best ways to see the historic centre of Guildford, look out for Dapdune Wharf National Trust visitor centre, Old Town Mill and Town Wharf – with a treadmill crane – as well as old lock workings. Hire boats at Guildford Boat House, Millbrook, Guildford, Surrey GU1 3XJ. Tel: 01483 504494, *www. guildfordboats.co.uk*. or take your own and launch at the Guildford Waterside Centre SU996511.

39 River Wey, Tilford, Surrey SU873436 Park by the bridge right next to the river and the village green. By the bridge the river widens and shallows making for perfect paddling and playing territory.

40 River Wey, Hankley Common/ Stock Bridge, Tilford, Surrey SU886430 Heading out of Tilford towards Rushmore after 500m a track to the left has a parking area leading off it. Follow the track towards Stockbridge ponds and then footpaths into Hankley Common. In less than a kilometre you reach the river with great rope swings and playing opportunities.

41 River Lambourne, Boxford, Berkshire, SU429713 Park near the church in Boxford and follow the river downstream. Look out for signal crayfish and fishermen.

THE THAMES

There are so many places you can stop off to see the Thames as well as great swimming and boating opportunities. These are a few particularly accessible ones but with a path along its length there's no need to be restricted.

42 River Thames, Lechlade, Gloucestershire SU213993 Park in the riverside car park and walk upstream or downstream on short cropped grazing meadows with access points along the way.

43 River Thames, Buscot Weir, Oxfordshire SU231980 Park in the car park in Buscot and walk the short distance to the lock, weir and river. There is a great rope swing into the weir pool downstream of the weir. Cross over the river and walk downstream for small beaches and further access to the water. You can walk all the way to Kelmscott Manor the country home of William Morris and the Arts and Crafts movement.

44 River Thames, Chimney Meadows, Oxfordshire SP345001 Park in limited parking at Tadpole Bridge and walk downstream on the north bank towards Duxford or upstream towards Radcot Lock.

45 River Thames, Duxford Ford, Oxfordshire SP370001 Park beside the road near Duxford Farm or swim or boat here. A lovely backwater of the Thames which bypasses Shifford Lock. A nice spot for a picnic and play in the ford.

46 River Thames or Isis, Port Meadow, Oxford SP499074 Port Meadow and the river are accessible from Wolvercote and the Trout Inn, Binsey and The Perch or North Oxford. The short-cropped bank on both sides is ideal for picnics, boats and playing. Bridge jumping and rope swings are popular at the Trout and near Fiddlers Island at the town end.

47 River Thames, Abingdon, Oxfordshire SU499968 Parking south of Abingdon Bridge is a good starting point as does the bridge itself. Walk either way from the bridge but downstream has a small sandy beach if you want to get down to the water.

48 River Thames, Clifton Hampden, Oxfordshire SU548952 Parking just south of the bridge which provides access to paths both upstream and downstream.

49 River Thames, Wallingford, Oxfordshire SU610903 Park just south of the bridge, cross over and walk along the riverside footpath. Drop down to the fishermens' stances if you want to get closer to the water and find unexpected privacy.

50 River Thames at Windsor, Berkshire SU975778 The river runs along the edge of Windsor Great Park, there are footpaths along most of the river here to take advantage of.

51 River Thames at Runnymede, Surrey SU995733 Parking here just by the river, have a look at Magna Carta Island.

52 River Thames at Chertsey Meads, Surrey SU060666 A nice rural seeming stretch of the Thames in this built up area. Beautiful arched bridge.

53 River Thames at Hampton Court Park, London TQ160680 Plenty of parking places as well as public transport to the Palace and Bushy Park. Lovely riverside footpath bounded by Hampton Court Park. Nice for picnics.

54 River Thames at Teddington Lock and Ham, London TQ168716 to TQ170732 An interesting stretch of surprisingly natural river margin. Park at Ham House and walk upstream to Teddington Lock, the freshwater limit of the Thames. Hire boats at Hammertons Ferry Boat House, Marble Hill Park (opposite Ham House), Twickenham TW1 3BL Tel: 0208 8929620, *www.hammertonsferry.co.uk* or Bridge Boat House, Riverside, Richmond, TW9 1TH (by the Old Richmond Bridge). Tel: 0208 948 8270, *www.richmondbridgeboathouses.co.uk*

55 The Lower Thames – Richmond, Kew, Chiswick, Barnes and on through centre of London to Greenwich and the tidal barrier. There is a path running adjacent to the river for all of this stretch with opportunities to get down to the water and paddle if you wish. Surprisingly large amounts of wildlife and birds all along the river with some nice parks and eateries.

EAST ANGLIA

56 River Stour, Flatford Mill to Dedham, Essex TM067336 Off the A12 north of Colchester. National Trust car park at Flatford Mill with a few 100m walk down to the river or start from Dedham and walk down to the bridge. You can hire rowing boats at Flatford and Dedham. A footpath along the river links the two places with a lovely walk, very rural peaceful countryside, lots of bird and wildlife. Shallow beach just by the bridge at Dedham for paddling. Good for picnics and can also swim. Hire rowing boats at Flatford Boats The Granary, Flatford, East Bergholt, Essex CO7 6UL. Tel: 01206 298 111, *www.flatfordboats.com* or Boathouse Restaurant, Mill Lane, Dedham, Colchester, CO7 6DH. Tel: 01206 323153, *www.dedhamboathouse.co.uk*

57 River Stour, Sudbury, Suffolk, TL872407 In the town centre the Stour wends its way through grazing meadows, a great place for a picnic by the river. You can go anywhere on the Sudbury Riverside, one option is to park at the end of Quay Lane behind the Quay Theatre. Cross the bridge by the Sudbury rowing club then turn right out onto open, mown riverside grass with boat access. Perfect for picnics and playing.

58 Little Ouse, Santon Downham, Thetford, Norfolk TL826873 There are two main options in Santon Downham. You can park by the Forestry Commission offices just by the bridge in the village. From the bridge there is a nice footpath alongside the river which takes you right in to Brandon (and in fact follows the river all the way to the Great Ouse), this stretch is good for swimming and boating. Alternatively over the bridge turn right following the picnic and parking signs. Half a mile down the small road is St Helen's picnic site and toilets. Perfect, open Breckland Heath lies alongside a lovely stretch of wide, knee-deep water. There are shelving beaches for access, nice walks, good picnicking and playing.

59 River Cam, Grantchester Meadows, Cambridge, Cambridgeshire TL448574 The whole stretch of river from Newnham to Grantchester is accessible to boats and swimmers and has nice open meadows for playing and sitting out. Deep enough for jumping in and sympathetic river users. Park in Newnham at the Paradise Nature Reserve car park at the end of a small lane – turn off the A603 where it takes a sharp turn just south of Cambridge. You can either go upstream to the rural Grantchester meadows or downstream through the 'Backs' smooth grassy riverside lawns behind the university colleges. Hire punts and Old Town canoes at **Granta Boat and Punt Company, Granta Moorings** (by Granta Riverside Pub, just a bit further up the A603 from the turn off to the parking), Newnham Road, Cambridge CB3 9EX. Tel: 01223 301845, *www.puntingincambridge.com*

60 River Stort, Sawbridgeworth, Hertfordshire TL489150 Park or train to the train station at Sawbridgeworth. Nice walking downstream along a surprisingly rural river. This stretch of the river is navigable so you can go by boat or swim as well.

61 River Waveney, Outney Common, Bungay, Suffolk TM324900 and TM334907 Car park just off the A143, turn off at the Outney Common Caravan Park sign but follow the road round left to the golf course and common car park. The river forms a loop around the common with access along its length. You can camp, hire canoes and bikes at the caravan park. Rope swings, swimming, paddling, canoeing, picnics, play. Camp at

Outney Meadow, Bungay, Suffolk NR35 1HG. Tel: 01986 892338, *www.outneymeadow.co.uk*.

62 River Waveney, Hoxne Weir, Norfolk TM183781 From the village follow the orange Mid Suffolk Footpath signs along the track marked 'Water Mill Lane, No Through Road'. Keep following the orange arrows to the left down to the river (actually the mill stream) and over a footbridge. Follow the mill stream to where it joins the main river at Hoxne Weir. Just upstream of here are open grazing fields with access to the water and a rope swing.

63 River Bure, Little Hautbois, Coltishall, Norfolk TG252217 Park by the bridge, the river is right there. Shelving access for playing and nice riverside walk, ideal for canoeing, swimming, investigating and playing, you can walk or canoe downstream to Coltishall.

64 River Bure, Buxton and Lammas, Norfolk TG237227 Park in the village by the play area and walk down to the river. Enjoy the beautiful old Mill while there is good playing and picnicking downstream on short-cropped grass. Nice walk and canoe upstream.

65 River Ant, How Hill, Ludham, Norfolk TG370192 Park at the How Hill study centre. Walk through the grounds to the adjacent Nature Reserve to see all that the river and its margins have to offer.

66 River Ant, Weyford Bridge, Wroxham, Norfolk TG347248 Park in the side road at Weyford Bridge. You can hire canoes from here. Go upstream past Broad Fen or Dilham or downstream towards Barton Broad. Some amazing wildlife to be seen. Hire boats at **Bank Boats,** Wayford Bridge, Norfolk, NR12 9LN.

Tel:01692 582457, *www.bankboats.co.uk*.

67 River Glaven, Letheringset Mill, Holt, Norfolk TG064388 The last flour producing water mill in Norfolk. Park up and have a look.

THE WEST INCLUDING WALES

68 River Wye, The Warren, Hay on Wye, Powys, Wales SO221426 There is parking down a rough track, 800m upstream of Hay. A white gravel beach on the inside of the river bend gives a shallow gravelly river for playing. Common meadowland beside the river is great for picnics. Alternatively a smaller beach is available immediately adjacent to and just downstream of the B4351 road bridge heading out of Hay on the Wye Valley walk. Hire boats from **Paddles and Pedals, Hay-on-Wye, Hereford** (just to the west of the B4351 road bridge in Hay). Tel: 01497 820604, *www.canoehire.co.uk*.

69 River Wye, Bycross, Herefordshire SO375426 There is camping and canoeing here, also some rapids fun and swimming, depending on the state of the river. There is canoe access as you enter the campsite and at the downstream end there are Monnington Falls for playing in tubes and mud flats that may or may not be exposed. Lots of bird life. Camp at Bycross Farm campsite, Moccas, Preston, Hereford, Herefordshire, HR2 9LJ. Tel:01981 500284.

70 River Wye, Wilton Bridge, Ross-on-Wye, Herefordshire SO590242 On the B4260 from Ross, there is some parking at the bridge or along Wye Street adjacent to the river in town. Upstream and downstream of the bridge are open parks with access to the river. You can launch canoes both sides of the bridge. Hire canoes from The River **Wye Canoe Hire Company, Ross Sports Centre, Wilton Road, Ross-on-Wye, Herefordshire HR9 5JA. Tel: 01600 890470**. You can also hire canoes at several canoe hire centres in Symonds Yat.

71 River Wye, Monmouth, Monmouthshire, Wales SO512129 All of the river Wye is swimmable and canoeable from Glasbury down to Monmouth and most has walking paths along the margins. Hire canoes from **Monmouth Canoes, Castle Yard, Old Dixton Road, Monmouth NP25 3DP. Tel: 01600 713 461**, *www.monmouthcanoe.co.uk*. Launch at Monmouth boat club, park on road behind, just off A40.

72 River Windrush, Minster Lovell, Wash Meadow, Oxfordshire SP319112 Park by the playing fields right next to the river.

73 River Windrush, Minster Lovell Hall, Oxfordshire SP325113 Dramatic ruins and tranquil waters. You can either park at Wash Meadow and walk along the river to the Hall (about one km) or park in the limited parking by the church just above the hall.

74 River Cherwell, Park Town, Oxford, Oxfordshire, SP516081 Turn off the Banbury Road A4165 almost opposite St Hughes College, down Bardwell Road, the Cherwell Boathouse is on the river bank at the end of this road. You can hire punts and eat at the riverside restaurant. Hire punts at **Cherwell Boat House, Bardwell Road, Oxford OX2 6ST. Tel: 01865 515978**, *www.cherwellboathouse.co.uk*

75 River Evenlode, Stonesfield, Oxfordshire SP393165 Park down the small roads behind the church and follow the lovely path down to the wooden bridge over the river. This is also a stock ford where the river has widened, perfect for playing with grazed banks for a nice picnic. You can swim for a km or two upstream with footpath access beside the river.

76 Wellow Brook, Wellow Nr Bath, Somerset ST741581 The Wellow Brook flows through its steep sided valley. There is footpath access to upstream and downstream of Wellow. Stay close to the village where there are nice places to stop and play where you can picnic on the open grazing land.

77 River Teme, Leintwardine, Herefordshire SO403738 Park by the bridge on the A4113. Nice grassy banks on the common, rope swings just 50m upstream, walk further up for shelving beaches

78 River Lugg, Lugg Meadows, Hereford, Herefordshire SO530414 Between Lugwardine Bridge on the A438 and Lugg Bridge on the A4103 are Lugg Meadows. At each bend is a shelving beach on the inside of the bend and deeper water on the outside. There's something for everyone – swimming, playing, picnicking. Park on one of the roads off A465 as you head out of Hereford and walk down to the river across the meadows.

79 River Monnow, Skenfrith Castle, Monmouthshire, Wales SO457202 Park by the castle on the B4521 from the A466 north of Monmouth. The river is on the other side of the castle, nice shallows and gravel beach to play in, stepping stones and good banks for picnicking and playing. Rope swing.

80 River Usk, Crickhowell, Powys, Wales SO215181 Park in Crickhowell and walk down to the medieval arched bridge. Stop there on the grassy banks or you can walk upstream for around 2km next to the river with access for paddling along the way.

81 River Conwy, Fairy Glen and the Conwy Falls, Betws-y-coed, Conwy, Wales SH801542 and SD809535 Park at the Conwy Falls car park a few kilometres upstream of Betws-y-Coed off the A5, you can take the footpath alongside the river downstream to reach the magical Fairy Glen. There are big boulders in the river channel to sit and contemplate and listen, also handy for dipping your feet.

82 River Llugwy, Swallow Falls, Betws-y-coed, Conwy, Wales SD766577 Park in the car park just off the A5 and walk the short distance to the falls. You actually get a better view if you park in the National Park Centre 1km further upstream but this requires a longer (1km) walk down the valley to reach the falls on the north bank.

YORKSHIRE

83 Goredale Beck, Janets Foss, Malham, Yorkshire Dales SD912634 Limited parking by Goredale Bridge. Walk down the footpath 100m to Janets Foss a beautiful waterfall and tranquil spot. Good for a dip and contemplating life.

84 Goredale Beck and Goredale Scar, Malham, Yorkshire Dales SD914635 Park by Goredale Bridge and walk up Goredale Beck through the baize greed fields of the campsite – a lovely place to stop and play even if you aren't camping. Keep going to the dramatic Goredale Scar, where peregrines nest. Contemplate the dramatic waterfall, then scale the rocks at the side to enjoy the jacuzzi pools upstream and see the classic limestone pavement scenery. Camp at

Goredale Scar Campsite, Gordale Farm, Malham, North Yorkshire BD23 4DL. Tel: 01729 830333.

85 River Aire, Newfield Bridge, Gargrave, Yorkshire Dales SD907580 On the road between Gargrave and Malham the road crosses the River Aire at Newfield Bridge. The Pennine Way follows the river at this point and there are open grazed river banks and shelving pebble beaches. A great place to stop and play.

86 River Ribble, Stainforth Force, Stainforth, Yorkshire Dales SD818673 Park in Stainforth and walk down the main road, across the railway track and down a small road, over the old packhorse bridge, to the river. Classic jumping location, flat stones to clamber on at the rivers edge and a nice waterfall to look at too.

87 Stainforth Beck, Catrigg Force, Stainforth, Yorkshire Dales SD833672 Park in Stainforth and walk 1km up good tracks to dramatic waterfalls. Rock slabs make good chutes as the water exits the waterfall plunge pools. Worth the walk.

88 River Lune, Devils Bridge, Kirby Lonsdale, Yorkshire Dales SD617783 The Devil's Bridge at Kirby Lonsdale is a beautiful and dramatic bridge. In *Waterlog* Roger Deakins tells of people jumping off but they must be mad. It is big, tall and rocky underneath. Upstream of the bridge are large pebbly beaches and shelving access to the water's edge. Downstream are sloping rock slabs at the river margin. The Lune Valley Ramble follows the river downstream for miles.

89 River Skirfare, Littondale, Yorkshire Dales SD943712 Park on Outgang lane and walk up the river to a shelving white pebble beach for great access to the river.

90 River Skirfare, Arncliffe, Yorkshire Dales SD934718 From the centre of Arncliffe find the church and follow the footpath behind the church alongside the river.

91 River Wharfe, Bolton Abbey, Yorkshire Dales SE075542 Park at Bolton Abbey and walk down to the river 200m or so. There are stepping stones and the Waterfall Bridge, good paddling and playing opportunities.

92 River Wharfe, The Strid, Bolton Abbey, Yorkshire Dales SE064566 Designated parking just off the B6160 then a 500m walk down to the cataracts. The river squeezed through a narrow channel is dramatic here, no chance to get in the water but it is good to look and marvel.

93 River Wharfe, Appletreewick, Yorkshire Dales SE053597 Lovely accessible river from the campsite, with islands and rope swings, lovely riverside walking too, upstream or downstream on the Dales Way. Nice campsite. Camp at **Mason's Campsite, Appletreewick, Skipton, North Yorkshire, BD23 6DD. Tel: 01756 720275.**

94 River Wharfe, Loup Scar, Burnsall, Yorkshire Dales SE029617 Park on the B6160 and take a lovely track down to the impressive suspension bridge and stepping stones. Walk back down the river to Loup Scar. Appealing short-cropped banks for picnics, rock climbing, swimming and playing. There is a very deep pool for jumping into. Alternatively park in Burnsall by the bridge and walk upstream.

95 River Wharfe, Ghaistrills Strid, Grassington, Yorkshire Dales SD991646 Park in Grassington and walk upstream half a kilometre to the Strid, rocky ledges rapids and pools.

THE NORTH WEST

96 Cald Beck and The Howk, Caldbeck, Lake District NY317398 Park by the bridge over Cald Beck in the village and walk upstream. You soon reach The Howk, site of an old bobbin mill with huge buildings and wooden water wheel still visible. Further upstream the river squeezes through a narrow limestone gorge with waterfalls known as the Fairy Kettle.

97 Cald Beck, St Mungo's Well, Caldbeck, Lake District NY326399 Behind St Kentigern's church in Caldbeck runs the Cald Beck. Just below the footbridge is St Mungo's Well, made holy by Kentigern, where early Christians were baptised in the sixth century AD.

98 River Caldew, Swineside, Mosedale, Lake District NY328327 From Mosedale, drive up past Swineside and park at the end of the road right beside the river. Gravel beaches, rocky pools and a sheep nibbled riverbank – perfect. The Cumbrian Way passes by here so you can follow the river valley all the way to the remote Skiddaw House Youth Hostel at the foot of Skiddaw.

99 Styhead Gill, Seathwaite, Borrowdale, Lake District NY235125 In Seathwaite there is camping and great watery opportunities in the Sour Mill Gill, Styhead Gill and Grains Gill. Camping at **Seathwaite Campsite and Camping Barn, Borrowdale, Cumbria. Tel: 017687 77394.**

100 Langstrath Beck, Black Moss Pot, Borrowdale, Lake District NY267114 Park as far as you can get in Stonethwaite and walk up the river on the clear footpaths on either bank. A 3km walk brings you to the small gorge and jumping cliffs of Black

Moss Pot. Good for jumping and swimming. Just Upstream of the Pot are shallow pebbly waters for paddling and playing and downstream are great chutes and pools for sliding and playing in.

101 Stonethwaite Beck, Galleny Force, Borrowdale, Lake District NY273131 On the walk out to Black Moss Pot is a campsite on the west bank and further up there are many great swimming pools of crystal clear waters and big boulders for hauling out on. Particularly beautiful areas are around the confluence of Langstrath Beck and Greenup Gill where they combine to form the Stonethwaite Beck. Explore. Camp at Stonethwaite Campsite, Stonethwaite, Borrowdale Valley, Cumbria. Tel: 017687 77234.

102 River Derwent, near Shepherds Crag, Lodore, Lake District NY260187 From the Lodore Hotel or landing stage walk down the B5289 200m and cut right across the water meadows to the footbridge. There is good playing here and jumping in when the water is high enough. Alternatively walk a short way along the river to find trees with small platforms for jumping into some of the deeper pools.

103 River Derwent, Grange, Lake District NY254176 All around the road bridge into Grange, the Derwent is shallow with pebble beaches – great for playing. Park in Grange or in the Bowderstone car park and walk down.

104 Easdale Beck, Grassmere, Lake District NY328083 1km to the northwest of Grassmere, New Bridge, along Easdale Beck, provides a perfect picnic and playing spot. Further up Easdale, Sour Milk Gill is impressive in full spate and off to the left Blind Tarn Gill has some

picturesque mini waterfalls and pools ideal for measurements and investigations as well as playing.

105 Skelwith Force, River Brathay, Skelwith, lake District NY342035 Some parking near Skelwith Bridge. Great waterfalls and nice walks up the river valley to Elterwater. Alternatively park in Elterwater and walk down.

106 River Rothay, Rothay Park, Ambleside, Lake District NY371046 From the centre of Ambleside walk west past the church and out through Rothay Park which leads you to a footbridge over the river (good for Pooh sticks). You can walk along the river round the park to enjoy the sights and sounds.

107 Yewdale Beck, Under Raven Crag, Tilberthwaite, Lake District NY311001 Limited parking but a great place to picnic and play in the braided, pebbled river.

108 Yewdale Beck, Low Tilberthwaite, Lake District NY306010 Good parking right by the bouldery river, great for picnics and scrambling.

109 Grizedale Beck, Grizedale Forest, Lake District SD334948 Near the Go Ape car park and running alongside the path to the main Grizedale centre runs Grizedale Beck, a nice rocky river running through great woodland, lots of opportunities for leaf sculptures and other games.

110 Scandal Beck, Smardale Viaducts and Smardale Bridge, Kirby Stephen, Cumbria NY720059 Park near Smardale Hall 3 miles west of Kirby Stephen. Walk down the disused railway track to Scandale Beck through the Smardale Gill NNR. There are two amazing Viaducts over the river. Smardale Viaduct (NY733082) is

still in use by the Carlisle to Settle line while the one further downstream, Smardale Gill Viaduct (NY729069), is now only used by the footpath. See also the disused lime quarries and huge old lime kiln. Down by Smardale Bridge (NY720059), the footbridge in the bottom of the valley, the river is ideal for pooh sticks, a picnic and play.

111 River Rawthey, Sedburgh, Cumbria SD666919 (LA10 5LQ) Park in Sedburgh and walk out to the Settlebeck Bridge on the A684. Walk upstream or downstream on the footpath alongside the river. About 100m upstream and downstream are extensive gravel beaches with grassy banks for picnics and good access to the river for playing. A short distance further upstream are attractive shallows and access to a bouldered river bed with plenty of interest, pools for stone skipping and good minibeasting.

THE NORTH EAST

112 River Tees, High Force, Barnard Castle, County Durham NY88128 Park on the B6277 at the Bowlees Visitor Centre. Follow the footpath to cross the river on Wynch Bridge, walk up the Pennine Way 1km to reach the waterfall.

113 River East Allen, Allendale, County Durham NY835557 There's plenty of parking in Allendale. Make you way to the river by the old Mill Bridge. You can walk some way along the river valley here with lots of opportunities to picnic and get into the water. There are lots of bridges for Pooh sticks as well.

114 River Coquet, Linshiels, Northumberland National Park, Northumberland NT894066 From Alnwick on the A1 head west into the

National Park. From the road bridge in Linshiels the River Coquet is a great place to be. Stop and play in Linshiels near the bridge or walk upstream to Shillmoor and then follow the Usway Burn on footpaths up into the hills.

115 North Tyne, Chesters Fort, Hadrians Wall, Northumberland NY912702 Behind the fort the route of Hadrian's Wall crossed the river at this point and boulders of the bridge remains are still scattered about the river. A shallow section of river for paddling and investigating. Just 3km up the road is Roman Broccolita where Coventina's Well can be found.

Sites with sacred wells

116 Alsia's Well, St Buryan, Cornwall SW394248 From St. Buryan take the B3283 SW for about half a mile, turn right on to a small lane and after half a mile Alsia Farm is on the left. Park just beyond the farm, hop over the stile and follow the public footpath around field to the well in the SW facing bank. This natural spring feeds a small stream which leads down to the Penberth Valley and out to sea. The spring is well tended and was believed to cure weak children.

117 Flaxley Brook, Wizards Well, Alderley Edge, Cheshire SJ858778 Originally believed to cure infertility the Wizards Well is off the B5087 Alderley Edge to Macclesfield Rd, follow the pathway signed to the Edge and turn left at the end. The Well is a natural spring near Castle Rock the water flows from under a rock with a carving of a wizards face on it and some writing.

118 St Dyfnog's Well, Llanhaedr, North Wales SJ081633 In the wood, behind St Dyfnog's church and graveyard, follow the stream right to find the springs. There are several springs that combine to form a large pool. Steps lead down into the pool for those who wish to pursue the healing properties of the holy springs.

119 St Seriol's Well, Porth Penmon, Anglesey, Wales SH631808 At Porth Penmon on the very eastern tip of Anglesey, just north of Bangor, are the remains of an Augustinian Priory. The well is a spring emerging from the cliff behind the church, it can be found from the car park, on the footpath leading past the fishponds.

120 River Skell, Robin Hood's Well, Fountains Abbey, Yorkshire, SE276683 4km southwest of Ripon on the south bank of the River Skell lies Robin Hood's Well, in the grounds of Fountains Abbey.

For more wells, look at *Sacred Wells* by Christina Martin – see page 223.

River-based wildlife centres

121 British Wildlife Centre, Lingfield, Surrey A rare chance to see many of our more elusive native creatures, including otters and water voles. Eastbourne Road (A22), Newchapel, Lingfield, Surrey RH7 6LF Tel: 01342 834658, *www.britishwildlifecentre.co.uk*

122 New Forest Wildlife Park, New Forest A large range of wildlife, mostly indigenous to the UK, in natural surroundings. New Forest Wildlife Park, Deerleap Lane, Longdown, Southampton SO40 4UH Tel: 02380 292408, *www.newforestwildlifepark.co.uk*

123 Butterfly and Otter Sanctuary, Buckfastleigh, Devon Lots of different species of otters, both native and non-native. Buckfast Butterflies & Dartmoor Otter Sanctuary, The Station, Buckfastleigh, Devon TQ11 0DZ Tel: 01364 642916, *www.ottersandbutterflies.co.uk*

124 Tamar Otter and Wildlife Sanctuary, Launceston, Cornwall A good place to see otters and other examples of local wildlife. Tamar Otter and Wildlife Sanctuary, North Petherwin, Launceston, Cornwall PL15 8GW. Tel: 01566 785646 *www.tamarotters.co.uk*

125 Wildwood Trust, Canterbury, Kent Native Wildlife Centre in woodland setting, lying between Canterbury and Herne Bay on the A291. Wildwood Trust, Herne Common, Herne Bay, Kent, CT6 7LQ *www.wildwoodtrust.org*

Access

Access to rivers is a hot topic and one that is less than clear-cut. In England and Wales, river access was left out of the Countryside Rights of Way Act when it was amended in 2000. So, while there is now an extensive 'right to roam' in England and Wales which allows you up to the edge of the water in much of the country – particularly in the National Parks and on National Trust, Wildlife Trusts and Forestry Commission land – there are no automatic rights to access if you want to get into the river to swim or boat. If you want to play in the river where you have a right of way on the bank there is no problem but if you want to get in to the water and travel up and down the river it is not so straightforward.

In Scotland, however, the Scottish Land Reform Act of 2003 gave the right to roam on all estates over 1000 acres. The right to roam included the rivers, so you can access all inland waters that you have a right of way to get to, as long as you uphold the Outdoor Access Code (a kind of Countryside Code).

In England and Wales there are special arrangements or laws on some rivers that allow navigation i.e. boating and swimming. There are also statute laws that allow a legal right of passage along any river that has historically been navigable to small boats – this has led to a growing body of support for the theory that this gives you the right to paddle or swim up virtually any river in this country.

At many sites, traditional bathing rights, based on historic usage, are respected by the local landowners, who allow swimming because it has gone on there for years.

If you want to get into the water then always access via a recognised right of way, never across private land, unless you have the consent of the landowner. Always be considerate and leave the water if asked. It is most unlikely if you access the river at a point where you have a legal right and just pass by quietly that anyone will ever challenge you.

If you want to canoe or boat in this country you will require a license for your boat and some rivers require a permit. Licenses can be obtained from British Waterways (www.britishwaterways.co.uk) or the Environment Agency (www.environment-agency.gov.uk). Alternatively if you are a member of Canoe England it will be included in your membership (www.canoe-england.org.uk/membership/).

Your licence will allow you to paddle in the following waters:

ENVIRONMENT AGENCY WATERS

River Thames (Cricklade Bridge to Teddington)

Bedford Ouse below Kempston, Bedford

Ancholme

Nene below Northampton

Welland and Glen

Little Ouse, Wissey, Lark and Cam (below Bottisham lock)

Suffolk Stour below Brundon, Sudbury

Medway below Tonbridge

BRITISH WATERWAYS LICENSED WATERS

River Trent below Derwentmouth

River Severn: Stourport to Gloucester

For the full list – see the British Waterways website as above.

WATERWAYS LICENSED BY OTHERS

Stratford Avon from Alverston to Tewkesbury

Basingstoke Canal (North West Region)

Rochdale Canal

Norfolk Broads

Wey and Godalming navigations

If you want to know where navigations rights are in place or have been negotiated then look at www.ukriversguidebook.co.uk or talk to one of the voluntary Local River Advisors from Canoe England – www.canoe-england.org.uk who may be able to advise you.

If you are particularly interested in the legal access situation look at the River and Lake Swimming Association website at www.river-swimming.co.uk or the Rivers' Access Code and Campaign at www.riversaccess.org which is lobbying to match the situation in England and Wales with that in Scotland.

Safety

Spending time outdoors by the river can be an inspiring and rewarding pastime. This book presents a whole range of activities in and around the river that can all be carried out safely but they all have their own risks and dangers associated with them.

The key to minimising the risks of accidents and injuries is understanding and respecting the power of the environment, your own abilities and the limitations of those you are with. The natural environment is dynamic and to a certain extent unpredictable; a safe situation one day with one group of people may change so that on another day, with a change in the weather or a group with different personalities and abilities it is no longer suitable for your plans. It is up to you to be responsible and to interpret the conditions whenever you are by the river so that you can act accordingly.

River hazards

Think about the weather conditions.

Has it been raining? If so, when? River levels can rise rapidly after heavy rainfall – on the River Wye the water levels can rise over 30cm an hour (Environment Agency Wales – Canoeist's Guide to the River Wye).

If you are concerned about the river levels the Environment Agency have an automated service – River Call – which provides information on levels in local rivers. Call 0906 619 77 then 22 for North East Region, 33 for North West, 44 for Midlands, 77 for Anglian or 55 for Wales.

● The bank conditions will change after rain. Expect slippery banks immediately after rain, but even after high water levels have subsided banks can become undercut and susceptible to collapse.

● In any conditions river rocks will be slippery, bare feet, rubber soles or socks over your shoes will give you the best grip.

● Keep off and out of rivers in flood.

● Children often lack fear and judgement – you will have to provide both for them.

● Take note of safety signs by rivers.

IN THE WATER

● Check out the hazards in the area before you get into the water (river depth, water currents, obstacles in the water, excessive weeds, other river users...) and enter cautiously.

● Conditions can change from one visit to the next. Even if you regularly visit a stretch of river, make sure it is still safe every time you go (boulders, submerged trees, dense growths of weeds and yes, even old bicycles and fridges may appear where you least expect them).

● Make sure you know where you can get out safely before you get in, ensuring there are no weirs or waterfalls downstream.

● Stay warm. Water temperatures below about 15°C suggest either a wet suit or a short swim. Look out for small children as they lose heat more quickly than adults. Take plenty of towels, warm layers and warm drinks for when you get out of the river – even on the warmest of summer days.

● Cold water will reduce your swimming strength and possibly even your judgement. Stay within your limits.

● Make sure you are happy with the water speed before you get in – don't be taken by surprise by the speed and strength of even an apparently slow flowing stream.

● Match the water speed to the activity. Make sure the weakest swimmers are strong enough to be in control in the conditions. Remember conditions change in rivers so don't assume that because it was fine last time it will be this time.

● Always make sure you are with at least one other person when you get in the water and make sure you know each other's swimming ability. Know your limits and stay within them.

● Watch out for boats: wear a brightly coloured hat to improve your visibility if you are swimming.

● Make sure everyone going into the water knows the defensive position in case they find themselves being taken by the current. To get into the defensive position roll on to your back, feet forward so you can see your toes. Stay in this position so you can see what is coming and fend off obstacles with your feet. If the current slows and you find you can swim for shore then roll over and go for it.

● Jumping and diving into water is exhilarating but dangerous. Check the depth, every time you go to the river – a mistake could paralyse you.

● Never drink alcohol if you plan to get into the water or are supervising others in the water. Many water related accidents, including drowning, occur when alcohol has been involved.

● There is more detailed safety information on currents and flow and the hazards they present to the swimmer at *www.wildswimming.com*.

ON BOATS AND OTHER CRAFT

● Wear appropriate bouyancy aids and helmets.

● Check your canoes, kayaks and inflatables to ensure they are safe and up to the task.

● Stay to the right where possible when passing other craft.

● Don't drag canoes at landing sites, try to carry them for the boat and the bank's integrity.

● Re'search the river conditions before you set out. Ensure there are no rapids or river features that are beyond your capabilities.

● Beware of Inflatables – they can be hard to manouvre and give a false sense of security so that you are carried downstream or into unsuitable conditions (deep water, rapids etc).

● Hail other river users if you need to get their attention or warn them of a hazard and don't take it as an insult if they hail you.

• Never go alone but if you must, ensure someone knows your plans and estimated timings. Always let them know when you have arrived.

• Avoid high flow conditions, weirs, sluices and complex currents and flows unless you are experienced enough to deal with them.

• As with all outdoor activities: Use your common sense, keep within your limits, and, if in doubt, don't!

SOME COLD WATER SCIENCE

Water conducts heat about 25 times better than air so heat will be conducted away from your body much more quickly in 10°C water than in 10°C air temperatures. The greater the body surface to weight ratio, the quicker you will lose heat. This is why it is so important to keep an eye on small children and thin people when you are in cold waters.

Also important is to watch out for people jumping in to cold water. The cold shock response causes you to gasp when you hit the cold, unfortunately if you are in a river this will turn out to be a lungful of water and it only takes a couple of gasps underwater to drown. It is best to get in to the water slowly when you first set off, in order to acclimatise the body more gently.

The second cold response of the body is to hyperventilate. When swimming you only breathe when you reach the right part of the stroke so breathlessness makes you inefficient and causes a problem for cold water swimmers.

Muscles find it harder to work immediately after exposure to water at 10°C – they have been shown to operate at 25 per cent lower force, in conjunction with this the body shivers to build up heat which affects coordination and again makes swimming harder. A good swimmer in the warm will be a weak swimmer in the cold and a weak swimmer in the cold could get into trouble.

The good news is that you can adapt to the cold, reducing the shock response and the shiver response. People who swim regularly in the cold are able to retain higher internal temperatures.

Swimming in the cold is not all negative. The benefits of cold water immersion are well documented with reports of higher libido and fertility as well as lower cholesterol, improved muscle recovery following exercise, great endorphine release and all sorts of other substantiated and unsubstantiated health and therapeutic benefits.

Health

• Check out the water quality if you plan to get into the water, especially if you are swimming. The Environment Agency website categorises all main river stretches in England and Wales. Anything between A–C is reasonable quality and should be fine to swim in.

• Water quality is likely to be worst after heavy rainfall – particularly following a long period of dry weather when everything gets washed into the river. Consider staying out of the water at these times.

• Try not to swallow river water.

• Cover cuts with waterproof plasters.

• Always wash your hands or clean with antiseptic gels after handling nature finds and certainly before eating on the riverbank.

• If you see a green algal scum in the water don't get in. These are more usually in standing waters and will be rare in rivers. Algal blooms can irritate your skin and eyes and make you sick if you swallow it.

• In the margins of slow flowing marshy rivers small snails living in the marginal reeds can cause swimmers itch. There is no treatment but it can last a couple of days.

WATER-BORNE DISEASES

Leptospirosis is a bacterial infection, with flu like symptoms and often conjunctivitis, easily treated with antibiotics. The bacterium is carried in the urine of infected rats and will get in to the water environment where they live. You can get infected through open wounds, mouth, nose or ears. Leptospirosis is rare and you reduce the risks if you keep cuts covered and stay out of urban rivers.

Weil's disease is a serious disease that can develop from Leptospirosis if it goes untreated. The symptoms start with those of Leptospirosis but then develop into jaundice and kidney failure. It is rare but potentially fatal so must be diagnosed and treated as quickly. If you feel unwell after being in the water see your doctor – particularly if you have flu like symptoms 3–13 days later.

Cryptosporidiosis is a gastroenteritis type illness caused by the Cryptosporidium parasite that lodges in the gut. This is a protozoan parasite that can be present in rivers, particularly rivers that receive run off from cattle grazing or farming areas. Anyone can get cryptosporidiosis but it most commonly affects children under 5 and can be a problem for people who are immuno-suppressed.

The symptoms are watery diarrhoea and stomach cramps, 3–12 days after contact with the parasite. Generally there is no treatment. Symptoms should subside within 12–14 days.

Liver flukes These tiny flatworms live in the liver ducts of sheep and cattle. They lay up to 500,000 eggs a day which are passed out of the host animal and can end up in river water clinging to vegetation in the stream. People can ingest liver fluke from eating wild water plants – this results in a condition known as fascioliasis. Symptoms are vomiting, diarrhoea, fever and abdominal pain. Wash water plants that may have been exposed to animals thoroughly and then cook them as this will kill any eggs present.

Links

ONLINE MAPPING
www.multimap.com

www.ordnancesurvey.co.uk/getamap
www.streetmap.co.uk

LAND ART
www.RichardShilling.co.uk

WATER MILLS
www.ukmills.com

CRAYFISH DISTRIBUTION
www.wildlifetrusts.org is the national body and has links to all the county wildlife trust sites most of which are the county name joined onto … wildlifetrust.org

www.jncc.defra.gov.uk/protectedsites/sacselection

PLACES TO SWIM
www.wildswimming.co.uk
www.outdoorswimmingsociety.com

SWIMMING HOLIDAYS
www.swimtrek.co.uk

CANOEING AND KAYAKING
www.bcu.org.uk
www.ukriversguidebook.co.uk

www.canoe-england.org.uk
www.environment-agency.gov.uk
www.britishwaterways.co.uk

BATS
Bat Conservation Trust – www.bats.org.uk

WATER QUALITY
www.environment-agency.gov.uk/maps

RIVER ACCESS ISSUES
Rivers and Lakes Swimming Association www.river-swimming.co.uk

Rivers' Access Code and Campaign at www.riversaccess.org

Scotland's Outdoor Access Code – www.outdoo ess-scotland.com

GENERAL RIVER INTEREST
www.caughtbytheriver.com
www.outdoornation.org.uk
www.UKRivers.net
www.Waterscape.com
www.ourrivers.org.uk

Code of conduct

❶ Be thoughtful of other river users; keep noise to a minimum if others are around.

❷ Don't disturb fishermen and if you have to, try to pass quickly, with as little disturbance a possible. Coarse fishermen (sitting on the bank, often with an umbrella) will have a float 5–10m out into the water. Fly fishermen (standing, often in the water) will move downstream as they fish and cast right across the water. Try to stay clear of the area opposite them and downstream

❸ If you are skinny dipping or getting changed, try and keep it private.

❹ Try to avoid damaging banks and gravel beds as well as vegetation. Only enter and exit from rivers at recognised, existing landing places.

❺ Don't disturb wildlife, crops or farm animals. If you think you may be causing a disturbance move on.

❻ Gravel shoals and islands are used by breeding birds, fish and otters so try to steer clear between April and August in particular.

❼ Ensure equipment is cleaned and dried between visits to different rivers to avoid transferring undesirable species and diseases. Don't drop litter and if you need the toilet stay well away from the river and paths and dig a shallow hole. (For more information read *How to Shit in the Woods* by Kathleen Meyer).

❽ Consider carrying a spare bag so you can even take away other peoples litter if you see it.

❾ Try to leave the riverside how you found it and take only loose and/or dead plant and animal remains that are common and found in abundance where you see them.

❿ If you drive, park considerately, without obstructing local residents and others.

⓫ Be friendly and polite to local residents and other river users – access often relies on landowners' permissions.